Bookkeeping and Accounting

Bookkeeping and Accounting

Harold Randall is a Chartered Accountant who has had extensive
experience in practice and industry and now lectures full-time at
Southgate Technical College. David Beckwith is a practising
Chartered Accountant and part-time lecturer at Southgate Technical
College.

Bookkeeping and Accounting

Harold Randall and
David Beckwith

***Chambers** Commerce Series*

Published by W & R Chambers Ltd Edinburgh, 1987

British Library Cataloguing in Publication Data

Beckwith, David
    Bookkeeping and Accounting — (Chambers commerce series)
    1. Accounting
    I. Title   II. Randall, Harold
    657   HF5635
ISBN 0 550 20708 2

Typeset by Blackwood Pillans & Wilson Ltd. Edinburgh and London

Printed in Great Britain by
Richard Clay Ltd, Bungay, Suffolk

Contents

Exe 5.

Chapter 18   The Accounts of Non-Commercial Organisations

Chapter 19   Incomplete Records

Chapter 20   Departmental Accounts

Chapter 21   Control Accounts

Preface

As professional accountants involved in education we are hoping to convey accounting as a real live subject. As teachers we know our students experience problems in understanding the intricacies of bookkeeping and accounting.

Accounting is a challenging prospect especially to the majority of students who have no background experience, since accounting (as with bookkeeping) is a precise subject and requires exacting standards. We hope this text will encourage students to persevere, helped by the clarity of the writing, REMEMBER boxes and examination hints.

```
┌─────────────────────────────────────────────────┐
│                   Remember                       │
│                                                  │
│        Accounting is a challenging subject       │
└─────────────────────────────────────────────────┘
```

We have used established techniques to teach this traditional subject. The style is that of a lecturer or teacher talking to a class. It is a friendly and informative style, supported by examples and illustrations. There are many traps for the unwary student and we have given advice on avoiding them.

Each chapter has several questions to check and consolidate the facts learned in the chapter.

Examinations

This book is primarily aimed at GCSE students and those studying examinations at a similar level, such as Royal Society of Arts, London Chamber of Commerce and Industry and the basic accounting syllabuses of professional bodies.

Detailed examinations hints, which should prove especially valuable when revising for examinations, are included in every chapter.

H.R.
D.B.

Acknowledgements

Documents which are Crown Copyright are reproduced with the permission of the Controller of Her Majesty's Stationery Office.

We wish to thank the following organisations for the use of documents as illustrations.

Barclays Bank PLC
Bennett & Starling Ltd

Permission of the following examining bodies is acknowledged for the use of examination papers.

The Association of Accounting Technicians (AAT)
The Associated Examining Board for the General Certificate of
    Education (AEB)
Joint Matriculation Board (JMB)
The London Chamber of Commerce and Industry (LCCI)
Northern Ireland (GCE Examinations) (NI)
Royal Society of Arts Examination Board (RSA)
University of Cambridge Local Examinations Syndicate
                                    (University of Camb.)
University of London (University of Lond.)
University of Oxford Delegacy of Local Examinations
                                    (University of Oxford)
Welsh Joint Education Committee (WJEC)

We must make it clear that answers given by us to questions set by the various examining bodies are the sole responsibility of us, the authors. The answers do not reflect either the views or thinking of the examining bodies.

We are indebted to our colleague Alan Brindley for his help, support and advice in completing this book.

Chapter 1
The Cash Book and Double-entry Bookkeeping

1.1 What Topics are Covered in this Chapter?

We begin by learning about the cash book and explain its use. Then we see how each entry in the cash book only partly records the transaction to which it relates and needs an entry elsewhere in another account to complete the picture. We learn how to balance accounts and some terms commonly used by accountants.

1.2 The Cash Book

Many people keep cash books in which to record money they receive and payments they make. We are concerned with cash books kept by businesses. The cash book contains the cash account. *Account* means history, and the cash account is a history of all cash received, or paid, by a business. It is convenient to separate receipts from payments so the account is divided down the middle into two parts. The left hand side is called the *debit* side and is the side on which we record cash received. The right hand side is called the *credit* side and we use it to record payments.

Fig. 1.1 *Cash Account Ruling*

	(Debit side)				(Credit side)		
Date	Details	Fo	£	Date	Details	Fo	£

The words Debit side and Credit side are not shown on the account in practice, but are printed in brackets in this example by way of explanation. Debit is often abbreviated to Dr and Credit to Cr.

1

Points to Note

(a) The account is headed Cash Account. Every account must be given a heading as we shall see later. (Section 1.4)

(b) Each side of the account has a column to record the date cash is received or paid, and a details column in which to record the sources from which cash is received, or the purpose for which it is paid.

The purpose of the columns marked Fo (short for folio) will be described later. (Section 1.4)

The money columns may be ruled for pounds and pence but it will be convenient in this book to keep all figures in the examples in pounds only. We also wish to demonstrate accounting principles clearly; to this end we shall use comparatively small sums of money in the figures and exercises so as not to bewilder you with unnecessarily large numbers.

1.3   Worked Example of Cash Book Entries

Fig. 1.2

January 2 Alec Brown starts a hardware business by paying £2,000 into it as capital.

3 Buys shop premises, £1,000.

4 Buys fixtures and fittings for the shop, £200, and a motor van, £300.

5 Purchases stock, £450.

6 Sells some of the stock for £75.

7 Receives loan for the business from John Blunt, £500.
Pays wages to assistant, £35.

9 Buys stationery for use in the business, £12.
Receives rent for part of premises he has sub-let, £24.

10 Pays rates, £56; telephone, £18.

Cash

19–			£	19–			£
Jan 2	Alec Brown— Capital		2,000	Jan 3	Shop premises		1,000
6	Sales		75	4	Fixtures and fittings		200
7	John Blunt— Loan		500		Motor Van		300
9	Rent receivable		24	5	Purchases		450
				7	Wages		35
				9	Stationery		12
				10	Rates		56
					Telephone		18

Points to note

(a) We have entered all money received by the business on the debit side and shown all payments on the credit side of the cash account.

(b) Purchases of stock (i.e. goods bought for resale), known as stock-in-trade, are described as *purchases* and not as *stock*. Do not describe these entries as stock as this word has a special use in book-keeping which will be explained in a later chapter. Similarly, sale of stock is described as *sales*.

(c) We have not recorded any personal expenses of Brown such as what he has spent on food, clothes or other household expenses, nor money he may have received from sources outside the business, eg Premium Bond Prizes, a legacy from his favourite aunt or even salary from another employment; they are not part of his business.

Remember

Record only transactions which affect the business

Now do Exercise 3 at the end of this chapter and compare your answer with that at the end of the book to see if you have understood the chapter so far.

Keep all your work neat and write all figures clearly.

Keep figures in columns under each other, units under units, tens under tens, hundreds under hundreds.

1.4   Completion of Double-entry

The cash account shows money which the business has received and money it has paid away. A debit entry for cash received implies that the person who has paid money to the business has recorded the payment on the credit side of his cash book. A credit entry in our cash book for a payment to somebody implies that the person receiving the money has entered the amount as a debit in his cash book as a receipt. Double-entry book-keeping recognises that there are two sides, or aspects, to every transaction – giving and receiving. In order to record both aspects of every transaction in the books of Alec Brown's business (Fig. 1.2) we must open additional accounts. We shall most easily understand the application of the principle of double-entry if we consider first the payments into the business by Brown (capital £2,000) and Blunt (loan £500). The debit entry for Brown's capital in the business cash account must be matched by a credit entry of the same amount in an account called *Alec Brown, Capital Account*. The ruling of the account will be similar to that of the cash account and the amount of capital paid by Brown will be credited to it. We shall also open a *John Blunt, Loan Account* and credit the amount of his loan to it. This completes the double-entry for these two items.

Fig. 1.3

Alec Brown — Capital

	£	19–			£
		Jan 2	Cash		2,000

John Blunt — Loan

	£	19–			£
		Jan 7	Cash		500

We complete the double-entry for the sales of £75 and rent receivable £24 by crediting them to accounts in similar manner.

Fig. 1.4

Sales

	£	19–			£
		Jan 6	Cash		75

Rent Receivable

	£	19–			£
		Jan 9	Cash		24

To complete the double-entry for payments on the credit side of the cash account, we make debit entries in accounts opened for those items.

Fig. 1.5

Shop Premises

19–			£		£
Jan 3	Cash		1,000		

Fixtures and Fittings

19–			£		£
Jan 4	Cash		200		

Motor Van

19–			£		£
Jan 4	Cash		300		

Purchases

19–			£		£
Jan 5	Cash		450		

Wages

19–			£		£
Jan 7	Cash		35		

Stationery

19–			£		£
Jan 9	Cash		12		

Rates

19–			£		£
Jan 10	Cash		56		

Telephone

19–			£		£
Jan 10	Cash		18		

Points to Note

(a) Show the name of the other account in which the corresponding double-entry is found in the detail column against each entry.

(b) Purchases and sales of stock are entered into accounts called *Purchases* and *Sales*, and not in a stock account. This follows from what has already been said in **Section 1.3** above. On the other hand, items bought for use in the business and not for resale are entered in accounts called *shop premises, fixtures and fittings, motor van* as the case may be and not in the purchases account.

Remember

Credit the account that gives

Debit the account that receives

Because of the large number of entries made in the cash account, we keep it in a separate book called the *cash book*. The other accounts are kept in another book called a *ledger*, usually one account to each page; the pages are numbered. For convenience, we enter in the folio column of the cash book the page number on which the corresponding entry will be found in the ledger. Similarly, we enter the appropriate cash book page number in the folio column of the ledger account whenever we make a ledger entry from the cash book. See Fig. 1.6. This makes it easy to trace entries between the cash book and the ledger. Any item in the cash book without an entry in the folio column indicates that we may have forgotten to post it to the ledger account. The process of making entries in the ledger accounts from the cash book is called *posting*.

Now try Exercise 4 at the end of this chapter.

1.5   Bank and Cash Accounts

Anyone starting a business usually opens a business bank account. This will be a separate bank account from his own private one. Most of the money of the business will be kept in the bank account; only sufficient money to meet day-to-day expenses will be kept as ready cash in the business. Cash surplus to the immediate needs of the business will be banked. If the cash balance becomes insufficient, it will be increased by money drawn from the bank account. Separate accounts must be kept in the cash book for cash at bank and cash in hand. When cash in hand is banked, it will appear as a payment on the credit side of the cash account and as a receipt on the debit side of the bank account. Cash drawn from the bank appears as a payment on the credit side of the bank account and as a receipt on the debit side of the cash account.

We will now work an example which includes all the principles covered so far.

Fig. 1.6

July 1 Mr A. Biswas started business as owner of a general stores by paying £6,000 into the business bank account.
Paid rent for shop by cheque, £300.

2 Drew £200 out of bank for use as cash float.
Bought stock costing £1,000 and paid by cheque.

3 Bought shop fittings, £350, and motor van, £400.
Paid for both by cheque.

4 Bought stationery, £75, and paid cash.
Bought more stock, £120, and paid cash.

5 Drew £200 out of bank for cash float.
Sold stock, £400, and banked takings immediately.

7 Paid insurance by cheque, £100.

8 Sold more stock, £270 for cash but did not bank takings.

9 Returned some of the shop fittings as unsuitable and received a refund by cheque, £80.

10 Banked cash, £275.

11 Drew £100 out of bank as personal living expenses.

12 Received refund of insurance by cheque, £10.

14 Returned motor van as it was unsuitable and received a refund by cheque, £400.

We start by entering the transactions in the bank and cash accounts as appropriate.

Fig. 1.7

Bank

19–			£	19–			£
July 1	Capital	L1	6,000	July 1	Rent	L2	300
5	Sales	L4	400	2	Cash	CB5	200
9	Shop				Purchases	L3	1,000
	fittings	L5	80	3	Shop		
10	Cash	CB5	275		fittings	L5	350
12	Insurance	L8	10		Motor van	L6	400
14	Motor van	L6	400	5	Cash	CB5	200
				7	Insurance	L8	100
				11	Drawings	L9	100
				14	Balance	c/d	4,515
			£7,165				£7,165
July 15	Balance	b/d	4,515				

Cash

19–			£	19–			£
July 2	Bank	CB1	200	July 4	Stationery	L7	75
5	Bank	CB1	200		Purchases	L3	120
8	Sales	L4	270	10	Bank	CB1	275
				14	Balance	c/d	200
			£670				£670
July 15	Balance	b/d	200				

We now post the items from the bank and cash accounts to the ledger accounts.

Fig. 1.8

A. Biswas—Capital

19–			£	19–			£
July 14	Balance	c/d	6,000	July 1	Bank	CB1	6,000
				July 15	Balance	b/d	6,000

A. Biswas—Drawings

19–			£	19–			£
July 11	Bank	CB1	100	July 14	Balance	c/d	100
July 15	Balance	b/d	100				

Purchases

19–			£	19–			£
July 2	Bank	CB1	1,000	July 14	Balance	c/d	1,120
July 4	Cash	CB5	120				
			1,120				1,120
July 15	Balance	b/d	1,120				

Sales

19–			£	19–			£
July 14	Balance	c/d	670	July 5	Bank	CB1	400
					Cash	CB5	270
			670				670
				July 15	Balance	b/d	670

Shop Fittings

19–			£	19–			£
July 3	Bank	CB1	350	July 9	Bank	CB1	80
					Balance	c/d	270
			350				350
July 15	Balance	b/d	270				

Motor Van

19–			£	19–			£
July 3	Bank	CB1	400	July 14	Bank	CB1	400

Rent

19–			£	19–			£
July 1	Bank	CB1	300	July 14	Balance	c/d	300
July 15	Balance	b/d	300				

Stationery

19–			£	19–			£
July 4	Cash	CB1	75	July 14	Balance	c/d	75
July 15	Balance	b/d	75				

Insurance

19–			£	19–			£
July 7	Bank	CB1	100	July 12	Bank	CB1	10
				July 14	Balance	c/d	90
			100				100
July 15	Balance	b/d	90				

Point to Note

The return of shop fittings and the motor van are recorded as credit entries in the same account as received the debit entries when those items were purchased.

Remember

Every debit entry must have a corresponding credit entry

Every credit entry must have a corresponding debit entry

Learn to think of every transaction in terms of its debit and credit entries

---

1.6 Balancing Accounts

Look again at the bank account in Fig. 1.7 and remember that debit entries show money which has been paid into the bank account and credit entries show payments away. You will understand that the amount by which the total of the debits exceeds the total of the credits should represent the bank balance.

This is called the balance on the account. To balance the bank account, we find the amount which must be inserted on the credit side to make it add up to the total of the debit side; this is £4,515.

Now proceed as follows:

(a) Insert the balance on the credit side of the bank account with the narrative 'Balance c/d' (c/d = carried down).
(b) Write the totals level with each other on either side and rule with a single line above and a double line underneath.
(c) Enter the balance below the total on the debit side with the narrative 'Balance b/d' (b/d = brought down) and dated the day following that at which the account is balanced. You will realise that this completes the double-entry for the item 'Balance c/d'.

Further Points to Note

(a) A balance carried down from the credit side to the debit side is called a debit balance. A balance carried down from the debit side to the credit side is a credit balance, as on the capital and sales accounts in our example.
(b) When an account has a single entry on one side, insert the balance level with it on the other side but do not enter totals. Doubly underline the original entry and the balance. See the rent, stationery, capital and drawings accounts in Fig. 1.8.
(c) If an account has one entry on either side and they balance each other, doubly underline both entries; do not insert totals. See motor vans account.
(d) Accounts may be balanced at any time; we have balanced ours at July 14 as a matter of convenience. In practice accounts are usually balanced at the month-end or even only at the year-end although cash and bank accounts will generally be balanced at more frequent intervals – weekly or even daily.
(e) A bank account may sometimes have a credit balance on it, when it is said to be overdrawn. You should never have a credit balance on a cash account.

Now do Exercise 5 at the end of this Chapter.

1.7   Definitions

Asset   Something owned by a business; one of its resources.
Fixed Assets   Assets acquired for use in a business and not for resale; e.g. shop premises, fixtures and fittings, motor vehicles, plant and machinery used in the business.

Current Assets Assets in which a business deals; those bought for resale; i.e. stock-in-trade, also consumable stores. It also includes other assets which are acquired in the course of trading, notably debtors (people who owe the business money) and cash at bank and in hand.

Capital The amount a business owes to its owner. We shall meet further definitions of this later in our studies.

Liability Amount owed by the business to somebody other than the owner.

Income (Revenue) Amounts received or receivable in the course of carrying on a business. Examples we have met so far are sales and rent receivable. It does not include the proceeds of a sale of a fixed asset.

Expenses Amounts paid or payable in the course of carrying on business. Examples:— purchases of stock, rent payable, rates, telephone, stationery, insurance, wages.

Assets and expenses are represented by debit entries.
Capital and liabilities are represented by credit entries.

1.8   Examination Hints

These will be regular features throughout the book. In later chapters they will have particular application to the topic being studied.
(a) Ensure your work is always neat and accurate.
(b) Keep figures in columns under each other.
(c) If you make a mistake, cross your error through with a single line and enter the correct amount above it. Never alter figures and avoid the use of corrective fluids.
(d) Tick each item of data or instruction in an exercise as you make the entries for it and check that all items are ticked by the time you have completed the exercise. This avoids missing things out!

1.9   What Should I Have Learned in this Chapter?

(a) Any business, club or other activity for which we keep accounts is distinct from its owner or members; it is said to have an existence of its own, to be a separate entity or being. This is known as the *Concept of Entity*. A concept is a basic assumption about something. Only transactions which affect the business are recorded in the accounts.

(b) Every transaction has two aspects, a giving and a receiving.

(c) The giving and receiving aspects of transactions are recorded in the accounts by credit and debit entries respectively of equal amounts.

(d) Following from (c) the total of the debit entries equals the total of the credit entries.

(e) Assets and expenses are represented by debit entries; capital and liabilities by credit entries.

(f) The amounts of assets and expenses may be reduced by credit entries to their accounts; capital and liabilities are reduced by debit entries to their accounts.

Exercises

1　(a) Which of the following would not be recorded in the accounts of a business?

　　(i) The owner pays £1,000 into the business as capital.

　　(ii) The owner receives a legacy of £500.

　　(iii) The owner draws £100 out of the business bank account for living expenses.

　　(iv) The owner gives his wife £50 for housekeeping.

　(b) Which of the following would not be an asset in a business?

　　(i) Motor vans.

　　(ii) Fixtures and fittings.

　　(iii) Loan from A. Brown.

　　(iv) Cash.

2　(a) Cash drawn from the bank for business use will be

　　(i) Debited to the bank account and credited to cash account.

　　(ii) Debited to bank account, credited to capital account.

　　(iii) Credited to cash account, debited to capital account.

　　(iv) Credited to bank account, debited to cash account.

　(b) Cash in hand paid into the bank will be

　　(i) Credited to bank account, debited to cash account.

　　(ii) Credited to cash account, debited to bank account.

　　(iii) Debited to capital account, credited to cash account.

　　(iv) Debited to bank account, credited to capital account.

3　On March 1 R. Smart started business as a dealer in video films with capital of £4,000 which he paid into the business. His other transactions were as follows:

　March　2　Rented shop and paid rent in advance £100.
　　　　　　　Purchased stock of video films £1,200.

    3   Bought shop fittings £600.
    5   Sold films £250.
    6   Bought stationery £40; postage stamps £15.
    8   Received business loan from A. Good £300.
    9   Sold more stock £170.
         Bought stock costing £300.
   10   Bought video equipment £900.

You are required to write up the cash account to record these transactions.

4 Complete the double-entry from the cash account in Exercise 3 by opening ledger accounts and making the relevant entries in them.

5 Sept 1 Ms H. Allen begins business by paying £10,000 into a bank account she has opened for the business.
            Draws £100 out of bank for office cash.
       2 Buys premises £4,000 and pays by cheque.
            Buys fixtures £700 paying by cheque.
       3 Buys stock £900 paying by cheque.
       5 Buys office equipment £75 paying cash.
       7 Buys more stock for £1,300 by cheque.
     10 Cashes a cheque for office cash float £150.
            Sells stock £300 and banks takings.
     11 Buys motor van and pays by cheque £1,000.
     12 Returns the office equipment because it is faulty and receives refund of £75 by cheque.
     14 B. Charlery lends £2,000 to the business by cheque.
     15 Buys more stock and pays by cheque £3,200.
     16 Sells stock £800 and is paid by cheque.
            Sells more stock £40 and is paid cash which is not banked.
     20 Buys petrol for motor van £10 and pays cash.
     22 Banks cash £100.
     23 Sells stock £1,000 and banks takings.
     24 Cashes a cheque for £50 for office cash.
            Sells more stock and banks takings £1,800.
     26 Pays wages by cash £40.
            Repairs to motor van £25 paid by cheque.
     29 Repays loan to B. Charlery £2,000 by cheque.
     30 Pays wages by cheque £20.
            Draws £50 out of bank for personal expenses.

You are required to enter the above transactions in Ms Allen's books and to balance the accounts as at 30 September.

6   State which accounts will be debited, and which credited, to record the following transactions

	Debit	*Credit*
(i) P. Singh pays £4,000 into bank as capital.		
(ii) Rent paid for shop by cheque.		
(iii) Purchase of shop fittings by cheque.		
(iv) Purchase of goods for resale by cheque.		
(v) Cash drawn from bank for business use.		
(vi) Wages paid by cash.		
(vii) Shop fittings returned and refund received by cheque.		
(viii) Insurance paid by cheque.		
(ix) Goods sold and proceeds banked.		
(x) Surplus cash banked.		

Chapter 2
Credit Transactions and Books of Prime Entry

2.1 What Topics are Covered in this Chapter?

Transactions not involving immediate payment of money; invoices and books of prime (or original) entry, monthly statements of account; the division of the ledger into separate sections, and some more definitions.

2.2 Credit Transactions

If possible people like to be paid at once for goods they sell. However, the object of a business is to make profit and it may sell more goods and make more profit if it allows customers to buy now and pay later, provided they do pay within a reasonable time. The firm is said to allow its customers *credit*.

2.3 Invoices

An invoice is a document setting out full particulars of a credit transaction. It is sent by a seller to the buyer. To the seller it is a sales invoice; to the buyer the same document is a purchase invoice. For a specimen see Fig. 2.1 on page 16.

Be prepared to produce an invoice from given information.

Points to Note

Details shown on an invoice:
  (i) Names and addresses of seller and buyer
 (ii) Serial number of invoice for reference and control purposes.
(iii) Customer's order number
 (iv) Quantities, unit prices and extended prices in total column
  (v) Total
 (vi) Trade discount, if any (see over)

Fig. 2.1 *Invoice*

BENNETT & STARLING LTD.	
WINDMILL HILL, ENFIELD, MIDDX. EN2 7AT	**INVOICE**

TELEPHONE: 01-366 4111 (Head Office, Printing Works)
01-367 0777 (Stationery & Furniture Sales)

VAT REG. 220 4760 01

	NUMBER	10030
	PAGE	1

INVOICE ADDRESS:	DELIVERY ADDRESS:	BY VAN	
A CUSTOMER LTD	YOUR WORKS AT MILLSEA	ORDER NO.	PO4092
253 STATION ROAD		ACCOUNT NO.	A429
WESTCHESTER			
WESSEX			
WE2 8EH		DATE	31.08.86

DESCRIPTION	CODE	VAT	PRICE	VALUE
1000 PRINTED ORDER SETS TO SPEC.		1	.66	660.00
10 FOOLSCAP BOX FILES		1	2.04	20.40
2 STORAGE CABINETS NO 79		1	80.00	160.00

——— VAT SUMMARY ———				TOTAL GOODS	840.40
CODE	%	GOODS	TAX	DISCOUNT	84.04
1	15.00	756.36	113.45	TOTAL VAT	113.45
				TOTAL £	869.81

Until payment of the contract price in full, all goods supplied by the Sellers remain the property of the Sellers.
No claim for shortages can be entertained unless noted on delivery note. Non-delivery must be advised within 3 days of invoice date.

B&S 31370 B1535   E.&O.E.   NETT MONTHLY ACCOUNT

  (vii) VAT Registration No. and VAT (value added tax) if
        applicable (see p. 17)
 (viii) Cash (or settlement) discount (see p. 17)

Trade Discount

Manufacturers and wholesalers issue catalogues and price lists
which show the prices at which they are prepared to sell to the
general public; but wholesalers and retailers must buy at prices
lower than their selling prices if they are to trade profitably. To
avoid having different catalogues and price lists for different types
of customers, manufacturers price all goods at catalogue price but
allow for wholesalers' and retailers' profit margins by giving them
trade discount. There will be one rate of discount for wholesale
customers and a lesser rate for retail customers. Similarly
wholesalers will allow trade discounts to retailers.

    Trade discounts are never recorded in the ledger accounts.

Cash Discount
Firms encourage customers to pay invoices promptly by allowing a cash (or settlement) discount to customers who pay within a certain time; e.g. invoice dated 15 June for £100, terms 2½% net 30 days; if customer pays on or before 15 July he pays only £97.50 and receives £2.50 discount. If the terms are 2½% monthly, payment should be made by the end of the following month to receive discount. Cash discount is always recorded in the ledger accounts i.e. in a *Discounts Allowed* account in the seller's ledger and in a *Discounts Received* account in the buyer's ledger.

Remember

Trade discounts are never recorded
in the Ledger Accounts
Cash discounts are always recorded

Value Added Tax (VAT)
This is a tax on goods or services which is borne ultimately by the consumer although it is collected in stages from manufacturers, importers, wholesalers and retailers. The present rate of tax is 15% and is added to sales invoices by the seller who must account for the tax (known as *output*) to HM Customs and Excise after deducting VAT he has already paid on his own supplies (*input*).

Some supplies such as food, fuel, books and newspapers are taxed at *zero rate*, which means that the supplier does not add VAT to his invoices and therefore does not have to account for output tax to HM Customs and Excise, but he may still claim a refund of his input tax.

Other items, notably insurance, postal services and education are exempt from VAT, and suppliers of these services neither have to account for output tax, nor may they claim relief or refunds for input tax. Very small businesses do not have to charge VAT to their customers, and, like suppliers of exempt goods, cannot claim for input tax.

There are two types of expenditure on which VAT may not be reclaimed as input tax.
1. The purchase of private motor cars unless they are bought for resale.
2. Entertainment expenses, unless incurred for the entertainment of an overseas visitor who is a customer but not a supplier of the business.

A more detailed study of VAT is in Chapter 25 but what is here is sufficient to enable you to understand the examples that follow in this chapter and to do the exercises intended to give you practice in recording VAT. Usually, examination questions ignore VAT but those set to test your knowledge of the subject sometimes assume a tax rate of 10% to simplify calculations. VAT applies to all transactions, whether for cash or on credit.

Traders should check invoices carefully before sending them to customers to ensure that the charges are correct, thus avoiding disputes and possible loss of revenue. Similarly, customers should check purchases invoices carefully before paying them to ensure that the goods have actually been received, correspond to the goods ordered, and that prices, discounts and arithmetic are correct.

2.4   Credit Sales and Double-entry Bookkeeping

Sales are recorded in the ledgers at the time of sale and not when payment is received, if that is later. This principle is known as the *Concept of Realisation*. A sale is deemed to have taken place when the ownership of goods passes from the seller to the buyer, regardless of the fact that the sale may be on credit terms and that the customer may not eventually pay for the goods. To ensure that all credit sales are recorded in the double-entry system, sales invoices are entered in numerical sequence in a *Sales Day Book* (sometimes called Sales Journal). The Sales Day Book itself is not part of the double-entry; it is known as a book of prime (or original) entry. Books of prime entry are a means of collecting all transactions of a similar nature in an orderly sequence before double-entry postings are made. In this case all the transactions are credit sales. A Sales Day Book in its simplest form would be ruled as shown below.

Fig. 2.2   *Sales Day Book*

Page 4

Date	Customer	Invoice No.	Fo.	£
19–				
Nov 1	H. Hamilton	1001	SL52	102
4	S. Malcolm	1002	SL149	1,745
6	W. Bruno	1003	SL31	978
7	H. Hamilton	1004	SL52	1,064
7	Transferred to Sales Account		GL23	3,889

Points to Note

(i) The details copied from the invoices are: invoice date, customer's name, invoice number and invoice total.

(ii) Invoice numbers are recorded in numerical sequence as this constitutes a control on the recording of all invoices. It also facilitates reference to filed copy invoices if further details of transactions recorded in the ledger accounts are required at a later date.

(iii) The folio column is required for posting purposes.

(iv) Do not record sales of fixed assets in the Sales Day Book.

As the Sales Day Book is not part of the double-entry we must now make debit and credit entries in the ledger. In Chapter 1 we credited cash sales to the Sales account; we now treat credit sales in the same way by crediting them to the Sales account. The Sales account will then record all sales. However, we do not need to post each credit sale individually to the Sales account as that would be inconvenient and make the Sales account cumbersome. We need post only daily totals of sales. In smaller businesses we could post weekly or even monthly totals. In the following example, post the weekly total of £3,889 to the credit of the Sales account; to complete the double-entry, open an account for each customer and debit the individual invoice amounts to those accounts. Remember to complete the folio column of the Sales Day Book by inserting the ledger page number on which the customer's account is to be found. In the folio column of the customer's account enter the page number of the Sales Day Book. (See Fig. 2.3 on page 20.)

Points to Note

(i) There is usually a large number of accounts for customers and they are therefore kept in a separate ledger called the *Sales Ledger*. It is sometimes called the *Debtors Ledger* because the customers are debtors of the business, as shown by debit balances on their accounts.

(ii) Only one account is kept for each customer; all invoices sent to that customer are debited to that account. Note that the two invoices for Hamilton are posted individually to his account and not added together before posting.

(iii) We have now recorded the sales by double-entry. The debit entries made to the customers' accounts equal the total credited to the Sales account.

Fig. 2.3   *Postings from Sales Day Book*

Sales Ledger

Page 31

W. Bruno

19–			£		£
Mar 6	Sales	SDB 4	978		

Page 52

H. Hamilton

19–			£		£
Mar 1	Sales	SDB 4	102		
7	Sales	SDB 4	1,064		

Page 149

S. Malcolm

19–			£		£
Mar 4	Sales	SDB 4	1,745		

General Ledger

Page 23

Sales

			19–			£
			Mar 7	Credit Sales for week	SDB 4	3,889

(iv) Debit balances on the customers' accounts show how much they owe the business. They are debtors to the business for those amounts.

2.5   Credit Purchases and Double-entry

As in the case of sales, purchases must be recorded when made and not later when paid for. The book of prime entry for purchases on credit is the *Purchases Day Book* (sometimes called *Purchases Journal*). Except in very small businesses, where the number of purchases may be few in number, all purchase invoices should be serially numbered as received. Special automatic metal-die stamps are available for such a purpose. When the invoices have been checked and found correct, they are entered in the Purchases Day Book in serial number order.

Fig. 2.4   *Entries for Credit Purchases*

Purchases Day Book

Page 2

Date	Supplier	Invoice No.	Fo.	£
19–				
Mar 1	I. Patel	1050	PL63	1,015
2	E. Knox	1051	PL27	914
5	S. Browne	1052	PL19	1,400
7	S. Browne	1053	PL19	248
7	Transferred to Purchases Account		GL30	3,577

Purchases Ledger

Page 19

S. Browne

							£
			19–				
			Mar 5	Purchases	PDB	2	1,400
			7	Purchases	PDB	2	248

Page 27

E. Knox

							£
			19–				
			Mar 2	Purchases	PDB	2	914

Page 63

I. Patel

							£
			19–				
			Mar 1	Purchases	PDB	2	1,015

General Ledger

Purchases

			£			£
19–						
Mar 7	Credit purchases for week	PDB	2	3,577		

Points to Note

   (i) Do not record purchases of fixed assets in the Purchases Day Book.

   (ii) The Purchases Day Book is a book of prime entry and not part of the double-entry system.

   (iii) Complete the double-entry for credit purchases by crediting the invoice amounts individually to accounts opened in the names of the suppliers, and debiting the periodic totals of the Purchases Day Book to the Purchases account in the General ledger.

   (iv) The ledger in which suppliers' accounts are kept is the Purchases (or Creditors') ledger. The suppliers are creditors of the business, as shown by credit balances on their accounts, until they are paid.

   (v) The Purchases ledger folios must be entered in the folio column of the Purchases Day Book as the items are posted to the suppliers' accounts; enter the Purchases Day Book page number in the folio column of the Purchases ledger accounts.

2.6 Summary of Procedures for Recording Sales and Purchases on Credit

	Sales	Purchases
Documents used	(Sales) invoices	(Purchases) invoices
Recorded in	Sales Day Book	Purchases Day Book
Invoices posted from Day Book individually to	Debit of customers' accounts in Sales ledger	Credit of suppliers' accounts in Purchases ledger
Periodic totals of Day Books posted to	Credit of Sales account in General ledger	Debit of Purchases account in General ledger

2.7 Sales Returns and Purchases Returns

Goods are sometimes found by the buyer to be defective or unsuitable. The goods will be returned to the seller with a document called a Debit Note which is an advice that the buyer intends to debit the seller's account in his or her books with the cost of goods returned. If, having inspected the goods, the seller allows the customer's complaint, he or she will send a credit note confirming that the customer's account has been credited with the cost of goods. (See Fig. 2.5.)

Goods returned by a business to its suppliers are recorded in a Purchases Returns Book from the suppliers' credit notes. Returned goods received by a business from its customers are recorded in a Sales Returns Book from copies of credit notes.

Fig. 2.5

Credit Note

BENNETT & STARLING LTD.
WINDMILL HILL, ENFIELD, MIDDX. EN2 7AT

Credit Note

TELEPHONE: 01-366 4111 (Head Office, Printing Works)
01-367 0777 (Stationery & Furniture Sales)

VAT REG. 220 4760 01

	NUMBER	C987
	PAGE	1

ADDRESS:

A CUSTOMER LTD   INCORRECTLY ORDERED
253 STATION ROAD
WESTCHESTER
WESSEX
WE2 8EH

ORDER NO. P04092
ACCOUNT NO. A429
DATE 01.09.86

DESCRIPTION	CODE	VAT	PRICE	VALUE
10 FOOLSCAP BOX FILES		1	2.01	20.10

VAT SUMMARY

CODE	%	GOODS	TAX
1	15.00	20.10	3.02

TOTAL GOODS	20.10
TOTAL VAT	3.02
TOTAL £	23.12

Fig. 2.6 shows how returns are entered in the seller's books.

Fig. 2.6

Entries for Returned Goods

(i) March 9. Some of the goods sold to W. Bruno (Fig. 2.3) are faulty and it is agreed to send him a credit note for £40. The goods had originally been obtained from I. Patel (Fig. 2.4) at a cost of £25 and are now returned to Patel.

(ii) March 11. S. Malcolm (Fig. 2.3) returns as unsuitable goods to the value of £72. These goods had been supplied by E. Knox at a cost of £48.

Seller's Books

Sales Returns Book

Date	Customer	Credit Note No.	Fo.	£
19–				
Mar 9	W. Bruno	97	SL31	40
11	S. Malcolm	98	SL149	72
11	Transferred to Sales Returns Account		GL27	112

Purchases Returns Book

Date	Supplier	Credit Note No.	Fo.	£
19–				
Mar 9	I. Patel	23	PL63	25
11	E. Knox	24	PL27	48
11	Transferred to Purchases Returns Account		GL35	73

Sales Ledger

W. Bruno

19–			£	19–				£
Mar 6	Sales	SDB 4	978	Mar 9	Sales Returns	SRB 3		40

S. Malcolm

19–			£	19–				£
Mar 4	Sales	SDB 4	1,745	Mar 9	Sales Returns	SRB 3		72

Purchases Ledger

E. Knox

19–			£	19–				£
Mar 11	Purchases Returns	PRB 6	48	Mar 2	Purchases	PDB 2		914

Page 63

I. Patel

19–			£	19–			£
Mar 9	Purchases Returns	PRB 6	25	Mar 1	Purchases	PDB 2	1,015

General Ledger

Page 27

Sales Returns

19–			£				
Mar 11	Sales Returns	SRB 3	112				

Page 35

Purchases Returns

				19–			£
				Mar 11	Purchases Returns	PRB 6	73

Points to Note

(i) Sales Returns are recorded in a Sales Returns account and not in the Sales account; Purchases Returns are recorded in a Purchases Returns account and not in the Purchases account.

(ii) The procedures for recording Sales Returns and Purchases Returns may be summarised as follows:

	Sales returned by customers	*Purchases returned to suppliers*
Document used	Credit note (copy)	Supplier's Credit note
Recorded in	Sales Returns Book	Purchases Returns Book
Items posted individually from Day Book to	Credit of customer's account in Sales ledger	Debit of supplier's account in Purchases ledger
Periodic totals of Returns Books posted to	Debit of Sales Returns (or Goods Inwards) account in General ledger	Credit of Purchases Returns (or Goods Outwards) account in General ledger

(iii) The Purchases Returns Book and the Sales Returns Book are books of prime entry and do not form part of the double-entry.

2.8 The Cash Book and Cash (or Settlement) Discounts

Cash received from customers
Dr: Cash Book
Cr: Customer's account in Sales ledger with actual amount of cash received.

Cash discount allowed to customers
Dr: Discounts Allowed account in General ledger.
Cr: Customer's account in Sales ledger with amount of discount.

Cash paid to suppliers
Dr: Supplier's account in Purchases ledger.
Cr: Cash Book with actual amount of payment.

Cash Discounts Received from suppliers
Dr: Supplier's account.
Cr: Discounts Received account in General ledger with amount of discount.

Fig. 2.7

Posting Cash and Discounts

Data as in Fig. 2.6. At March 31st, the following transactions take place: Bruno pays £920, taking £18 discount; Malcolm pays £1,640, taking £33 discount. We settle Knox's account, taking £20 discount and Patel's account, taking £25 discount.

Cash Book

Page 7

19–			£	19–			£
Mar 31	W. Bruno	SL31	920	Mar 31	E. Knox	PL27	846
	S. Malcolm	SL149	1,640		I. Patel	PL63	965

Sales Ledger

Page 31

W. Bruno

19–			£	19–			£
Mar 6	Sales	SDB	978	Mar 09	Sales	SRB	40
					Returns	3	
				31	Cash	CB7	920
					Discount	GL40	18
			978				978

S. Malcolm

19–			£	19–			£
Mar 4	Sales	SDP 4	1,745	Mar 11	Sales Returns	SRB 3	72
				31	Cash	CB7	1,640
					Discount	GL40	33
			1,745				1,745

Purchases Ledger

E. Knox

19–			£	19–			£
Mar 11	Purchases Returns	PRB 6	48	Mar 2	Purchases	PDB 2	914
31	Cash	CB7	846				
	Discount	GL42	20				
			914				914

I. Patel

19–			£	19–			£
Mar 9	Purchases Returns	PRB 6	25	Mar 1	Purchases	PDB 2	1,015
Mar 31	Cash	CB7	965				
	Discount	GL42	25				
			1,015				1,015

General Ledger

Discounts Allowed

19–			£				£
Mar 31	W. Bruno	SL31	18				
	S. Malcolm	SL149	33				

Discounts Received

				19–			£
				Mar 31	E. Knox	PL27	20
				Mar 31	I. Patel	PL63	25

Points to Note

  (i) Use separate accounts for discounts allowed and discounts received.

  (ii) The cash book is both a book of prime entry and part of the double-entry system. It is the only book that combines both functions.

Remember

The Cash Book is the only book of prime entry
which is also a Ledger account

2.9 Analysed Day Books

We have already seen that purchase invoices often include the cost of transporting goods to the buyer's premises; this is known as *carriage inwards*. Sales invoices may include the cost of sending goods to the customer; that is *carriage outwards*. Carriage inwards must be debited to a Carriage Inwards account and not to the Purchases account. Similarly Carriage outwards must be credited to a Carriage Outwards account and not to Sales account; it represents a recovery from customers of delivery charges paid to carriers by the seller on behalf of the customers. VAT outputs must be credited to a VAT account and not to sales.

VAT inputs of a firm not selling exempt supplies must be debited to the VAT account and not to Purchases. It is convenient if the Day Books have additional columns so that invoices can be analysed before the postings are made to the ledger accounts.

Fig. 2.8   *Postings from Analysed Day Books*

Analysed Purchase Day Book

Page 14

Date	Supplier	Inv. No.	Fo.	Total	Purchases	Carriage	VAT
19–				£	£	£	£
Apr 10	J. Smith	1021	PL41	115	98	2	15
Apr 11	L. Bains	1022	PL17	69	57	3	9
				184	155	5	24
					GL 10	GL 23	GL 52

Purchases Ledger

Page 17

L. Bains

				£	19–			£
					Apr 10	Purchases	PDB 14	69

Page 41

J. Smith

					19–			£
					Apr 11	Purchases	PDB 14	115

General Ledger

Page 10

Purchases

19–			£					
Apr 11	Purchases	PDB 14	155					

Page 23

Carriage Inwards

19–			£					
Apr 11	Purchases	PDB 14	5					

Analysed Sales Day Book

Page 22

Date	Customer	Inv. No.	Fo.	Total	Sales	Carriage	VAT
19–				£	£	£	£
Apr 10	F. Brown	942	SL16	230	185	15	30
	H. Kahn	943	SL39	1,150	997	3	150
				1,380	1,182	18	180
					GL 16	GL 24	GL 52

Sales Ledger

F. Brown

19–			£				£
Apr 11	Sales	SDB 22	230				

H. Kahn

19–			£				£
Apr 11	Sales	SDB 14	1,150				

General Ledger

Sales

			£	19–			£
				Apr 11	Sales	SDB 22	1,182

Carriage Outwards

19–			£	19–			£
Apr 2	Cash	CB 76	90	Apr 11	Sales	SDB 22	18

Value Added Tax

19–			£	19–			£
Apr 11	Purchases	PDB 14	24	Apr 11	Sales	SDB 22	180

Points to Note

(i) Enter the total of each invoice to the total column of the appropriate Day Book. Enter the amount of the purchases or sales before carriage and VAT into the Purchases or Sales column as appropriate and then enter carriage and VAT into their respective columns. As you enter each invoice make sure that the amount entered in the total column equals the sum of the amounts entered in the Purchases or Sales, carriage and VAT columns.

(ii) Post each amount in the total column of the Purchases Day Book to the credit of the supplier's account in the Purchases ledger. Post the periodic totals of the Purchases, Carriage and VAT columns to the debit sides of the Purchases, Carriage Inwards and VAT accounts. That completes the double-entry for purchases.

(iii) Post each amount in the total column of the Sales Day Book to the debit of the customer's account in the Sales ledger. Post the periodic totals of the Sales, Carriage and VAT columns to the credit sides of the Sales, Carriage Outwards and VAT accounts. That completes the double-entry for sales.

(iv) The debit of £90 cash in the Carriage Outwards account in our example represents cash already paid by the business for carriage on goods sold. The credit of £18 is the amount of carriage charges the business is recovering from customers.

(v) The business must account to HM Customs and Excise for £180 credited to the VAT account less the debit of £24, i.e. £156.

2.10 Accounts with Running Balances

Ledger accounts as we have shown them are called T accounts, describing their appearance. When accounting is done by machines or computers, the principles of double-entry remain unchanged but the ledger accounts are designed to give continuous or *running balances* after every transaction. The debit and credit entries may be printed in adjacent columns and the balance in a third column. It is more usual nowadays with computers for debit and credit entries to be printed in the same column, credit entries being distinguished by – or CR.

Fig. 2.9a

Account with three columns and running balance

H. Evans			
	Dr.	Cr.	Bal.
1 Dec 19– Sales	2,740		2,740 Dr
4 Dec 19– Sales	1,396		4,136 Dr
6 Dec 19– Returns		752	3,384 Dr
9 Dec 19– Cash		1,956	1,428 Dr
Discount		32	1,396 Dr

Fig. 2.9b   *Running balance with two columns*

H. Evans		
		Bal.
1 Dec 19– Sales	2,740	2,740
4 Dec 19– Sales	1,396	4,136
6 Dec 19– Returns	752 –	3,384
9 Dec 19– Cash	1,956 –	1,428
Discount	32 –	1,396

2.11   Statements

All accounts in the sales ledger should be balanced monthly and a copy of each account sent to the customer. This copy is called a *statement*. The purpose of the statement is to enable the customer to check his records against the statement and to query any matter in dispute. It is also a reminder to the customer to pay.

Statements received from suppliers must be checked to the Purchases Ledger accounts as soon as possible and any discrepancies referred to the supplier.

Fig. 2.10   *Statement*

Bennett & Starling Ltd

COLOUR PRINTERS ENFIELD EN2 7AT

Telephone: 01-366 4111

A CUSTOMER LTD   Account A429   31 Aug 1986   Page 1
253 STATION ROAD
WESTCHESTER
WESSEX   **STATEMENT**
WE2 8EH

Bankers: Midland Bank plc. 1 The Town, Enfield, Middx EN2 6LD Code 40 20 23
Account 80149470

DATE	TYPE	REFERENCE	STATUS	DEBIT	CREDIT	BALANCE
31.08.86	Invoice	10028		969.62		
31.08.86	Invoice	10029		966.46		
31.08.86	Invoice	10031		966.46		
31.08.86	Invoice	10032		866.98		

THREE MONTHS & OVER	TWO MONTHS	ONE MONTH	CURRENT MONTH	TOTAL DUE	
.00	.00	.00	3769.52		3769.52

CASH RECEIVED AFTER DATE WILL BE SHOWN ON YOUR NEXT STATEMENT

B&S 25730 B1384

2.12   Division of Ledger

We have noted that the number of ledger accounts is generally too great to be contained in a single ledger. Customer accounts are therefore kept in a Sales (or Debtors') ledger and suppliers' accounts in a Purchases (or Creditors' or *Bought*) ledger. The cash book is really part of the ledger containing the cash and bank accounts as well as being a book of prime entry.

The remaining accounts are kept in a General (or *Nominal*) ledger, although a few accounts of a confidential nature, such as the owner's capital account, drawings account and the accounts showing the trading results and profits and losses of the business are usually kept in a *Private* ledger, access to which is restricted to the owner and perhaps a trustworthy senior employee.

Division of the ledger in this fashion also enables two or more people to work simultaneously on posting sales, purchases and cash items, which is important where the amount of work is too great for one person. When the work is done by two or more people, the work of one person forms a cross-check on the work of another, and this reduces the risk of errors, and even of fraud, remaining undetected for long. This is known as *internal check*.

2.13   Definitions

Debtor A person who owes money; one on whose account in a firm's ledger there is a debit balance.

Creditor A person to whom money is owed; his account has a credit balance on it.

Personal account A ledger account for a person i.e. debtor or creditor.

Impersonal account Any ledger account other than a personal account. Impersonal accounts are either real accounts or nominal accounts.

Real accounts Ledger accounts for the assets of a business, e.g. property, machinery, vehicles, furniture.

Nominal accounts Ledger accounts for income, expenses, gains, losses, e.g. sales, purchases, rent receivable, rent and rates payable, salaries and wages.

Tangible assets Assets which can be seen and touched, e.g. land and buildings, plant and machinery, cash, etc.

Intangible assets Assets other than tangible ones, e.g. goodwill, book debts.

Capital expenditure Expenditure which results in the acquisition of a fixed asset or an addition or improvement to an existing fixed asset.

Revenue expenditure All other expenditure including that required to maintain existing fixed assets in their present state, the acquisition of current assets, selling and distribution expenses and other day-to-day expenses of running a business, e.g. wages, rent, stationery and postage.

We shall see later that it is most important to distinguish between capital and revenue expenditure in order to arrive at a proper calculation of business profits or losses and a correct statement of the assets of a business. In the meantime, always exercise great care to debit expenditure to the correct accounts, e.g. the purchase of a motor van for use in a business to Motor Vehicles account and not to Motor Running Expenses account. Petrol, oil, motor repairs, licences, etc. must be debited to Motor Running Expenses account and not to the fixed asset account for motor vehicles. These and similar items are pitfalls for the unwary student!

(In practice, capital expenditure which is *not material* is usually treated by businesses as revenue expenditure. Not material means that the expenditure is insignificant, when compared to the total capital expenditure of the business.)

2.14 Examination Hints

(i) Improve the presentation of your answers by grouping your accounts according to type, e.g. Sales ledger, Purchases ledger, General ledger. A preliminary reading of a question should give an indication of the accounts required and the amount of space needed for each. Too many students spoil their work by leaving insufficient space between accounts to write them up and balance them.

(ii) If in doubt, check your entries by asking yourself such questions as:

    (a) 'Does this transaction result in the business owing somebody money?' If it does, a credit entry must be made in that person's account.

    (b) 'Does the transaction result in somebody owing money to the business?' Then a debit entry must be made in that person's account.

(c) 'Is the business paying a creditor?' The payment must be credited in the cash book to reduce the business cash (bank) balance, and be matched by a debit entry in the creditor's account to reduce the credit balance there.

(d) 'Has somebody paid money to the business?' The debit entry in the cash book requires a corresponding credit entry in the payer's account.

Remember

Maintain the principle of Double-Entry
for every transaction

(iii) Be careful to distinguish between capital and revenue expenditure.

(iv) Always do your work neatly and tidily.

2.15 What Should I Have Learned in this Chapter?

(i) The Concept of Realisation means that transactions are recorded in the accounts when they become legally binding and not when payment passes, if that is later.

(ii) Sales Day Books, Purchases Day Books, Sales Returns Books and Purchases Returns Books are books of prime (or original) entry intended to ensure that all credit transactions are recorded in the firm's books.

The cash book is also a book of prime entry.

(iii) Books of prime entry (except the cash book) are not part of the double-entry book-keeping; only the cash book is also a ledger account.

(iv) Trade discount is never recorded in the ledger accounts, but cash discount is always recorded.

(v) Credit sales create debtors in the Sales ledger because the sales are recorded by debit entries in the customers' accounts.

(vi) The periodic totals of the Sales Day Book are posted to the credit of the Sales account.

(vii) Purchases on credit create creditors in the Purchases ledger because the purchases are recorded by credit entries in the suppliers' accounts.

(viii) The periodic totals of the Purchases Day Book are posted to the debit of the Purchases account.

  (ix) Statements are copies of ledger accounts sent at monthly or
       other intervals to customers who should check them to the
       accounts in their Purchases ledger.
   (x) Internal check is the division of duties between two or more
       persons (if the size of business permits) in such a way as to
       ensure that errors are discovered without delay and fraud is
       discouraged.

Exercises

1 Which of the following documents does the book-keeper of a
   firm need to record a purchase of goods in the Purchases Day
   Book?
   (a) his firm's debit note
   (b) a credit note
   (c) a statement
   (d) an invoice

2 A firm received an invoice from A. Ogdon Ltd for 250 packs of
   audio cassettes at £4 per pack, less 25% trade discount. The
   goods were for resale and bought on credit. The entries to
   record the purchase correctly in the firm's books are:
   (a) Debit A. Ogdon, credit Purchases—£1,000
   (b) Debit Purchases, credit A. Ogdon—£750
   (c) Debit Purchases, credit Cash—£1,000
   (d) Debit A. Ogdon, credit Purchases—£750

3 Enter the following transactions in the Purchases Day Book
   and Purchases Returns Book. Then post them to the accounts
   in the Purchases ledger and show the transfers to the General
   ledger. Finally balance the accounts.
   19—
   Oct.   1 Purchase of goods on credit from H. Bloom £145
          2 Purchase of goods on credit from T. White £96
          4 Purchase of goods on credit from F. Lilley £206
          7 Goods returned to H. Bloom £32
          9 Purchase of goods on credit from T. White £244
         10 Purchase of goods on credit from K. Jones £54
         11 Purchase of goods on credit from H. Bloom £216
         12 Goods returned to F. Lilley £26
         14 Purchase of goods on credit from T. White £104
         15 Goods returned to T. White £42

4 Enter the following transactions in the Sales Day Book and Sales Returns Book. Post them to the accounts in the Sales ledger and show the transfers to the General ledger, then balance the accounts.

19—

Mar. 1 Sold goods on credit to P. Singh £240
3 Sold goods on credit to D. Massey £470
4 Sold goods on credit to B. Matthews £190
5 P. Singh returned goods £72
7 Sold goods on credit to I. Webster £64
10 Sold goods on credit to P. Singh £136
11 Sold goods on credit to B. Matthews £510
11 Sold goods on credit to D. Massey £348
13 D. Massey returned goods £102
14 Sold goods on credit to I. Webster £420

5 Enter the following transactions into the appropriate books of prime entry, post to the ledger accounts and balance the accounts.

19—

July 1 Paid £6,000 into bank as capital
2 Drew £200 from bank for use as cash in business
Bought goods on credit: C. Williams £1,000; P. Stephens £840
3 Sold goods on credit to A. Briers £128
4 Purchased goods £775; paid by cheque
5 Sold goods on credit to N. Goodyear £600
6 Bought goods on credit from D. Tong £660
7 Goods sold for cash £125 (not banked)
8 Sold goods on credit to L. Cannock £1,270
Sold goods for £220, received cash (not banked)
Sold goods for £400, received cheque
10 L. Cannock returned goods £150
Purchased goods for cash £60
11 Bought goods on credit from P. Stephens £315; D. Tong £570
Banked cash £180
12 Sold goods on credit to A. Briers £470
Goods returned to P. Stephens £40
Goods returned to D. Tong £55
13 Returned goods which had been bought for cash; received cheque £170

    14 Goods which had been sold for cash now returned; gave cash refund £5

    15 A. Briers returned goods £80

    16 Sold goods to L. Thorne on credit £360

6 Enter the following into the books of prime entry as appropriate, post to the ledger accounts and balance the accounts.

19—

Oct. 1 Paid £10,000 into bank as capital

    2 Drew £400 from bank as cash for the business

    3 Bought delivery van for use in business £3,000, paying by cheque

       Bought business equipment from H. Larbey & Co. £2,000 to be paid for later

    4 Purchased goods on credit: P. Bickers £2,000; R. Sandy £1,700; H. Stone £900

    5 Purchased goods, paying by cheque £140

       Purchased further goods, paying cash £110

    6 Returned some of the equipment to H. Larbey & Co. as it was unsuitable £200

    7 Sold goods on credit: L. Blake £600; J. Snow £420; F. Coker £340

       Goods sold for cash £184. Cash not banked

    8 Purchased goods on credit: H. Stone £300; T. Butcher £800; D. Epworth £160

    9 Sold goods on credit: M. Callaghan £100; N. Short £80; P. O'Donnell £500

       Received cheque for goods sold for cash £420

   10 Sold some surplus business equipment to H. Woolley on credit £300

   11 M. Callaghan returned goods as unsuitable £50

       P. O'Donnell returned goods as defective £80

   12 We return goods as defective to H. Stone £40; D. Epworth £25

       We return goods for which we have paid cash and receive a refund of £50 in cash

   13 Banked cash £350

   14 Received cheques from: L. Blake £600; J. Snow £300; N. Short £80; P. O'Donnell £320; H. Woolley £300

15 Paid wages £40, insurance £30, petrol for van £20, all from cash
Sent cheques to H. Larbey £1,800; P. Bickers £1,000; R. Sandy £850; H. Stone £1,060; T. Butcher £800

7 Rewrite the bank and cash accounts in Exercise 7 so as to show running balances.

8 Enter the following transactions into Analysed Purchases and Sales Day Books. Post the items to the Sales and Purchases ledger accounts and show the transfers to the General ledger. Finally balance the accounts (calculate VAT at 10%).
19—
Dec. 1 Purchased goods from D. Bolton for £400 less trade discount 25%, plus carriage £10 and VAT.
      3 Purchased goods from E. Burnley for £700 less trade discount 20%, plus carriage £20 and VAT.
      4 Sold goods to F. Shefford for £1,000, plus carriage £20 and VAT.
      7 Sold goods to A. Bedford for £700, plus carriage £30 and VAT.
      8 Sold goods to P. Northam for £200, plus carriage £10 and VAT.
     10 Purchased goods from P. Hastings for £200 less trade discount 15%, plus VAT (no charge for carriage).

Chapter 3
Bank Accounts and Bank Reconciliation Statements

3.1 What Topics are Covered in this Chapter?

The differences between current and deposit accounts; the relationship between a banker and his customer, and the nature and purpose of bank statements. Various ways of paying money into, and out of, current accounts. The reasons why the balance on the bank account in our cash book may differ sometimes from that shown by the bank statement. The reconciliation of the cash book and bank statement balances.

3.2 Current and Deposit Accounts

Most bank accounts are current accounts from which money may be withdrawn, or paid to somebody else without prior notice being given to the bank. Current accounts are therefore the normal working accounts of individuals and businesses. Provided a minimum balance is kept in a current account a bank will not usually make any charges to the customer for operating the account. If a minimum balance is not maintained, the bank will usually make a small charge each time money is paid into or withdrawn from the account.

The main banks do not pay interest on money in current accounts. People who want their bank balances to earn interest must open deposit accounts and give the bank seven days notice in advance of their intention to make withdrawals. Money can be withdrawn if necessary in an emergency without giving notice to the bank but then only with the loss of interest. Deposit accounts cannot be used in the same way as current accounts to make payments to third parties.

The remainder of this chapter will be concerned with current accounts.

40

3.3   Paying-in Books

These books contain a number of paying-in slips with counterfoils.

The customer completes the slips by inserting the name and identifying number of his bank account, a summary of notes and coins and details of cheques being paid in. These details are copied

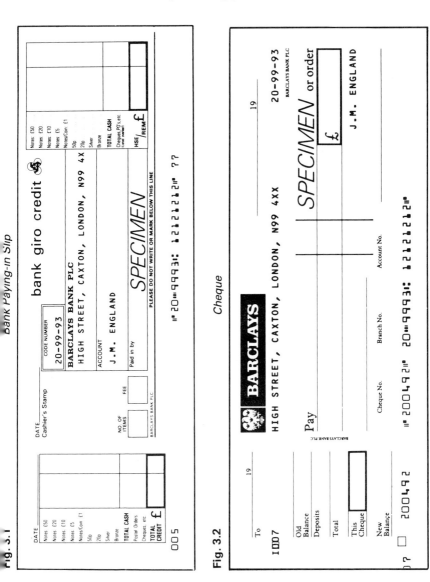

Fig. 3.1   Bank Paying-in Slip

Fig. 3.2   Cheque

on to the counterfoils. The slips are retained by the bank and the customer keeps the counterfoils to support the debit entries in his cash book.

3.4   Cheque Books

A person wishing to transfer money from a current account to somebody else will generally do so by sending a cheque. A cheque is an instruction to the bank to pay the amount stated on the cheque to the person who is to receive the money and must be signed by the customer.

Points to Note

   (i) Name of bank and address of branch printed on cheque.
  (ii) Every branch of each bank has its own sorting code number printed in the top right hand corner of the cheque and repeated in magnetic characters along the bottom edge to make automatic cheque-sorting possible.
 (iii) Every cheque must be dated as banks will not pay 'stale' cheques, i.e. out of date cheques (those over six months old).
  (iv) Name the payee (the person to be paid).
   (v) Amount of the cheque in words.
  (vi) Amount of the cheque in figures. Words and figures must agree or the branch will refuse payment.
 (vii) Signature of drawer (person instructing the bank to pay; the bank is technically called the drawee).
(viii) Serial number of the cheque in magnetic characters.
  (ix) Customer's account number in magnetic characters.
   (x) Crossing (See Section **3.5** below).

3.5   Cheque Crossings

A cheque without a crossing is an open cheque. The payee may present such a cheque at the branch of the bank on which it is drawn and obtain cash for it over the counter. If the payee loses the cheque before presenting it for payment, any person finding it can take it to the bank and obtain the money. Open cheques are therefore not a satisfactory way of making most payments and will usually only be used when the payee has no bank account of his own. An open cheque made payable to 'cash' may be used by the drawer to withdraw cash from his own account.

Fig. 3.3   *Cheque Crossings*

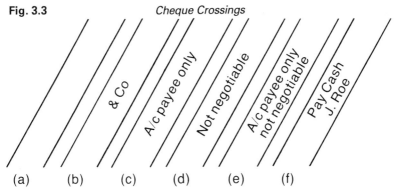

(a)   (b)   (c)   (d)   (e)   (f)

If a cheque is crossed as shown in (a), (b), (c), (d) and (e) in Fig. 3.3 it cannot be cashed over the counter of a bank but must be paid into another bank account, normally that of the payee. This offers some protection against theft of the cheque, and the protection can be further improved by additions to the crossing.

A crossed cheque may be *opened* to enable the drawer to use it to withdraw cash from his account. This is done by the addition of the words *Pay cash* and the drawer's signature to the crossing. See (f) in Fig. 3.3.

3.6   The   Banker/Customer   Relationship   and   Bank Statements

If J. Brown pays £100 into his bank account, he will debit the bank account in his cash book with £100. The cash book is where he records his dealings with his banker in the same way as the personal accounts in his Sales and Purchases ledgers record his dealings with his debtors and creditors. So long as Brown's cash book shows a debit balance on the bank account, the bank is one of his debtors, and that situation exactly describes the normal relationship between a banker and his customers, i.e. it is a debtor/creditor relationship. It also follows that if the bank is a debtor in its customers' books, the customers must be creditors in the bank's books.

We shall see later that the situation is reversed if the customer owes money to the bank, i.e. he has an overdraft with the bank, but for the moment we shall ignore that circumstance.

In Chapter 2, we saw that creditors send monthly statements of account to their debtors and logically we might expect the same thing to happen between customers and their banker. In fact, it is always the banker who sends statements to his customers. This may be at monthly, quarterly or six monthly intervals, although for large businesses, when a large number of items is being paid into or out of the accounts every day, the bank may supply statements on a weekly or even a daily basis.

Fig. 3.4

Bank Statement

THRIFTYSAVERS BANK PLC
Cashmere Street, Silvertown, Stirlingshire

Mr J. Brown
9 The Avenue
Silvertown
Stirling

Statement of Account

Details	Payments	Receipts	Date	Balance
Balance forward			Mar 1	201.58
0034	10.78		2	190.80
0035	54.90		13	135.90
Counter Credit		100.00	20	235.90
0037	113.48		21	122.42
0036	42.00			80.42
Dividend		15.00	26	95.42
Charges	6.00		31	89.42

A *bank statement* is a copy of a customer's account in the bank's books. The £100 which Brown paid into the bank and debited in his cash book (see above) will have been debited in the bank's cash book and credited to Brown's account in their ledger. It follows that the £100 debited in Brown's cash book will appear as a credit in his bank statement. As you would expect, payments credited in Brown's cash book will appear as debits in his bank statements. The bank statements could be described as a mirror version of the cash book with everything appearing on opposite sides. This is a principle the student must grasp in order to understand the remainder of this chapter and many examination questions require candidates to explain this principle.

Notice that bank statements show *running balances*. Unfortunately the use of computers by banks has resulted in cheque numbers and not names being shown on statements, and no details of lodgments. Unless cheque numbers are recorded in the cash book, it may be necessary to refer to cheque counterfoils to identify items of similar amounts in the statements.

The purpose of bank statements is to enable people to check their cash books against their accounts in the bank ledgers and to enquire into differences.

3.7 Differences between Cash Book and Bank Statements

When we draw a cheque and enter it in our cash book then send the cheque to a creditor, a few days may elapse between the date of the entry in our cash book and the time the creditor banks the cheque. A further three days delay will usually occur before the bank debits the cheque in our bank statement. At any particular date, therefore, our cash book balance may not agree with that on the bank statement.

The bank may also enter receipts or payments on our statements before we enter them in our cash book e.g. interest or dividends paid directly into our bank account by the paying company or standing orders we have given the bank to make regular payments from our account on particular dates e.g. building society repayments on the first day of each month.

3.8 Bank Overdrafts

When a person has insufficient money in his bank account to cover all his payments as they fall due, he may make arrangements with his bank manager to *overdraw* on his account. This means that his account in the bank ledger will have a debit balance instead of a credit one on it. The normal bank/customer relationship will then be reversed with the bank as creditor and the customer as debtor.

3.9 Necessity for Bank Reconciliation Statements

Three reasons why the cash book balance may differ from that on the bank statements at the same date are:

(i) Delays which occur before items appear on the bank statements.

(ii) Items in the bank statement which have been omitted from the cash book.

(iii) The same item may appear as different amounts in the cash book and bank statements. For example, a cheque may be entered in the cash book as £104 and in the bank statements as £140. Either we or the bank have made an error. You will now realise how important it is to compare the cash book with the bank statements to ensure that we have included all items in the cash book. When we have brought the cash book up to date by including missing items, any difference remaining between that and the statement should relate to items which have not yet appeared on the statements. We prove that to be the case by preparing a bank reconciliation statement.

3.10   Bank Reconciliation Statement

The steps required are:

(i) Check the amounts paid into the bank as shown on the debit side of the cash book with the credit entries in the bank statements. Tick the items in both cash book and bank statements as you go. See Fig. 3.5a. Unticked items remaining will represent lodgments (amounts banked) in the cash book, not yet credited in the statements, or credits in the statements which have been omitted from the cash book.

(ii) Check the payments side of the cash book to the debit entries in the statements ticking both records as you go. See Fig. 3.5a. Items remaining unticked in the cash book should represent cheques sent to creditors which have not yet been cleared through the bank statements. Unticked items in the bank statements will represent payments which have been omitted from the cash book, such as standing orders, direct debits, bank charges, etc.

(iii) Bring the cash book up to date by entering all items which have been omitted, i.e. the unticked items in the bank statements, as described in (i) and (ii) above, and calculate the new balance. See Fig. 3.5b.

(iv) Prepare bank reconciliation statement. See Fig. 3.5b.

Fig. 3.5a   *Steps (i) and (ii) in a Bank Reconciliation*

Cash Book

Bank

19–		£	19–		£
April 2	E. Slater	√ 540	April 2	F. Keeble	√ 24
12	B. Brocklebank	√ 600	7	J. Wesley	√ 252
20	R. Young	√ 926	14	J. Bull	√ 74
27	K. Palmer	√ 69	26	B. Rogers	418
30	J. Boucher	700	29	A. Homewood	370
				Balance c/d	1,697
		£2,835			£2,835
May 1	Balance b/d	1,697			

Bank Statement

19–		Dr.	Cr.	Bal.
		£	£	£
April 2	E. Slater		540 √	540 Cr
6	F. Keeble	24 √		516 Cr
11	J. Wesley	252 √		264 Cr
	s/o W. Byrd	100		164 Cr
13	B. Brocklebank		600 √	764 Cr
17	J. Bull	74 √		690 Cr
	D/d W. Ebb	125		565 Cr
20	R. Young		926 √	1,491 Cr
	C/T K. Roberts		50	1,541 Cr
27	K. Palmer		69 √	1,610 Cr
30	Bank Charges	10		1,600 Cr
	K. Palmer – cheque returned	69		1,531 Cr

Points to Note

(i) Abbreviations: S/O = standing order; D/d = direct debit; C/T = credit transfer.

(ii) Do not rewrite the whole cash book in your exercises; time would not permit that in an examination and we would certainly not do it in real life. Starting with the cash book balance, enter the additional receipts and payments and calculate the new balance.

> **Remember**
>
> All entries must be made in the Cash Book before the reconciliation is compiled

Fig. 3.5b   *Steps (iii) and (iv) in a Bank Reconciliation*

Cash Book

Bank

19–			£	19–			£
May 1	Balance	b/d	1,697	April 11	W. Byrd		100
April 20	C/T –			17	W. Ebb		125
	K. Roberts		50	30	Bank Charges		10
					K. Palmer– cheque returned		69
					Balance		1,443
			£1,747				£1,747
May 1	Balance	b/d	1,443				

Bank Reconciliation Statement

as at 30 April 19–

	£	£
Balance per bank statement		1,531
Add lodgement not credited, 30/4 J. Boucher *see*		700
		2,231
Deduct cheques not presented –		
26/4 B. Rodgers *payments*	418	
29/4 A. Homewood	370	
	—	788
Balance per cash book		£1,443

3.11   Bank Overdrafts and Bank Reconciliations

These sometimes cause students difficulty but there is no reason why they should, provided you think about the effects of outstanding lodgments and cheques upon the overdrawn balance on the statements. When the bank balance is overdrawn, it appears as a debit balance on the statements and is indicated by Dr printed after the balance. Payments into the bank account will be credited in the statements and reduce the debit balance; therefore deduct outstanding lodgments from the overdrawn balance on the statements. Outstanding cheques will be debited in the statements in due course and increase the debit balance; therefore add uncleared cheques to the statement balance. In other words, the adjustments which would be made to a credit balance on the bank statements are reversed when the balance on the statement is a debit one.

Remember

A debit balance on the bank statements
indicates an overdraft
Add unpresented cheques: deduct uncleared lodgments

3.12   Examination Hints

  (i) Always give the bank reconciliation statement a proper heading and describe it as being 'as at (date)'.
 (ii) Follow the steps in sequence (See Section **3.10**).
(iii) If the bank statement balance is a credit, add outstanding lodgments and deduct unpresented cheques. If the bank statement balance is a debit (overdrawn), deduct outstanding lodgments and add unpresented cheques.
 (iv) If in doubt about the treatment of any outstanding item, ask yourself what effect it will have on the bank balance when it appears on the statements. There is no substitute for commonsense in solving most accounting problems, which is why you should make sure you thoroughly understand all the basic principles.

3.13   What Should I Have Learned in this Chapter?

  (i) The normal banker/customer relationship is that of debtor/creditor.
 (ii) A bank statement is a copy of a customer's account in the bank's ledger.
(iii) A balance at bank is represented by a debit balance in the cash book but by a credit balance in the bank statements.
 (iv) A debit balance on bank statements shows that the bank account is overdrawn (i.e. the customer owes money to the bank) and will be represented by a credit balance in the cash book. The banker/customer relationship is then one of creditor/debtor.

(v) The steps in producing a bank reconciliation statement are:
   (a) Check the cash book against the bank statements.
   (b) Bring the cash book up to date by entering the items which have been omitted.
   (c) Prepare the reconciliation by adjusting the bank statement balance for items which have not cleared through the bank.

Exercises

1   Reconcile the balance in Ms William's cash book with the balance on her bank statement:

	£
Bank balance in cash book	800
Amount paid in not yet credited	260
Dividend paid direct into bank not yet debited in cash book	140
Standing orders in statements but not yet entered in cash book	80
Cheques paid to suppliers, not presented	310

The bank balance is
   A £960
   B £910
   C £860
   D £740

2   Mrs Patel's cash book indicates that she has an overdraft of £36. When she receives her bank statements, she finds that she has wrongly entered a cheque drawn for £51 as £15. Another cheque for £70 which she sent to Mr Biswas has not yet been presented.

   The final balance on Mrs Patel's bank statement is
   A £70 (debit)
   B £70 (credit)
   C £2 (credit)
   D £2 (debit)

3   Mr Barnes, a café proprietor, had an overdraft at the bank on 1 March 1982 of £800. On 3 March 1982, he was notified by the bank that a cheque for £120, which Barnes had lodged in February, had been returned unpaid because the drawer had

no funds. On 7 March 1982, the bank paid a standing order of £400 òn his behalf. During the month he lodged cash and cheques amounting to £1,900 and made payments by cheque amounting to £1,250. On 31 March 1982, the bank debited interest on his account of £120.

Prepare a statement of account to show the amount of Mr Barnes' overdraft on 31 March 1982. (Northern Ireland 'O' level, 1982.)

4   Kay Rogan's cash book at 30 November 1982 showed an overdrawn position of £3,630 although her bank statement showed only £2,118 overdrawn. Detailed examination of the two records revealed the following:

(a) The debit side of the cash book had been undercast by £300.

(b) A cheque for £1,560 in favour of Z Suppliers Ltd had been omitted by the bank from its statement, the cheque having been debited to another customer's account.

(c) A cheque for £182 drawn in payment of the telephone account had been entered in the cash book as £128 but was shown correctly on the bank statement.

(d) A cheque for £210 from A. Brooks having been paid into the bank was dishonoured and shown as such on the bank statement although no entry relating to the dishonour had been made in the cash book.

(e) The bank had debited a cheque for £126 to Kay's account in error; it should have been debited by them to Ray Kogan's account.

(f) A dividend of £90 on Kay's holding of Ordinary Shares has been paid direct to her bank account and no entry made in the cash book.

(g) Cheques totalling £1,260 drawn on 29 November had not been presented for payment.

(h) A lodgment of £1,080 on 30 November had not been credited by the bank.

(i) Interest amounting to £228 had been debited by the bank but not entered in the cash book.

You are required to:
(i) make any necessary entries in the cash book;
(ii) prepare a statement reconciling Kay Rogan's corrected cash book with her bank statement at 30 November 1982 and

(iii) state what further action would be necessary as a result of your examination of Kay's cash book and bank statement. (AAT 1982)

5   Jim Duddy received a statement from his bank at 30 April 1983, showing a balance of £1,420 in his favour. The differences between his cash book and bank statement balances at 30 April are given below.

(1) An amount of £421 paid into bank on 29 April has not been entered by the bank.

(2) Two cheques drawn by Duddy were not presented for payment until after 30 April: C. Walker £206, P. Higgins £39.

(3) The bank made standing order payments amounting to £168 on behalf of Duddy. This had not been recorded in the cash book.

(4) On 23 April 1983 Duddy received from V. Bennett a cheque for £306 which he paid to bank on the same day. The bank statement showed that this cheque was dishonoured on 28 April 1983.

(5) On 24 April Duddy paid into bank a cheque for £360 which was received from a customer in full settlement of a debt of £375. This item was shown correctly in the bank statement but Duddy had entered the full £375 in the bank column of his cash book.

(6) J. Elliss, a debtor, had made a payment of £292 direct to the bank but this entry had not been entered in Duddy's cash book.

Required:

(a) A statement showing the corrected bank statement balance.

(b) The cash book (bank columns only) showing the opening balance at 30 April, the additional entries now made necessary and closing with the corrected balance.

(c) An explanation of why a credit balance on a bank statement represents an asset to the firm concerned. (AEB 'O' level, 1983.)

6   A. Smith's cash book (bank columns only) for the month of
May 1985 was as follows:—

Dr. 1985		£	1985			Cheque Number	Cr. £
May 1	Balance	600	May 9	A. Rock		11241	125
5	Cash	198	16	Tax Collector		11242	250
14	C. Grant	72	27	J. Bird		11243	27
14	W. Dean	48	31	Balance		c/d	656
22	Cash	80					
31	Cash	60					
		£1,058					£1,058

The following bank statement was received at the beginning of
June 1985:

1985	Details	Payments £	Receipts £	Balance £
May 1	Balance brought forward			600
6	Cash		198	798
12	11241	125		673
14	Cheques		120	793
15	Dividend		52	845
18	Unpaid cheque – Dean	48		797
23	Cash		80	877
24	11242	250		627
31	Standing Order – Midas Finance	45		582

You are required to:

(a) Bring the cash book up to date starting with the balance
carried down of £656 on 31 May 1985. (There is *no* need to
copy down the whole cash book as shown above.)

(b) Prepare a statement, under its proper title, to reconcile the
difference between your amended cash book balance and
the balance in the bank statement on 31 May 1985.
(Cambridge 'O' level 1985)

7   The following information relates to the Bywater School Fund
for the month of March 1984.

Cash Book (Bank Account Extract)

		£		Cheque No.	£
29.2.84	Total Receipts	2,200	29.2.84 Total Payments		2,600
	Balance c/d	400			
		£2,600			£2,600

		£			Cheque No.	£
1.3.84	Balance b/d	400	2.3.84	Flyn	123	10
5.3.84	Tote Money	150	5.3.84	Ned	124	20
9.3.84	Sponsored Walk	400	6.3.84	Hay	125	50
12.3.84	Tote Money	325	7.3.84	Bedford	126	100
14.3.84	Donation	1,000	9.3.84	Smith Press	127	500
19.3.84	Tote Money	100	14.3.84	Joy	128	40
23.3.84	Coffee Evening	175	15.3.84	Morris Ltd	129	150
26.3.84	Tote Money	250	19.3.84	Henley	130	60
31.3.84	Staff Dance	200	20.3.84	Waters	131	25
			21.3.84	Richey	132	5
			23.3.84	Oxford Ltd	133	250
			30.3.84	Petty Cash	134	30
			31.3.84	Balance c/d		1,420
		£3,010				£3,010
1.4.84	Balance b/d	1,420				

Notes:

(1) The Bank Account Extract was compiled by the Treasurer from his own records. It contains some arithmetical errors, and no adjustments have been made to it.

(2) As at 29 February 1984 a cheque for £550 (cheque number 122) had not been credited by the bank.

A copy of the Bank Statement is shown below.

Bank Statement (Copy)

Details	Payments	Receipts	Date	Balance
			1.3.84	150
Counter Credit		150	5.3.84	300
Bank Charges	10			290
Counter Credit		400	9.3.84	690
124	20		12.3.84	
Counter Credit		325		995
127	500		13.3.84	495
Counter Credit		1,000	14.3.84	1,495
Standing Order	45		15.3.84	1,450
Counter Credit		100	19.3.84	
Returned Cheque	15			1,535
126	100		21.3.84	1,435
Direct Debit	120		22.3.84	1,315
Counter Credit		175	23.3.84	1,490
131	25		24.3.84	
130	60			1,405
Counter Credit		250	26.3.84	1,655
132	5		27.3.84	
123	10			1,640
Transfer to Deposit	75		30.3.84	1,565
128	40		31.3.84	
122	550			
129	150			
Refund of Bank Charges		10		835

You are required to:

(a) calculate the correct cash book balance as at 31 March 1984 and
(b) prepare a bank reconciliation statement as at that date. (AAT 1984)

Chapter 4
Two- and Three-Column Cash Books

4.1 What Topics are Covered in this Chapter?

The cash account and bank account in the cash book may conveniently be kept in columnar form. We extend the principle of 'columnar' accounts by adding further columns to record cash discounts allowed and received.

4.2 The Cash Book

The cash book contains the accounts for cash in hand and cash at bank.

The two accounts may be kept side by side, the cash book being ruled with two cash columns on the debit side and two on the credit side.

Fig. 4.1 *Two-Column Cash Book*

19–			Cash £	Bank £	19–			Cash £	Bank £
Jan 2	Balances	b/d	120	2,150	Jan 3	Van			
3	A. Timms			200		expenses		40	
4	G. Barker			95	4	Rent			300
	L. Pitt			360		Purchases			1,000
5	Sales		200		5	Office			
6	Cash	C		100		expenses		15	
7	Sales			700		Wages		35	
10	Bank	C	50		6	Bank	C	100	
						Rates			120
						Telephone			40
						Purchases		60	
					10	Cash	C		50
						Balances	c/d	120	2,095
			370	3,605				370	3,605
Jan 11	Balances	b/d	120	2,095					

56

Points to Note

(i) There are two cash columns on the debit side and two on the credit side. It is customary to make the left-hand column of each pair *cash account* and the right-hand column *bank account*.

(ii) Cheques received from Timms, Barker and Pitt have been debited in the bank column. Cheques drawn for rent, purchases, rates and telephone have been credited in the bank column. In other words, the entries are the same as they would have been if the bank account had been kept as a separate account in the cash book.

(iii) Cash received from sales and not banked has been debited in the cash column, and van expenses, office expenses, wages and purchases paid by cash have been credited in the cash column exactly as they would have been if the cash account had been kept separately.

(iv) When cash surplus to office requirements is banked, credit the cash column and debit the bank column. If a cheque is cashed to increase the cash in hand, credit the bank column and debit the cash column. In such cases, the letter C is entered in the folio column against each entry. C is short for *contra*, a Latin word meaning against or on the other side. It tells the reader that the double entry is to be found on the other side of the account.

(v) Notice how the cash and bank balances carried down (c/d) and brought down (b/d), when both are debit balances, are entered on the same line, the one word *balances* serving for both.

(vi) If the bank balance is overdrawn, you should have a credit balance on the bank account, but the balance on the cash account should always be a debit one.

Remember

Take care to enter each item in the correct column

4.3 Cash Discounts and Three-Column Cash Books

You will recall that in Chapter 2 we saw that the entries for discounts allowed to customers are:

Debit: Discounts allowed
Credit: Customers' personal accounts

and that entries for discounts received from suppliers are:

Debit: Suppliers' personal accounts
Credit: Discounts receivable

If we make these entries individually for every discount allowed or received it could entail a large number of entries in the discount accounts. It may also have occurred to you that although other transactions are collected together in books of prime entry, we have not so far mentioned one for discounts. The answer is that the cash book may be used for this purpose.

You will remember that the cash book is both a book of prime entry for cash and bank and, in its dual role, as a ledger account, is also part of the double-entry. But, as far as discounts are concerned, it serves as a book of prime entry only and not as a ledger account. It is not therefore part of the double-entry for discounts which must be posted as periodic totals to the discount allowed and discount received accounts in the nominal ledger. The posting of periodic totals reduces the number of postings to those accounts.

To record discounts in the cash book, it is necessary to have a third column on each side of the book.

Fig. 4.2

Worked Example using Three-Column Cash Book

March 1 Allen paid his account by cheque £148; discount allowed £10.
Brown paid his account by cash £90; discount allowed £10.
Charlery paid his account by cheque £245; discount allowed £35.
2 We pay Deveraux his account for £200 by cheque after deducting 2 ½ per cent discount.
We pay Edwardes's account for £75 by cash after deducting 4 per cent discount.
We pay Fernando's account for £120 by cheque after deducting 5 per cent discount.

Cash Book

19-			Discount £	Cash £	Bank £	19-				Discount £	Cash £	Bank £
Mar 1	Allen		10		148	March 2	Deveraux			5		195
	Brown		10	90			Edwardes			3	72	
	Charlery		35		245		Fernando			6		114
							Balances	c/d			18	84
			55	90	393					14	90	393
Mar 3	Balances	b/d		18	84							

Sales Ledger

Allen

19–			£	19–			£
Mar 1	Balance	b/f	158	Mar 1	Bank		148
					Discount		10
			158				158

Brown

19–			£	19–			£
Mar 1	Balance	b/f	100	Mar 1	Cash		90
					Discount		10
			100				100

Charlery

19–			£	19–			£
Mar 1	Balance	b/f	280	Mar 1	Bank		245
					Discount		35
			280				280

Purchases Ledger

Deveraux

19–			£	19–			£
Mar 2	Bank		195	Mar 1	Balance	b/f	200
	Discount		5				
			200				200

Edwardes

19–			£	19–			£
Mar 2	Cash		72	Mar 1	Balance	b/f	75
	Discount		3				
			75				75

Fernando

19–			£	19–			£
Mar 2	Bank		114	Mar 1	Balance	b/f	120
	Discount		6				
			120				120

General Ledger

Discounts Allowed

19–		£					
Mar 2	Cash Book	55					

Discounts Received

				19–			£
				Mar 2	Cash Book		14

Points to Note

(i) Enter discounts allowed on the debit side of the cash book next to the money received. Enter discounts received on the credit side of the cash book next to the payments.

(ii) Whereas the receipts and payments in the cash book are part of the double-entry, the discount columns are not part of the double-entry. They are memorandum columns only.

(iii) Balance the cash and bank columns but do not balance the discount columns which must be totalled only.

(iv) Complete the double-entry for discounts entered in the personal accounts by debiting the total of the discount allowed column (on debit side of cash book) to Discounts Allowed account; credit the total of the discounts received column on the credit side of the cash book to the Discounts Received account.

(v) You must remember that the totals of the discount columns are the only items that are posted from the debit side of the cash book to the debit of an account or from the credit side of the cash book to the credit side of an account. You should also be clear in your own mind that the reason for this is because the discount columns in the cash book are memorandum columns only and not part of the double entry.

Remember

Debit the total of the Discounts Allowed column to the Discounts Allowed account

Credit the total of the Discounts Received column to the Discounts Received account

---

4.4 Examination Hints

(i) Take care to enter each item in the correct column of the cash book.

(ii) Be prepared to explain how the cash and bank columns are part of the double-entry, but the discount columns are memorandum ones only.

(iii) Make sure you show both contra entries to record transfers between cash and bank.

(iv) Balance the cash and bank columns and remember to bring the balances down in the cash book; you could lose marks if you fail to do this.

(v) Never balance the discount columns. Transfer the totals of the columns to the Discount Allowed or Discount Received account as appropriate.

(vi) The balance on the bank columns will generally be a debit one but it will be a credit balance if the bank account becomes overdrawn. In the latter case, it would be as well to recheck that the credit balance has not arisen simply because you have entered a bank receipt in the cash column or a cash payment in the bank column.

The balance on the cash account should always be a debit one.

4.5 What Should I Have Learned in this Chapter?

(i) The bank and cash accounts may conveniently be kept in columnar form. We shall meet columnar accounts again in our studies when we come to partnership accounts and departmental accounts.

(ii) The addition of extra memorandum columns in the cash book enables it to be used also as a book of prime entry for cash discounts.

Exercises

1 Walter Gardner, a sole trader, enters all his cash and bank transactions in a three-column Cash Book. His transactions for the month of February 1984 were as follows:

Feb. 1 Cash in hand £37. Cash at bank £194.

4 Received cash from H. Robins £47 in full settlement of a debt of £51.

10 Paid by cheque to F. Johnson the sum of £152, in full settlement of a debt of £160.

11 Received from N. Wilson a cheque for £32, in full settlement of a debt of £37. This cheque was paid into the bank the same day.

12 Paid wages in cash £44.

22 Drew a cheque for £50 for office cash.

25 Drew a cheque for £60 in favour of *self*, being in respect of drawings.

26 Paid wages in cash £42.

29 Paid salaries by cheque £51.

29 Paid by cheque to R. Church the sum of £65 in full settlement of a debt of £70.

Required:

(i) Draw up the three-column Cash Book of Gardner to record the above transactions.

(ii) Balance the Cash Book as at 29 February 1984 and carry down the balances.

(iii) Total the two discount columns and state to which accounts in the ledger these should be posted and also on which side of the ledger each entry should be made.

Note: Ledger Accounts are *not* required.

(LCCI 1984)

2   Abel Cass is a sole trader who keeps records of his cash and bank transactions in a three-column Cash Book. His transactions for the month of February 1985 were as follows:

Feb.   1 Cash in hand £37. Cash at bank £244.

6 Received cash £39 from D. Young in full settlement of a debt of £42.

11 Paid wages in cash £41.

15 Paid by cheque £68 to J. Edwards in full settlement of a debt of £75.

19 Received from H. Shipley a cheque for £63. This was paid directly into the bank. The cheque was in full settlement of a debt of £68 due from Shipley.

21 Paid salaries by cheque £74.

23 Drew £50 from the bank for office cash.

23 Paid wages in cash £40.

28 Paid by cheque £60 to F. Gill in full settlement of a debt of £65.

Required:
  (i) Enter the above transactions in the three-column Cash
      Book of A. Cass and balance the Cash and Bank
      columns.
 (ii) Carry down the balances of the Cash and Bank columns.
(iii) Total the two Discount columns and state to which
      account in the ledger each total should be posted and
      also which side.

(LCCI 1985)

3 (a) A sole trader who keeps his books of account on the
   double-entry system wishes to subdivide his ledger. His
   business transactions include a substantial number involving
   cash and bank and he also buys and sells on credit.
       (i) State into what *four* divisions the trader could split his
           ledger assuming that a Private ledger would not be
           required.
      (ii) What two functions does the Cash Book fulfil within the
           double-entry system?
   (b) A trader keeps a three-column Cash Book. The following
   transactions occurred during April:
   April 1 Sold goods for cash £150.
         2 Received a cheque for £198 from P. Hyde, a debtor,
            having allowed him cash discount of £2.
         3 Paid by cheque the amount owing to C. Small £240
            less cash discount of 2½ %.
         4 Paid wages by cash £560.
         7 Drew and cashed a cheque for office use £50.
   State in which ledger accounts you would enter the above
   transactions and indicate whether the entries are debit or
   credit. Set out your answer in the form of a table as below:

Date	Ledger Account	*Amount*	
		Debit	*Credit*
		£	£

(RSA I 1986)

Chapter 5
Petty Cash and Analysed Petty Cash Books

5.1   What Topics are Covered in this Chapter?

Small, incidental business expenses are usually paid from a petty cash float kept on an Imprest system. We explain the use of an analysed petty cash book.

5.2   Petty Cash Floats

Most businesses have to make numerous small cash payments for incidental day-to-day expenses. The cashier is usually a fairly senior member of the staff who is kept busy controlling the bank account and the main cash account in addition to performing other duties. His time is too valuable to allow him to be interrupted constantly to make minor cash payments. These may be made by a more junior member of staff from a small cash float kept under his or her control. This small float is known as the *petty cash*, and the person looking after it is the petty cashier.

5.3   Imprest System

Control is best exercised over the petty cashier and his float if the latter is kept on the *Imprest system*. This means that the float is a fixed amount which is initially drawn from the bank for the purpose or it may be part of the main cash balance. It would hardly be satisfactory to allow the petty cashier to authorise his own expenditure, so all expenditure should be authorised by a manager or other responsible person before it is paid. The petty cashier must always obtain a properly authorised voucher for every item of expenditure. At any point in time, therefore, the imprest petty cash float should be represented by the cash in hand plus vouchers.

Fig. 5.1 *Petty Cash Voucher*

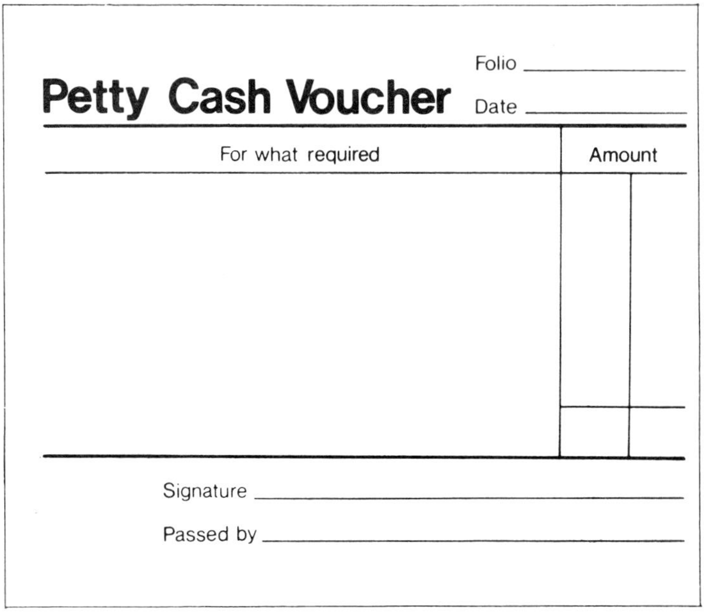

Petty Cash Voucher

Folio ____________

Date ____________

For what required	Amount	

Signature ____________________

Passed by ____________________

At regular intervals, the petty cashier should produce his petty cash float, vouchers and petty cash book to the main cashier who should check the float, vouchers and book before giving the petty cashier more cash to make his float up to the full amount again. You will realise that the amount of this reimbursement should equal the total of the vouchers for cash spent.

5.4 Petty Cash Book

This book is similar to the cash book and contains the petty cash account; it is therefore part of the double-entry system. Amounts given to the petty cashier for his float are credited in the main cash book and debited in the petty cash book. Petty cash expenditure is credited in the petty cash book and debited to the appropriate ledger accounts.

Petty cash expenses are relatively small amounts, may be numerous, and generally represent a large variety of items such as staff fares, subsistence (staff expenses when away on business), motor expenses, stationery, postages, cleaning expenses, customer entertainment, etc. Posting these individually to the nominal ledger accounts can be time-consuming and result in overloading those accounts with entries. We require some means of reducing the work by arriving at periodic totals of each type of expenditure which can be posted to the ledger accounts. The answer is to use an analysed petty cash book.

5.5   Analysed Petty Cash Book

The analysis of petty cash expenditure depends entirely upon the requirement of each individual business, and that will decide the form of petty cash book used. Our example could be typical of many businesses and serves to show the double-entry principles involved, which are the same for all businesses.

Points to Note

(i) Only one date column and one detail column are required; these serve for debit and credit entries.

(ii) The main cash book folio is entered against the amounts received for the petty cash float.

(iii) The petty cash vouchers are serially numbered and the numbers entered in the petty cash book next to the Total column. The vouchers should be filed in the same order to support the entries.

(iv) Each payment is entered in the Total column and extended into one or more of the analysis columns as appropriate.

Fig. 5.2

Worked Example of a Petty Cash Book

You are the petty cashier for your firm. On 1 January the cashier gives you a float of £100. You make the following payments in January:

2 S. Peters £10 (Fares £8; lunch while away on business £2).
4 Cleaning expenses £3.
5 J. Kirk, office messenger, fares £5.
6 Alpha Garage, petrol £8.
8 Purchase of postage stamps £5.
9 A. Roberts (lunch while away on business) £4.
11 Cleaning expenses £3.
    Refund to P. Smith (customer) £6.
12 Purchase of stationery £2.
14. Alpha Garage, petrol £7.
19 S. Peters £12. (Fares £10; lunch while away on business £2).
23 A. Roberts, fares £5.
27 Sundry telephone calls £4.

Enter these transactions in an analysed petty cash book and show the reimbursement of cash spent.

Page 1

Analysed Petty Cash Book

Cash Received £	Folio	Date	Details	Voucher No	Total £	Sub- sistence £	Staff Travelling Expenses £	Cleaning £	Motor Expenses £	Postages and Stationery £	Folio	Ledger £
100	CB5	Jan 1	Cash									
		2	S. Peters	1	10	2	8					
		4	Cleaning	2	3			3				
		5	J. Kirk	3	5		5					
		6	Alpha Garage	4	8				8			
		8	Postage Stamps	5	5					5		
		9	A. Roberts	6	4	4						
		11	Cleaning	7	3			3				
			Refund to P. Smith (cash customer)	8	6						NL32	6
		12	Stationery	9	2					2		
		14	Alpha Garage	10	7				7			
		19	S. Peters	11	12	2	10					
		23	A. Roberts	12	5		5					
		27	Telephone calls	13	4						NL18	4
					74	8	28	6	15	7		10
		31	Balance	c/d	26	NL5	NL6	NL27	NL36	NL37		
100					100							
26	b/d	Feb 1	Balance									
74	CB11		Cash									

Page 5

Cash Book

				£		19–			£
						Jan 1	Petty Cash	PCB1	100
						Feb 1	Petty Cash	PCB1	74

Nominal Ledger

Page 5

Subsistence

19–			£				£
Jan 31	Petty Cash	PCB1	8				

Page 6

Staff Travelling Expenses

19–			£				£
Jan 31	Petty Cash	PCB1	28				

Page 18

Telephones

19–			£				£
Jan 31	Petty Cash	PCB1	4				

Page 27

Cleaning

19– Jan 31	Petty Cash	PCB1	£ 6				£

Page 32

Sales Returns

19– Jan 31	Petty Cash	PCB1	£ 6				£

Page 36

Motor Expenses

19– Jan 31	Petty Cash	PCB1	£ 15				£

Page 37

Postage and Stationery

19– Jan 31	Petty Cash	PCB1	£ 7				£

(v) Provision is made for items which do not occur regularly or are of an unusual nature by the ledger column. This column must have a folio column next to it.

(vi) At the end of each week or month, the petty cash book columns are totalled. It is essential to prove the accuracy of the entries at this stage by:

    (a) making sure the Total column equals the sum of the totals of the analysis columns (ie £74 = £(8 + 28 + 6 + 15 + 7 + 10).

    (b) the petty cash vouchers add up to the amount of the Total column.

> **Remember**
>
> The Analysis columns must add up to the Total column

(vii) Insert the balance in the Total column to make it add up to the original float and carry it down into the Cash Received column. Check that this balance is equal to the actual cash in hand.

(viii) Enter the amount received from the cashier to restore the float to its full amount in the Cash Received column.

(ix) Post the totals of the analysis columns (but not that of the ledger column) to the debit of the appropriate ledger accounts and write the nominal ledger folios under each column.

(x) Post the items in the ledger column to the debit of the appropriate accounts, entering the appropriate ledger folios in the folio column.

Remember

Post the totals of the Analysis columns to the debit of the nominal ledger accounts: but post the items in the Ledger column individually

---

5.6 Examination Hints

(i) Analysed petty cash books and the imprest system are common examination topics. Make sure you understand (a) the method of completing the double-entry from the petty cash book and can explain what is meant by imprest systems, (b) how such floats are represented at any one time by the cash in hand and the expenditure vouchers, and (c) the checks that may be made upon the accuracy of the petty cash book.

(ii) Read the question carefully for any instructions as to the columns required in the petty cash book and follow them carefully. If the question does not contain any such instructions, use your judgment to produce what you think would be a useful analysis.

5.7 What Should I Have Learned in this Chapter?

(i) The Imprest system is a method of exercising control over the petty cash float.

(ii) The petty cashier should be able to account for the imprest float at any time by producing the balance of cash in hand plus authorised petty cash vouchers for expenditure.

(iii) A petty cash book is part of the double-entry book-keeping system.

(iv) An analysed petty cash book enables the petty cashier to analyse expenditure as he enters it in the book and avoids much unnecessary posting of detail to ledger accounts.

Exercises

1   Evans & Co have decided to introduce into their accounting system an analysed petty cash book which will be kept on the Imprest System. You are asked to provide a specimen ruling for this book, with four analysis columns, and to give a list of instructions for the person who will be the petty cashier. (Oxford 'O' level 1984).

2   (a) For what purposes does a business keep a petty cash book?
(b) Explain the Imprest System of keeping petty cash.
(c) Explain how the petty cash book would be balanced at the end of the accounting period. Where would the petty cash book closing balance be shown at the end of the financial year?
(d) Explain what happens to the total of the postage and stationery column.
(e) Explain what happens to the items in the column headed Ledger Accounts.
(AEB 'O' level 1983)

3   (i) Explain how the Imprest System of controlling petty cash operates.
(ii) Enter the following items under suitable headings under the Imprest System, for the month of May. Show the balance in hand and the amount reimbursed to the petty cashier at the end of May and the balance brought down at the beginning of June.

			£
May	1	Cash balance (Imprest) in hand	80.00
	3	Postage stamps	10.00
	8	Stationery	3.50
	10	Fares	2.20
	16	Window cleaning	6.80
	18	Tips to delivery men	2.60
	20	Postage stamps	10.00
	26	Fares	5.80
	28	Stationery	12.00

(Welsh Joint Education Committee 'O' level 1983)

4 Walter Holmes is a sole trader who keeps his petty cash on the Imprest System, the Imprest amount being £40. For the month of December 1983 his petty cash transactions were as follows:

1983			£
December	1	Petty cash in hand	3.47
	1	Petty cash restored to the Imprest amount	
	4	Stamps purchased	3.96
	8	Envelopes purchased	4.15
	10	Paid wages	6.30
	14	Paid to Alfred Jackson, a creditor	5.60
	19	Stamps purchased	4.29
	21	Typing paper purchased	3.70
	24	Paid wages	7.10
	31	Stamps purchased	2.00

Required:
   (i) Draw up the Petty Cash Book of Walter Holmes and enter the above transactions in it.
   (ii) Balance the Petty Cash Book as at the close of business on 31 December 1983 and carry down the balance.
   (iii) Give the entry necessary on 1 January 1984 to restore the petty cash to the Imprest amount.

Note: Your analysis columns should be postages, stationery, wages and ledger. (LCCI 1984)

5 The following is a summary of the petty cash transactions of Jockfield Ltd. for May 1982.

May 1 Received from cashier £300 as petty cash float

			£
	2	Postages	18
	3	Travelling	12
	4	Cleaning	15
	7	Petrol for delivery van	22
	8	Travelling	25
	9	Stationery	17
	11	Cleaning	18
	14	Postage	5
	15	Travelling	8
	18	Stationery	9
	18	Cleaning	23
	20	Postage	13

		£
24	Delivery van 5,000 mile service	43
26	Petrol	18
27	Cleaning	21
29	Postage	5
30	Petrol	14

You are required to:

(1) Rule up a suitable petty cash book with analysis columns for expenditure on cleaning, motor expenses, postage, stationery, travelling.

(2) Enter the month's transactions.

(3) Enter the receipt of the amount necessary to restore the Imprest and carry down the balance for the commencement of the following month.

(4) State how the double-entry for the expenditure is completed. (AAT 1982)

Chapter 6

Bills of Exchange

6.1 What Topics are Covered in this Chapter?

We study the nature and function of bills of exchange and how they are used. We learn how bills of exchange are recorded in ledger accounts.

6.2 Credit Transactions and Bills of Exchange

In Chapter 2 we discussed the reason for buying and selling goods on credit (see Section **2.2**). A seller of goods on credit may need the money from a sale before his customer is due to pay. He may, if he wishes, send the customer a written request requiring that customer to pay him (or some other person) the amount of the debt, either now or at a certain future date. The document containing this request is called a *bill of exchange.* Generally the time

Fig. 6.1

Bill of Exchange

Alfred Regis owes John Bognor £1,000 for goods received. Bognor draws a bill of exchange on Regis.

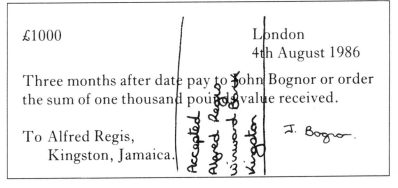

expressed for payment will be sufficiently in the future to allow the customer the agreed period of credit. The customer, on receiving the bill, should *accept* it by signing his name across it. He may add the name and address of his bank to show where the bill should be presented at maturity (when it is due for payment) and this is called *domiciling* the bill; otherwise the bill should be presented for payment at the customer's normal place of business. Having accepted the bill, the customer returns it to the seller. The seller now has a *bill receivable* which he may keep until maturity but, if he needs the money earlier, he can discount the bill with his bank (see Section **6.3**) or negotiate it for money to somebody else.

To the acceptor of a bill, it is a *bill payable*.

Bills of exchange are now used mainly in overseas trade.

Points to Note

   (i) The amount is shown in words and figures.

  (ii) The bill is payable three months after date, ie 4 November 1986.

 (iii) The money is to be paid to Bognor or, if he has passed the bill to somebody else in the meantime, to his order.

 (iv) The words *value received* indicate that Regis is a debtor to Bognor for the amount, and this is confirmed by Regis when he accepts the bill.

  (v) Regis has *accepted* the bill by writing accepted and signing his name across it.

 (vi) Regis has *domiciled* the bill by adding the name and address of his bank to the crossing; that is where it should be presented for payment on 4 November.

(vii) Bognor is the drawer of the bill and Regis was the *drawee*; when Regis accepted it, he became the *acceptor*.

6.3   Discounting Bills

If, in our example, Bognor keeps the bill until it is due for payment, he will not get his money until 4 November. However, he presumably drew the bill of exchange on Regis because he needed the money before then. He can pay the bill into his bank as though it were a cheque. Indeed, a cheque is a bill of exchange drawn on a bank and payable on demand. The bank will not be able to collect the amount of the bill from Regis until 4 November but will nevertheless credit the bill to Bognor's account now. It is in effect lending the money to Bognor for three months. When banks lend money they charge interest. In the case of bills of exchange the charge is *discount* which is deducted from the proceeds of the bill before they are credited to Bognor's account. The discount is calculated on the amount of the bill. Suppose the discount rate is 10% p.a., the discount on a bill for £1,000 with three months to run would be £25, leaving £975 to be credited to Bognor's account. (You must not confuse discount and interest; a loan of £975 producing interest of £25 in three months would bear interest at the rate of 10.256% p.a.)

Instead of discounting the bill with his bank, Bognor could discount it with a firm who specialise in discounting bills; such firms are known as discount houses.

6.4 Transfer and Endorsement

Bognor may owe £1,000 to somebody else; he can transfer the bill which has been accepted by Regis to that other person instead of discounting it. Had the bill been made payable to 'John Bognor or bearer', Bognor could have given it to his creditor without doing anything more to it; but the bill has been made payable to 'John Bognor or order' and he must endorse it on the back before paying it into his bank or giving it to somebody else.

6.5 Dishonour

If, on 4 November, Regis or his bank fail to pay the money to the person presenting it for payment, he is said to dishonour it. The person who holds the bill may require further evidence to show that the bill has been dishonoured before taking further action to recover the money from Regis. He can do this by giving it to a Notary Public for representation, who, when the bill has been dishonoured the second time, notes that fact on the bill with the addition of the amount of his charges. Since these charges have been incurred as a result of Regis' failure to honour the bill, they will be added to the amount that he now owes Bognor.

6.6   Worked Example of Accounting Entries

Event	In drawer's books	In drawee's/ acceptor's books	With
(i) Bill drawn	None	None	
(ii) Bill accepted	Dr Bills receivable	Dr Drawer	Amount of Bill
	Cr Acceptor	Cr Bills Payable	Amount of Bill
(iii) Bill held until	Dr Bank	Dr Bills Payable	Amount of Bill
maturity	Cr Bills receivable	Cr Bank	Amount of Bill
(iv) Bill discounted	Dr Bank	None	Amount of Bill
before maturity	Cr Bills receivable	None	Amount of Bill
	Dr Discounts	None	Discount
	Cr Bank	None	Discount
OR	Dr Bank	None	Amount received
	Dr Discounts	None	Discount
	Cr Bills receivable	None	Amount of Bill
(v) Bill	Dr Acceptor's	Dr Bills Payable	Amount of Bill
dishonoured before	account		
being discounted	Cr Bills receivable	Cr Drawer	Amount of Bill
(vi) Bill	Dr Acceptor	As (v) above	Amount of Bill
dishonoured after	Cr Bank		
being discounted			

6.7   Examination Hint

Our table of book-keeping entries in Section 6.6 above looks more complicated than it is, but you should not attempt to learn it parrot-fashion. Common sense should enable you to work out the entries required in any question on bills of exchange provided you take the time to think carefully and clearly.

Remember

The rules of double entry

Debit the account that receives and credit the account that gives. There must be a debit for every credit and vice versa

---

6.8   What Should I Have Learned in this Chapter?

(i) Bills of exchange enable a creditor to obtain his money early and still allow his customer a period of credit.

(ii) A bill of exchange is drawn by a creditor who is called the drawer. The customer is the drawee and when he accepts the bill, he becomes the acceptor.

(iii) A bill receivable may be held until maturity (due date), discounted (usually with a bank) or transferred to a third party.

(iv) A dishonoured bill is one that is not paid on maturity by the acceptor or his banker.

Exercises

In all the multiple-choice questions the student is required to select the correct answer from the lettered alternatives.

1 On 1 October Mr Singh draws a bill of exchange on Mr Koh for £1,500 for three months and discounts it on the same day with his bank. The net amount credited in his bank statement was £1,455. The annual rate of discount is:
   (a) 3.09%
   (b) 12.37%
   (c) 12%
   (d) 3%

2 On 1 March Mr Bradman accepted a bill of exchange for £1,000 payable in two months, which had been drawn on him by Mr Larwood. On 1 April Mr Bradman retired the bill, paying his debt by cheque. Mr Larwood allowed Mr Bradman discount at the rate of 7½% p.a. in consideration of early payment. The amount Mr Bradman paid by cheque was:
   (a) £987.50
   (b) £993.75
   (c) £930.23
   (d) £994.19

3 On 31 March 1984 Harold Ives, a sole trader, had the following balances in his ledger:
   W. Adams   £470   Dr balance
   F. Brown   £260   Dr balance
   M. Church   £339   Cr balance
   During the month of April 1984 Ives had the following transactions:
   April 1 Drew a bill of exchange for £400 on W. Adams at one month after date (Bill No 1). This was accepted by Adams.
         10 Discounted Bill No 1 with his bank. Bank interest £20.

    17 Church drew a bill of exchange on Ives at one month after date (Bill No 2). This was for £300 and was in full settlement of the amount due by Ives to Church. The bill was accepted by Ives.

    24 Drew a bill of exchange for £260 on Brown at one month after date (Bill No 3). This was accepted by Brown.

Bills 1 and 2 were paid on the due dates but Bill No 3 was dishonoured when presented for payment.

Required:

(a) Draw up the ledger accounts of Adams, Brown and Church as they should appear in Ives' ledger to record all the above transactions.

(b) Draw up the appropriate Cash Book entries.

(c) Draw up the Bills Receivable Account and Bills Payable Account as they should appear in Ives' ledger.

(LCCI Elem)

Chapter 7

The Trial Balance

7.1 What Topics are Covered in this Chapter?

The nature and purpose of trial balances and how they are produced. We learn what types of error do not affect trial balances.

7.2 What a Trial Balance Is and What It Does

This book is about double-entry book-keeping. A single entry system would consist of personal accounts only; with such a system we would record transactions only as they affect the debtors and creditors of the business. Double-entry book-keeping not only does that but it also records transactions as they affect the business, that is, the acquisition of assets, income, gains, expenses and losses. Because of this we are able to produce financial statements about the business, showing the profits or losses as a result of carrying on the business, and the financial state of the business at any particular time. We shall come to these in Chapters 9 and 10. In Chapter 12 we shall see that not all the information necessary to produce correct statements about the business has been included in the accounts and further adjustments to some accounts may be necessary to enable us to produce reliable statements. Meanwhile, our accounting information is scattered over numerous accounts in various ledgers and the cash book and this is not the most convenient situation in which to produce financial statements of any kind.

The solution to these problems is to make a summary of all the accounts. The summary does not include all the individual debit and credit entries in the accounts, otherwise it would not be a summary! Instead it lists the balances on the accounts, using two columns, one for debit balances, the other for credit balances. It follows from this that accounts with no balance are not included in the trial balance. To illustrate the method, here is a trial balance extracted from the books of Mr Biswas as given in Figs. 1.6–1.8.

Fig. 7.1

Mr A. Biswas Trial Balance at 14 July 19-

	Fo.	Dr. £	Cr. £
Bank	CB1	4,515	
Cash	CB1	200	
A. Biswas—capital	L1		6,000
Rent	L2	300	
Purchases	L3	1,120	
Sales	L4		670
Shop fittings	L5	270	
Stationery	L7	75	
Insurance	L8	90	
A. Biswas—drawings	L9	100	
		£6,670	£6,670

Points to Note

(i) The trial balance is properly headed with the name of the business or its owner and described as 'Trial balance at (date)'.

(ii) The correct layout of the trial balance, showing the name of each account, the cash book or ledger folio, and the balances in two adjacent columns, according to whether they are debit or credit balances.

(iii) The cash columns are totalled and the totals should be the same. (See p. 81.)

(iv) A trial balance is not part of the double entry system; it is only a list of balances on the accounts.

Remember the rules of double-entry; every debit must have a corresponding credit, and every credit a corresponding debit. It follows that:

(a) If we have made all our postings correctly the total of the debit entries should equal the total of the credit entries.

(b) It follows from (a) that if we have balanced the accounts correctly the total of the debit balances must equal the total of the credit balances.

(c) If we have taken proper care in copying all balances into the correct columns of the trial balance, the two columns of that should also agree in total.

If the trial balance does agree, we shall have succeeded in summarising our accounts in a convenient form and in proving that our postings in the accounts are arithmetically correct but that does not necessarily mean that each account is in itself correct. We say that the accounts are *prima facie* correct, i.e. they appear at first sight to be correct. They may still contain some errors which do not prevent the trial balance from balancing, or agreeing, as we usually describe it. We shall look at these types of errors in **Section 7.3**.

Our example above did not contain any debtors or creditors but, had it done so, as trial balances usually do, and the debtors and creditors had been more than one or two in number, we could have shown them as total amounts in each case.

Now use your answer to Exercise 5 of Chapter 2 to compile a trial balance from those accounts as at 16 July 19—.

Compare your trial balance with Fig. 7.2.

Fig.7.2

Trial Balance as at 16 July 19-

	Dr. £	Cr. £
Capital		6,000
Sales		3,573
Sales returns	235	
Trade creditors		3,290
Bank	5,775	
Cash	300	
Purchases	4,220	
Purchases returns		265
Trade debtors	2,598	
	£13,128	£13,128

Trade creditors: Williams £1,000; Stephens £1,115; Tong £1,175.
Trade debtors: Briers £518; Goodyear £600; Cannock £1,120; Thorne £360.

7.3 Errors Not Affecting the Trial Balance

If the trial balance is only *prima facie* evidence that the book-keeping has been performed correctly, we need to know what errors may be made without affecting the trial balance. These are any errors which do not contradict the rules of double-entry which are that every debit entry must have a corresponding credit entry, and every credit entry must have a corresponding debit entry so that the total of the debit entries equals the total of the credit entries.

There are six types of error which do not affect the trial balance and you should learn them and make sure you fully understand them.

(i) *Errors of omission*

Any transaction which is completely omitted from the books, e.g. a purchase invoice omitted from the Purchases Day Book will not be posted to the credit of the supplier's account in the Purchases Ledger, nor as part of the period total of the Day Book to the debit of Purchases account in the nominal ledger. Both sides of the trial balance will be short by the same amount.

(ii) *Errors of commission*

An amount posted to a wrong account but to one of the same type as the correct account, e.g. a payment of £10 credited in the cash book and debited to J. Webb's account instead of to D. Webb's account. Both accounts are personal accounts in the Purchases Ledger; the double-entry has been completed.

(iii) *Errors of principle*

An amount posted not merely to the wrong account but to one of the wrong type, e.g. purchase of a motor van posted to motor expenses (nominal account) instead of motor van account (real account). Capital expenditure has been wrongly treated as revenue expenditure, but the double-entry is complete.

(iv) *Errors of original entry*

For example, an invoice for goods sold to D. Elliott for £105 entered in the Sales Day Book as £150. Elliott's account will be debited with £150 and the same amount included in the period total of the Sales Day Book credited to Sales account. Both Elliott's and the Sales accounts are overstated by the same amount, £45.

(v) *Complete reversal of entries*

The correct amount is posted to the proper accounts, but to the wrong side in each case, e.g. goods returned by Jones, a customer, are debited to his account and credited to the Sales Returns account. The debit balance on Jones' account will be too big and that on the Sales Returns account (also a debit balance) will be too small.

(vi) *Compensating errors*

One error is cancelled out by another of the same magnitude, e.g. Salaries account is overcast by £100. The Purchases Day Book is undercast by £100. The debit balance on the Salaries account is £100 too much; £100 too little has been transferred from the Purchases Day Book to the debit of Purchases account so that the debit balance on that account is £100 too little. The errors cancel each other out and the total of the debit column of the trial balance will still be correct.

7.4 Examination Hints

(i) Take care over your work, write your figures clearly and keep them underneath each other in columns. Do not alter wrong figures; cross them through and rewrite the correct figures above them. Check your additions; double check figures you copy from the question paper or other parts of your answer. It is better to avoid errors than to have to spend time looking for them. 'Prevention is better than cure.'

(ii) If a trial balance fails to agree, do not panic. They often do not agree first time in real life as the examiner well knows. Carefully work through the procedure for finding errors in the time available. If you cannot find your error in the time allowed for the question, leave it and go on to the next. You must attempt all questions in the time if you are going to pass.

(iii) Learn thoroughly the types of error that do not affect the trial balance and make sure you can recognise them and can give examples of them.

7.5 What Should I Have Learned in this Chapter?

(i) A trial balance is *prima facie* evidence that accounts are arithmetically correct.

(ii) A trial balance is a list of balances; it is not part of the double-entry.

(iii) To find a difference on a trial balance, begin by checking the additions of the trial balance, then the extraction of balances from the accounts, followed by the correctness of the balances themselves and finally if necessary the postings to the accounts.

(iv) The six types of error that do not affect trial balances are: Commission. Omission. Principle. Compensating. Original entry. Reversal of entries.

Exercises

1   Which one of the following items in a trial balance is incorrect?
(a) Discounts allowed as a debit balance.
(b) Discounts received as a credit balance.
(c) Carriage outwards as a debit balance.
(d) Carriage inwards as a credit balance.

2   Which of the following errors should be revealed by a trial balance?
(a) A credit sale entered in B. Cannock's account instead of C. Bannock's account.
(b) A sales invoice not entered in the Sales Day Book.
(c) A purchase of goods on credit entered in the personal account only.
(d) Motor repairs debited to Motor Vehicles (capital) account.

3   (a) Define a trial balance and state what you understand to be its basic purposes.
(b) Give examples of six different types of errors which would not affect a trial balance.

4   The business transactions of T. Cornish during April 1986 were as follows:

April   1   Commenced business with the transfer of £8,000 to the firm's bank account.
2   Bought goods on credit from H. Duckworth £280; E. Locket £330.
3   Paid £350 by cheque for general expenses.
4   Bought goods and paid by cheque £220.
5   Sold goods on credit to E. McBay £510.
7   Returned goods to H. Duckworth £50.
8   Cash sales paid into bank £980.
10   Bought display fittings £412 paying by cheque.
11   Paid by cheque general expenses £196.
14   T. Cornish paid a further sum of £2,500 into the bank account.
19   Sold goods to E. McBay £175.
21   Paid E. Locket £200 on account by cheque.

22 Cheque for £25 was received following the return to the suppliers of some of the fittings purchased on 10 April found to be faulty.

25 Received cheque from E. McBay for the goods sold to him on 5 April.

Required:

(a) Enter the above transactions in the ledger of T. Cornish. The bank account is kept in the ledger.

(b) Balance the accounts and extract a trial balance as on 30 April 1986.

Note: Day Books are *not* required.

(RSA Stage 1 April 1986)

5   Mr J. Ockey commenced trading as a wholesale stationer on 1 May 1984 with a capital of £5,000 with which he opened a bank account for the business.

During May the following transactions took place:

May   1 Bought shop fittings and fixtures on credit from Store Fitments Ltd. for £2,000.

2 Purchased goods on credit from Abel £650.

4 Sold goods on credit to Bruce £700.

9 Purchased goods on credit from Green £300.

11 Sold goods on credit to Hill £580.

13 Cash sales paid intact into bank £200.

16 Received cheque from Bruce in settlement of his account.

17 Purchased goods on credit from Kaye £800.

18 Sold goods on credit to Nailor £360.

19 Sent cheque to Abel in settlement of his account.

20 Paid rent by cheque £200.

21 Paid delivery expenses by cheque £50.

24 Received cheque from Hill £200 on account.

30 Drew cheques for personal expenses £200 and assistant's wages, £320.

31 Settled the accounts of Green and Store Fitments Ltd.

You are required to:

(a) Record the foregoing in appropriate books of original entry.

(b) Post the entries to the ledger accounts.

(c) Balance the ledger accounts where necessary.

(d) Extract a trial balance at 31 May 1984.

(AAT June 1984)

6   The following cases refer to different trial balances. In each case an error has been made and the trial balance does not agree. The error in each case arises from one transaction only and all additions and subtractions are correct.

   You are asked to state what you think caused the error in each case.

   (i) Trial balance totals: Dr £2,006   Cr £2,036
      There is a transaction of £15.
   (ii) Trial balance totals: Dr £3,200   Cr £3,020
      There is a transaction of £200.
   (iii) Trial balance totals: Dr £1,600   Cr £2,150
      There is a transaction of £550.
   (iv) Trial balance totals: Dr £2,100   Cr £2,170
      There is a transaction of £35.

(Northern Ireland 'O' level 1982)

7   The following trial balance relating to Len Shackleton's business failed to agree. One of the major causes of this disagreement appeared to be the failure to post the following day book totals to the ledger: purchases £1,562; sales £2,941; returns inward £98; and returns outward £46. In addition the petty cash balance of £18 was omitted and some of the items inadvertently placed on the wrong side of the trial balance.

Trial Balance of Len Shackleton as at 31 May 1983

	Debit £	Credit £
Premises	25,000	
Purchases	1,398	
Sales		3,975
Bank overdraft	621	
Discount allowed		45
Rates	91	
Lighting and heating	96	
Bank charges	14	
Stock at 1 May 1983	823	
Debtors	960	
Creditors		840
Capital		21,682
	29,003	26,542

Required:
(a) Preparation of a corrected trial balance as at 31 May 1983.
(b) (i) Two types of error which would not prevent trial balance totals from agreeing.
    (ii) An explanation, using an example in each case, of why the trial balance totals would still be in agreement despite the existence of such errors.

(AEB 'O' level November 1984)

Chapter 8

The Journal

8.1 What Topics are Covered in this Chapter?

The journal, the remaining book of prime entry, is introduced and its form and uses are demonstrated. The calculation of capital from opening journal entries introduces the accounting equation, a most important topic of great relevance to the remainder of your accounting studies.

8.2 The Journal

One book remains to be introduced. It is found in every accounting system and features as an important topic in nearly every examination. It is *the journal*.

The journal is the book of prime entry for all ledger postings for which there is no other day book. Such entries relate to:
  (i) correction of errors
 (ii) purchases and sales of fixed assets on credit
(iii) recording the opening entries in a new set of books
(iv) making transfers between accounts.

8.3 Form of Journal

Memorise the form of journal ruling and be sure to reproduce it exactly when required.

Fig. 8.1   *Journal layout*

Date		Fo.	Dr. £	Cr. £
Date	Account to be debited Account to be credited Narrative			
Date	Account to be debited Account to be credited Narrative			

Points to Note

- (i) All entries should be dated.
- (ii) The name of the account to be debited is always entered before the name of the account to be credited. (Many students put these the wrong way round but the correct order is important.) Only one column is provided for the account names.
- (iii) The name of the account to be credited should be inset a little to the right, under the name of the account being debited.
- (iv) A folio column is an essential part of the ruling to record the ledger folios of the postings.
- (v) Separate cash columns are provided for debits and credits; these are placed next to each other.
- (vi) Every entry must have a brief narrative which provides a concise description of the entry. Reference should be made to whatever documentary evidence exists to support the entry, e.g. invoices, management instructions, correspondence, minute books, etc.

8.4 Examples of Journal Entries

Fig. 8.2

Journal entry to correct error

19–			Dr. £	Cr. £
Apr 1	L. Green	SL14	100	
	D. Green	SL12		100
	Correction of sale debited to			
	D. Green instead of L. Green.			
	Sales Invoice No. 1003			

Points to Note

- (i) The incorrect entry will mean that D. Green's account has been debited with £100.
- (ii) To correct the error, D. Green's account will need to be credited with £100.
- (iii) At the same time, a debit to L. Green's account will ensure that the books are now correct.

Fig. 8.3

*Journal to record purchase and
sale of fixed assets on credit*

		Dr. £	Cr. £
Oct 1	Motor Vans	5,000	
	A. Morris		5,000
	Purchase of motor van regd. no. —		
	from A. Morris. Capital invoice no.		
Oct 4	P. Winchester	200	
	Machinery		200
	Sale of machine no. 1234		
	P. Winchester, Asset Sales		
	invoice no. 987		

Fig. 8.4

*Journal recording opening entries
in a new set of books*

Ms Taylor has been in business as a florist for many years but she has not maintained any accounting records. She has now asked you to write up books of account for her. At 1 January she had a stock of florist's sundries worth £40; shop fixtures and fittings which cost £500. Apart from cash of £10 her bank statements showed that she had £300 in the business account. Unpaid invoices from suppliers totalled £160 and she was owed £75 by customers.

		Dr. £	Cr. £
Jan 1	Florist sundries — stock	40	
	Fixtures and fittings	500	
	Cash in hand	10	
	Bank	300	
	Debtors	75	
	Creditors		160
	Capital — Ms Taylor		765
		925	925
	Assets and liabilities of Ms Taylor's		
	business at 1 January 19– per		
	schedule produced by Ms Taylor		

Points to Note

  (i) This is an example of a composite journal entry which may be required on occasions. Care must be taken to ensure that both sides add up to the same amount.

  (ii) Cash at bank and in hand are journalised in this instance although the cash book itself is a book of prime entry.

(iii) Ms Taylor's capital invested in the business is represented by the amount required to be inserted in the credit column of the journal to make both columns add to the same amount.

8.5 Examination Hints

  (i) You must be prepared to draft journal entries in correct form with suitable narratives.

  (ii) Examiners often require answers to be shown in the form of journal entries rather than as ledger accounts. Take special care to note whether or not:

    (a) Narratives are required; examiners sometimes dispense with these to save time.

    (b) Cash book items are to be included as journal entries. Normally they should not be, but examiners often require them to be journalised to test your knowledge of double-entry principles.

(iii) When in difficulty do rough T accounts on a separate sheet of paper, pencilling in the debit and credit entries as required. When you are satisfied that the entries look correct, you can draft the necessary journal entries. (Always attach all working papers to your answers.)

(iv) Make sure you understand the accounting equation and can explain it. Be prepared to apply it whenever necessary.

8.6 What Should I Have Learned in this Chapter?

The journal is the book of prime entry for all transactions for which there is no other book of prime entry.

Exercises

1 Which of the following books is part of the double-entry system?

  (a) Purchases Day Book

  (b) Sales Day Book

(c) Journal

(d) Cash Book.

2   State in which subsidiary book of account you would make the original entry for each of the following:

(a) purchase of goods for re-sale on credit

(b) correction of error in posting a sales invoice to the wrong personal account

(c) purchase on credit of typewriter for office use

(d) an allowance made for overcharging a debtor

(e) cash discount allowed.

3   During the month of April, C. Williams & Co had the following transactions:

April   5   Purchase of goods for resale costing £500 posted from Purchases Day Book to credit of R. Doe's account instead of D. Roe's account. Error corrected.

10   Purchased office equipment from Broadwood Office Furniture (Putney) Ltd on credit £1,000.

15   Sold motor van on credit to D. Lowe £1,400.

20   Informed by L. Walker that a discount of £20 we had taken on a payment to him was not allowed.

Prepare the necessary journal entries to record the above transactions with appropriate narratives.

4   M. Michael has been in business for some years but has not kept accounting records. He has asked you to act as his book-keeper and, at 1 April last, his business consisted of: Motor van £3,000; stock of goods for resale £1,600; equipment £300, and cash in hand £40. His bank statements showed an overdraft of £150. Unpaid invoices from suppliers amounted to £200. Amounts owing to Michael by customers £75.

Show the journal entries required to open the books at 1 April.

5   The following balances have been extracted from Sarah Brown's books on 31 December 19—:

	£
Purchases	9,000
Drawings	2,100
Sales	1,600
Purchases returns	500
Sales returns	400

	£
Premises	10,000
Sundry debtors	2,800
Sundry creditors	1,700
Discounts received	750
Discounts allowed	375
Cash in hand	25
Cash at bank (Dr)	1,400
Equipment	1,600

The following errors have been made in the ledger postings before the above balances were extracted:

(i) Goods purchased for Sarah Brown's private use in the sum of £140 have been debited to Purchases.

(ii) Goods returned by a customer treated as Purchases £100.

(iii) Sale of equipment treated as Sales £200.

Required:

(a) Draft journal entries in proper form to correct the errors (i)–(iii) above.

(b) Prepare a trial balance from the corrected figures, showing the amount of Sarah Brown's capital.

Chapter 9
Trading and Profit and Loss Accounts of Sole Traders

9.1 What Topics are Covered in this Chapter?

The calculation of gross profit in the Trading account and the calculation of net profit in the Profit and Loss account.

9.2 The Trading Account

The purpose of the Trading account is to show the gross profit on the sale of goods. Gross profit is the difference between the sale proceeds of goods and what those goods cost the seller to buy, or cost of sales. The cost of sales for this purpose includes the amount which has been debited for them to the Purchases account plus the cost of getting them to the place of sale, which is usually the seller's premises, i.e. the carriage inwards on those goods.

The balance on the Purchases account, however, is the cost of all goods which have been purchased during the period but almost certainly, not all those goods will have been sold. Some of them will still be in stock at the end of the period. We call that the *closing stock*. The goods which were available for sale consist of goods in stock at the beginning of the period plus the purchases made in the period. The goods sold in the period were those which were available for sale less the closing stock.

In order to arrive at the closing stock figure, all the unsold items at the end of the period must be counted and listed, and priced at cost, or *net realisable value* if that is less. We shall explain what we mean by net realisable value later in Chapter 15.

We must open a Stock account in the ledger in which to record the amount of closing stock, and the entries will become clear in what follows.

9.3 Preparing a Trading Account

(i) The first step is to transfer the balance on the Sales account to the Trading account:
Dr Sales a/c; Cr Trading a/c

(ii) Next, debit the Trading account with the cost of goods sold, starting with the opening stock.
Dr Trading a/c; Cr Stock a/c.
The opening stock is obviously the same as the closing stock of the previous period; in the first year of trading of course, there will be no opening stock.

(iii) The balance on Purchases account is then transferred to the Trading a/c and added to the opening stock figure.
Dr Trading a/c; Cr Purchases a/c.

(iv) Transfer any balance on Carriage Inwards account to Trading account.
Dr Trading a/c; Cr Carriage Inwards a/c.
Add the carriage to the total arrived at in (iii) above. This gives the total cost of goods available for sale.

(v) Deduct the value of closing stock from the cost of goods available for sale. Any item deducted from the debit side of an account is, in effect, credited to the account. Deducting closing stock from the debit side of the Trading account is therefore crediting it to that account. The corresponding double-entry will therefore be to the debit of Stock account:
Dr Stock a/c; Cr Trading a/c (by deduction from the debit side).
We have now arrived at the cost of sales.

(vi) The balance on the Trading account will be the difference between sales and cost of sales, i.e. gross profit, which is carried down to the Profit and Loss account.

Point to Note

The debit to Stock account for closing stock is the value of the current asset of closing stock which will be included in the balance sheet (see Chapter 10). When the opening stock is credited to the Stock account in the next period, it will balance off the Stock account.

9.4 Net Sales (Turnover) and Net Purchases

Goods which have been returned by customers are represented by a debit balance on the Sales Return account. This must be transferred to the Trading account, otherwise the sales and gross profit in that account will both be overstated.

Following the same reasoning that allows us to deduct closing stock on the debit side of the Trading account we may deduct the debit balance on the Sales Returns account from the sales credited in the Trading account. In this way, we show the net sales for the year. Net sales are known as *turnover*. Similarly we show the credit

Fig. 9.1

Preparation of Trading Account

The following balances are included in the trial balance of K. Smith at 31 December 19-8.

	Dr. £	Cr. £
Sales		21,000
Purchases	14,000	
Sales Returns	2,000	
Purchases Returns		1,500
Stock at 1.1.19-8	2,000	
Carriage Inwards	700	

Stock at 31 December 19-8: £3,000.

Journal entries (narratives not shown)

19-8		Dr. £	Dr. £
Dec 31	Sales	21,000	
	Trading a/c		21,000
	Trading a/c	2,000	
	Sales Returns		2,000
	Trading a/c	2,000	
	Stock		2,000
	Purchases Returns	1,500	
	Trading a/c		1,500
	Trading a/c	700	
	Carriage inwards		700
	Stock	3,000	
	Trading a/c		3,000
	Trading a/c	14,000	
	Purchases		14,000

K. Smith

Trading Account for the year ended 31 December 19-8

	£	£		£	£
Stock at Jan 1		2,000	Sales	21,000	
Purchases	14,000		*less* sales returns	2,000	
less purchases					19,000
returns	1,500				
		12,500			
Carriage inwards		700			
		15,200			
less stock Dec 31		3,000			
		12,200			
Gross profit c/d		6,800			
		19,000			19,000
			Gross profit b/d		6,800

balance on Purchases Returns account as a deduction from purchases in the Trading account to show the net cost of purchases. Goods which have been returned to suppliers must not be included in the cost of sales. See Fig. 9.1.

Point to Note

The order of items is most important. Sales returns must be deducted from sales; purchases returns must be deducted from purchases; carriage inwards, if any, must be debited in the account before closing stock is deducted.

9.5 Profit and Loss Account

The remaining nominal accounts in the ledger represent non-trading income, gains and profits of the business in the case of credit balances, e.g. rent, discount and interest receivable. Debit balances represent expenses and losses of the business and are known as *overheads*, e.g. salaries and wages, rent and rates payable, lighting, heating, cleaning and sundry office expenses. These must now be transferred to the profit and loss account so that we can calculate the net profit of the business from all its activities.

Fig. 9.2

Preparation of Trading, Profit and Loss Account

The following trial balance has been extracted from the ledger of K. Smith at 31 December 19-7.

	£	£	
Sales		21,000	T
Sales Returns	2,000		T
Stock at 1 January	2,000		T
Purchases	14,000		T
Purchase Returns		1,500	T
Rent Receivable		900	P
Discounts allowed	900		P
Discounts received		1,300	P
Carriage inwards	700		T
Carriage outwards	750		P
Salaries and wages	2,300		P
Bonus and commission	700		P
Rent	1,000		P
Rates	300		P
Telephone and postages	500		P
Sundry expenses	150		P
Interest on loan	350		P
Premises	10,000		B
Equipment	5,000		B
Motor vehicles	3,000		B
Trade debtors	1,700		B
Trade creditors		1,300	B
Loan—A. J. Cook		4,000	B
Drawings	2,550		B
Bank	2,000		B
Cash	100		B
Capital		20,000	B
	50,000	50,000	

At 31 December closing stock was valued at £3,000.
The loan from A. J. Cook is repayable in 19-9.

K. Smith

**Trading and Profit and Loss Account
for the year ended 31 December 19-7**

	£	£		£	£
Stock at Jan 1		2,000	Sales	21,000	
Purchases	14,000		*less* sales returns	2,000	
less purchases					19,000
returns	1,500				
		12,500			
Carriage inwards		700			
		15,200			
less stock Dec 31		3,000			
Cost of sales		12,200			
Gross profit					
carried down		6,800			
		19,000			19,000
Salaries and			Gross profit		
wages		2,300	brought down		6,800
Bonus and			Rent receivable		900
commission		700	Discounts		
Rent		1,000	received		1,300
Rates		300			
Telephone,					
postages		500			
Discounts allowed		900			
Carriage outwards		750			
Sundry expenses		150			
Interest on loan		350			
Net profit carried					
to capital					
account		2,050			
		9,000			9,000

Points to Note

(i) Trading and profit and loss accounts are prepared for the benefit of business owners (amongst others) and, within certain limits, will be prepared to suit their requirements and the types of business concerned. For example, a trading account will not be prepared for a business which is not buying and selling goods, e.g. solicitors, accountants, doctors and dentists. Only a profit and loss account will be prepared in these instances.

(ii) It is customary to put one heading 'Trading and Profit and Loss Account for the (period) ended (date)' at the top of the trading account. Do not put a separate heading between the trading account and the profit and loss account. The balance on the trading account is carried straight down to the profit and loss account.

(iii) There are no set rules for the order of items in the profit and loss account, but good presentation depends upon style and the following suggestions will help:

(a) Place important items before those of lesser importance. Costs of employing staff are usually the biggest single item, so you may start with these. Costs of occupying premises, usually come next. After that, the order is probably not so important but *Sundry expenses* (sometimes called Miscellaneous or General expenses) usually denote a pool of minor or non-recurring items and are generally placed low in the order.

(b) Group items of a similar nature together, e.g. staff bonuses and commissions should be grouped with salaries and wages. Rent, rates, heat and light, insurance, etc. can be grouped together as property expenses.

The object of observing such principles as those above is to convey the most important facts about the business activities in a way that is quickly and easily understood.

(iv) Net profit is the balance required to make the debit side of the profit and loss account equal the credit side. The double-entry is completed by crediting the net profit to the owner's Capital account. Profit increases capital.

(v) If the total of the debits in the profit and loss account exceeds the credits, the overheads have exceeded the income and the business has made a net loss represented by a debit balance.

The balancing figure will be entered on the credit side of the profit and loss account and debited to capital account. Losses decrease capital.

Remember
Net profits increase capital
Net losses decrease capital

(vi) In practice, the balances are usually pencilled in the nominal accounts until the trading and profit and loss account has been finalised. As you will see later, in Chapters 11 and 12, it is possible that some of the balances will need to be adjusted for good reasons.

9.6   Definitions

Turnover   Net sales excluding trade discounts and VAT.

Cost of sales (or *cost of goods sold*)   The total cost to the business of making or buying goods that have been sold, including the cost of bringing them to the place of sale.

Gross profit (or *trading profit*, or *margin*)   Turnover less cost of sales.

Overheads   Expenses which are not part of the cost of sales. (This definition only applies to a trading concern; it is not appropriate for a manufacturing concern. See Chapter 23.)

Net profit   Gross profit plus all other non-trading income, profits and gains, less overheads.

9.7   Examination Hints

(i) Examiners usually require final accounts (Trading and Profit and Loss accounts) and Balance Sheets to be produced from given trial balances. You must therefore assume that all the book-keeping and balancing of accounts has already been done.

(ii) Be careful to give the Trading and Profit and Loss account a proper heading.

(iii) Before you prepare a Trading and Profit and Loss account, look at the trial balance carefully two or three times until you have familiarised yourself with its contents.

(iv) Recall the outline of a typical Trading and Profit and Loss account with its contents in order, and mark against each nominal account in the trial balance T for Trading account,

P for Profit and Loss account (see Fig. 9.2). Do not overlook the closing stock which will be found as a footnote to the trial balance.

(v) Compile the Trading and Profit and Loss account from the trial balance, ticking each item on the trial balance as you proceed.

(vi) Re-check the trial balance to see that all items marked T or P have been ticked. Then total the Trading and Profit and Loss account and insert the balances of gross and net profit, not forgetting to bring the gross profit down to the Profit and Loss account and to carry the net profit (loss) to Capital account.

(vii) Be careful to include only revenue items in the Profit and Loss account. Do not debit it with capital expenditure, i.e. cost of increasing the fixed assets of the business. The owner's drawings must not be debited in the Profit and Loss account since they are a reduction of the capital invested in the business and not an expense of carrying on the business.

9.8 What Should I Have Learned in this Chapter?

(i) Trading and Profit and Loss accounts are part of the double-entry system and show the profits or losses resulting from trading and non-trading activities.

(ii) A Trading account shows the turnover, cost of sales and gross profit.

A Profit and Loss account shows the gross profit plus non-trading income, and the net profit remaining after the deduction of all overheads.

Exercises

In all the multiple-choice questions the student is required to select the correct answer from the lettered alternatives.

1   Closing stock has been undervalued by £1,000. The effect is:
    (a) To understate cost of sales by £1,000
    (b) To overstate cost of sales by £1,000
    (c) To overstate gross profit by £1,000 or
    (d) To overstate net profit by £1,000.

2   Which of the following would you not expect to be debited in the profit and loss account?
(a) Discounts allowed
(b) Sundry expenses
(c) Carriage inwards
(d) Carriage outwards

3   Which of the following would you expect to be debited in the profit and loss account?
(a) Purchase of a motor van
(b) Drawings
(c) Discounts received
(d) Rent payable

4   The following trial balance has been extracted from the books of I. Cutler at 31 December 19-6:

	Dr £	Cr £
Sales		7,000
Purchases	3,500	
Stock at 1.1.-6	1,000	
Wages	1,200	
Rent and rates	800	
Electricity	340	
Sundry expenses	50	
Fixtures and fittings	1,500	
Motor van	2,000	
Debtors	700	
Creditors		400
Cash at bank	960	
Cash in hand	35	
Drawings	1,015	
Capital		5,700
	13,100	13,100

Stock on hand at 31 December 19-6 was £1,300.
Prepare a Trading and Profit and Loss account for the year to 31 December 19-6.
(Keep your answer. It will be needed again in Chapter 10.)

5   The following trial balance has been extracted from the books
of P. Catchpole at 31 December 19-6:

	Dr £	Cr £
Capital		17,000
Drawings	2,475	
Loan—A. Forster (repayable in two years)		7,500
Premises	10,000	
Plant and machinery	4,000	
Motor vehicles	3,600	
Cash at bank	2,750	
Cash in hand	104	
Debtors	1,223	
Creditors		997
Stock at 1.1.-6	2,400	
Purchases	4,650	
Sales		11,290
Purchases returns		415
Sales returns	620	
Postages and stationery	420	
Sundry expenses	610	
Salaries and wages	2,610	
Rent and rates	1,740	
	37,202	37,202

Stock on hand at 31 December 19-6 was £2,100.
Prepare a Trading and Profit and Loss account for the year
ended 31 December 19-6.
(Keep your answer. It will be needed again in Chapter 10.)

6   The following trial balance has been extracted from the books
of Bob Arrend at 31 March 19-7:

	Dr £	Cr £
Purchases	5,950	
Purchases returns		97
Sales		9,460
Sales returns	215	
Stock at 1.4.-6	2,400	
Discounts allowed	542	
Discounts received		840

	Dr	Cr
	£	£
Carriage outwards	415	
Carriage inwards	620	
Wages	1,200	
Rent payable	750	
Rent receivable		400
Postage and stationery	64	
Heating, lighting and cleaning	100	
Sundry expenses	120	
Insurance	75	
Plant and equipment	2,000	
Fixtures and fittings	1,400	
Debtors	820	
Creditors		610
Cash at bank and in hand	530	
Drawings	1,206	
Capital		7,000
	18,407	18,407

Closing stock was valued at £1,200.

Prepare a Trading and Profit and Loss account for the year ended 31 March 19–7.

(Keep your answer. It will be needed again in Chapter 10.)

Chapter 10
The Balance Sheet of a Sole Trader

10.1 What Topics are Covered in this Chapter?

The balance sheet is described. We learn how to prepare a balance sheet and some more definitions.

10.2 Balance Sheet

At any time, we should be able to produce a statement of the assets, liabilities and capital of a business to show what it owns and what it owes to other people. Such a statement is known as a *balance sheet* because it is a summary of all the balances remaining in the ledger after the Trading and Profit and Loss account has been prepared. As a statement, or summary, it is not part of the double-entry system; ledger balances are not transferred to it as they are to the Trading and Profit and Loss account.

Remember

Balance sheets are not part of the double-entry system

Until 1981, it was customary to show capital and liabilities on the left-hand side of the balance sheet and assets on the right-hand side. Then the Companies Act 1981 required limited companies which prepared two-sided balance sheets to reverse the sides, with assets on the left and capital and liabilities on the right. Although the Companies Acts do not apply to sole traders or partnerships, we shall be consistent and prepare all two-sided balance sheets with the assets on the left side and capital and liabilities on the right. You will not then be confused with two different styles. If you consult some other books, you may find balance sheets prepared the other way round, but providing you understand this chapter, you should have no difficulty with balance sheets produced either way.

One further principle you need to understand is that the accounting equation requires the two sides of the balance sheet to add to the same total because assets = capital + liabilities.

10.3 Order of Items in Balance Sheet

The order in which items should be shown in the balance sheet is:

(i) Assets

(a) *Fixed* (most permanent assets shown first)
Freehold property
Leasehold property
Plant and machinery
Furniture and fittings
Motor vehicles
(b) *Current* (inverse order of liquidity—see below)
Stock
Debtors
Cash at bank
Cash in hand
Liquid assets are those which are in the form of cash or can readily be converted into cash. Placing them in inverse order of liquidity means putting the least liquid assets first. Cash at bank can become cash in hand just as quickly as it takes to go to the bank and draw money out. It takes longer to obtain money from debtors while stock has not even been sold yet.

(ii) Capital and liabilities

(a) *Capital*, showing capital at beginning of period, new capital introduced during the period, profit/loss for the period and drawings.
(b) *Long term liabilities* (those not due to be settled within the next 12 months).
(c) *Current liabilities* (those falling due for settlement within the next 12 months).

10.4 Specimen Balance Sheet

Applying the above principles, we can now produce a balance sheet from the trial balance shown as Fig. 9.2 in Chapter 9.

We have already marked the balance sheet items in that figure with B.

Fig. 10.1   *Preparation of Balance Sheet*

K. Smith

Balance Sheet as at 31 December 19-7

	£	£		£	£
Fixed Assets:			Capital		
Premises	10,000		Balance at		
Equipment	5,000		1.1.-7		20,000
Motor vehicles	3,000		Add profit for		
	------	18,000	year	2,050	
			less drawings	2,550	
				------	(500)
					19,500
Current Assets:			Long term liability:		
Stock	3,000		Loan A. J. Cook		4,000
Trade debtors	1,700		Current liabilities:		
Cash at bank	2,000		Trade creditors		1,300
Cash in hand	100				
	------	6,800			
		24,800			24,800

Points to Note

(i) Heading. Always include the name of the business and describe the balance sheet 'as at (date)'. It does not cover a period of time but is sometimes likened to a 'snapshot' of a business at a particular moment.

(ii) The order of items is important. As the loan from A. J. Cook is not repayable within 12 months of the date of the balance sheet, it is shown as a long term liability.

(iii) The capital account shows additions (profit) to, and deductions (drawings) from the balance of capital at the beginning of the year. There is a net reduction of £500 shown in brackets.

(iv) Show sub-totals for fixed and current assets and for long term and current liabilities where appropriate.

(v) The closing stock figure which was credited in the trading account and debited in the stock account is included in the balance sheet as a current asset.

10.5   Net Worth

This term is used to express the worth of a business to its owner. In Fig. 10.1 the fixed and current assets total £24,800. The business owes Cook £4,000, and a further £1,300 to trade creditors. The net worth of the business is £24,800 – £(4,000 + 1,300) = £19,500. This is the same as the owner's capital and is exactly what we would expect from the accounting equation:

Capital = assets – liabilities.

10.6   Working Capital

This is the term given to net current assets, or total current assets less total current liabilities. In Fig. 10.1, the working capital is:

	£
Current assets	6,800
Less current liabilities	1,300
Working capital	5,500

Working capital is important because it is the fund of ready resources that a business has in excess of the amount required to pay its current liabilities as they fall due. All too often businesses fail through shortage of working capital. We shall study working capital more fully later. In the meantime we will show how this important piece of information may be shown more clearly in the balance sheet by actually deducting the current liabilities from current assets. We can redraft the balance sheet in Fig. 10.1 as shown in Fig. 10.2 (see page 110).

10.7   The Going-Concern Concept

Our balance at 31 December 19–7 shows the assets at the amounts they are recorded in the ledger. Unless the asset accounts have already been adjusted to revalue the assets, the ledger balances show the assets at cost. If the business were to be discontinued on the next day, the assets would be unlikely to fetch the same price as that at which they were purchased. We are all familiar with the greatly reduced prices in 'closing down' sales, for instance. If we had known the business was to close down, we would have produced a misleading balance sheet by showing the assets at their cost. It would have been more realistic to show them at the price we would expect to receive if we sold them. Most balance sheets however are prepared in the expectation that the business will continue to trade for the foreseeable future. This is known as the *Going-concern concept*. It is a fundamental principle that balance sheets are prepared on the going-concern basis unless the business is expected to be discontinued in the foreseeable future.

Fig. 10.2

Preparation of Balance Sheet to show calculation of working capital

K. Smith

Balance Sheet as at 31 December 19-7

	£	£		£	£
Fixed Assets:			Capital		
Premises	10,000		Balance at		
Equipment	5,000		1.1.-7		20,000
Motor vehicles	3,000		Add profit for		
		18,000	year	2,050	
			less drawings	2,550	
					(500)
					19,500
Current Assets:			Long term liability		
Stock	3,000		Loan A. J. Cook		4,000
Trade debtors	1,700				
Cash at bank	2,000				
Cash in hand	100				
	6,800				
less					
Current liabilities:					
Trade creditors	1,300				
Working capital		5,500			
		23,500			23,500

10.8   Final Accounts

The Trading and Profit and Loss accounts and the Balance Sheet are collectively known as Final Accounts even though the Balance Sheet is not an account.

10.9 Examination Hints

(i) Give every balance sheet a proper heading in correct form.

(ii) In these early stages of your studies, mark the asset and liability accounts in the trial balance with B for Balance Sheet.

(iii) Tick each item in the trial balance as you copy it on to the Balance Sheet. Before totalling the Balance Sheet, check that all items in the trial balance have been ticked.

(iv) Show sub-totals for fixed assets, current assets, capital, long term liabilities and current liabilities. Inset the details in inner columns where necessary.

(v) Do not insert totals in the Balance Sheet if they do not agree. You have made an error; do not make things worse by misleading the examiner into thinking you do not know that both sides of the balance sheet should agree in total.

10.10 What Should I Have Learned in this Chapter?

(i) Balance sheets are not part of the double-entry. The balances remain on the asset and liability accounts.

(ii) Assets and liabilities should be placed in the generally accepted order within their proper categories.

(iii) The meanings of net worth, working capital, and going-concern concept.

Exercises

1 A balance sheet is prepared by:
   (a) transferring all the balances on the nominal accounts to it;
   (b) transferring all the real and personal account balances to it;
   (c) transferring to it all balances remaining on the ledger accounts after the Trading and Profit and Loss account has been prepared;
   (d) extracting from the ledger all the balances on accounts after the Trading and Profit and Loss account has been prepared.
   Which of the above is correct?

2 Hawkins & Sons deal in typewriters and accessories.
   (a) State whether the following items are capital or revenue expenditure, giving reasons for your answers:
      (i) The purchase of fourteen typewriters as stock in trade.

   (ii) The purchase of four new tyres for the firm's delivery
        van.
   (iii) The payment of an insurance premium on the firm's
        premises.
   (iv) The payment of an annual Christmas bonus to the staff.
   (v) The purchase of two new electric typewriters for office
        use.
   (b) The firm's Profit and Loss account includes an item of
   £2,100 for repairs, redecoration and alterations to their
   freehold premises. If it is decided to charge two thirds of this
   sum as capital expenditure, what effect would this have on the
   firm's Balance Sheet?
   (RSA 1 1982)

3 Mr Brown has recently started in business on his own account
   and is puzzled by the terms Capital Expenditure and Revenue
   Expenditure.
   (a) Explain to him what Capital Expenditure is.
   (b) Mr Brown has purchased a new van, the details of the
       account were as follows:

	£
Van	3,000
Seat Belts	24
Delivery charges	42
Number Plates	15
Road Tax	90
Insurance	220
	3,391

   He has also received an account from his local builder, details
   of which are as follows:

	£
Redecorate shop front	400
Erect shelves in stock room	90
	490

   You are required to list the items from both invoices under
   their respective headings of Capital and Revenue Expenditure. (RSA 1 1984)

4 Prepare the balance sheet of I. Cutler as at 31 December 19–6
   from the trial balance in Exercise 4 of Chapter 9.

5   Prepare the balance sheet of P. Catchpole as at 31 December 19-6 from the trial balance in Exercise 5 of Chapter 9.

6   Prepare the balance sheet of Bob Arrend as at 31 March 19-7 from the trial balance in Exercise 6 of Chapter 9.

Chapter 11
Adjustments to the Trial Balance
I: Accruals and Prepayments

11.1 What Topics are Covered in this Chapter?

We consider the concept of matching expenditure with revenue. We learn about adjustments to be made to figures in the trial balance and the accounting entries necessary to reflect the adjustments.

11.2 Why Adjustments Are Necessary

At any point in time, a business will have incurred overhead costs for which it has not yet paid. It is quite likely, for instance, that electricity consumed in the last quarter before the end of the financial year will not have been paid for and will not have been debited to the Electricity account. The firm might have taken delivery of stores such as packing materials, office stationery or heating fuel in the last few days before the date of the trial balance and not paid for them. On the other hand, some expenses such as rent, rates and insurance may have been paid in advance.

It is a fundamental principle of accounting that not only should all revenue earned in the year be credited to the Trading and Profit and Loss accounts, but all the costs incurred in earning that revenue should also be included to make sure that net profit is correctly calculated. Expenditure which has been incurred to secure future benefits for the firm (e.g. rent, rates, insurance), which have been paid in advance must be excluded from the Profit and Loss account.

Remember

Expenditure and revenue must be matched in the period to which they relate

---

114

11.3 Accrued Expenditure

Accrued expenditure (*accruals*) represents costs which have been incurred but not yet paid for; the business owes money to somebody for goods or services it has received. That somebody is a creditor and should be represented in the appropriate expense account by a credit balance carried down at the year end.

Fig. 11.1 *Electricity Account adjusted for accrued charges*

Cash paid for electricity in the year to 31 December 19-7: £300. Amount owing for electricity at 31 December: £100.

Electricity

19-7 Dec 31			£	19-7 Dec 31			£
	Sundry payments	CB	300		Profit and Loss A/c	J	400
	Accrual	c/d	100				
			400				400
19-8				19-8 Jan 1	Balance	b/d	100

Point to Note

The charge for the year for electricity has been increased by £100 to £400, and is compensated on the credit side by a creditor for £100 which will be shown in the balance sheet as an expense creditor.

Remember

Complete the double-entry for every adjustment by bringing the balance down

---

11.4 Prepayments

An expense may sometimes be paid in advance, i.e. prepaid. This means that the business has paid for a benefit it has not received yet. In other words, somebody owes the business for the value of the prepayment; that somebody is a debtor of the business and should be represented in the appropriate expense account by a debit balance carried down at the year end.

Fig. 11.2

Insurance Account adjusted for prepaid premium

Insurance premiums paid on 1 January 19-7 for eighteen months to 30 June 19-8: £600. Amount of premium for 12 months to 31 December 19-7: $12/18 \times £600 = £400$. Amount prepaid at 31 December $19-7 = £(600 - 400) = £200$.

Insurance

19-7			£	19-7				£
Jan 1	Bank	CB	600	Dec 31	Profit and			
					Loss A/c	J	400	
					Prepayment	c/d	200	
			600					600
19-8				19-8				
Jan 1	Balance	b/d	200					

Point to Note

The debit balance will be shown as a prepayment in the balance sheet immediately under trade debtors.

11.5   Accruals and Prepayments on the Same Account

Sometimes one account will be used to record two or more items of expense. For example, a Rent and Rates account is often used for rent payable and rates.

Fig. 11.3 shows the adjustments made to a Rent and Rates account to allow for rent paid in advance, £50, and rates accrued, £65.

Fig. 11.3

Rent and Rates Account adjusted for an accrual and a prepayment

Rent and Rates

19-7			£	19-7				£
Dec 31	Sundry-rent	CB	400	Dec 31	Profit and			
	Sundry-rates	CB	300		Loss A/c	J	715	
	Accrued				Prepaid rent	c/d	50	
	rates	c/d	65					
			765					765
19-8				19-8				
Jan 1	Balance	b/d	50	Jan 1	Balance	b/d	65

Point to Note

The accrual for rates must not be offset against the prepayment of rent so that only a credit balance of £15 is carried down. The liability for rates cannot be reduced by rent paid in advance; the two items are separate and both must show as balances on the account.

11.6 Income Received in Arrears or in Advance

Rent received in arrear. Arrears of rent receivable at the year end will be credited to Rents Receivable account and carried down as a debit balance as the tenant is a debtor of the business.

Fig. 11.4

Rent Receivable Account adjusted for arrears of rent

Rent receivable in year: £1,000. Three quarters' rent received to 30 September 19-7; fourth quarter's rent outstanding at 31 December 19-).

Rent Receivable

19-7			£	19-7			£
Dec 31	Profit and Loss A/c	J	1,000	Jan 1	Cash	CB	250
				Apr 1	Cash	CB	250
				July 1	Cash	CB	250
				Dec 31	Balance due	c/d	250
			1,000				1,000
19-8							
Jan 1	Balance	b/d	250				

Rent received in advance. This will be carried down as a credit balance on Rent Receivable account as the tenant is a creditor for the prepaid rent. (See Fig. 11.5 on page 118.)

Other income accounts may be adjusted similarly.

11.7 Year-end Stocks of Stationery and Other Consumable Stores

At the end of the year, there may be stocks of stationery, fuel, canteen supplies or other consumable stores on hand. If these are not material they may be ignored but if they are material, it would be incorrect to treat them as expenses of a period in which they had not been used. In such cases, credit the account concerned with the value of such stores and carry it down as a debit balance.

Fig. 11.5

Rent Receivable Account adjusted for rent in advance

Annual rent receivable: £1,000. Rents received for quarter in advance of 1.1.-7; 1.4.-7; 1.7.-7; 1.10.-7; 31.12.07.

Rent Receivable

19-7			£	19-7			£
Dec 31	Profit and	J	1,000	Jan 1	Cash	CB	250
	Loss A/c			Apr 1	Cash	CB	250
	Balance in			July 1	Cash	CB	250
	advance	c/d	250	Oct 1	Cash	CB	250
				Dec 31	Cash	CB	250
			1,250				1,250
				19-8			
				Jan 1	Balance	b/d	250

Fig. 11.6

Stationery Account to record year-end stock

John Roe paid £120 on 15 December 19-7 for office stationery; his previous purchases in the year amounted to £800. At 31 December he still had £110 of his latest purchase of stationery in stock.

Stationery

19-7			£	19-7			£
Dec 1	Sundry	CB	800	Dec 31	Profit and		
15	Bank	CB	120		Loss		
					Account	J	810
					Stock on		
					hand	c/d	110
			920				920
19-8							
Jan 1	Balance	b/d	110				

Points to Note

(i) The debit balance will appear as an asset in the balance sheet. Compare this with the debit balance of closing stock on the Stock account.

(ii) Stocks of consumable stores should not be added to stock-in-trade in the balance sheet, but either shown separately or added to other prepayments.

11.8 Examination Hint

Examiners frequently leave a piece of information out of a question but give sufficient other information to enable you to calculate the missing piece. When you have calculated the missing figure, decide whether or not it looks sensible and fits in with any other facts given in the question. This is a useful cross-check.

11.9 What Should I Have Learned in this Chapter?

(i) The matching concept requires expenditure to be matched against revenue.
(ii) All the revenue of a period should be credited in the Trading and Profit and Loss account but it must not be overstated.
(iii) The expenditure debited in the Trading and Profit and Loss account should be, as near as possible, the expenditure actually incurred in earning the revenue (the matching concept).
(iv) Accrued expenditure is entered on the debit side of an expense account and carried down as a creditor to be included in the balance sheet.
(v) Prepaid expenditure is credited in the appropriate expense account and carried down as a debit balance to be included as a prepayment in the balance sheet.
(vi) Stocks of consumable stores at the year end are treated as prepayments. They are not added to stock-in-trade in the balance sheet.

Exercises

1 At 1 January 19-7, Jones had a credit balance brought forward on his telephone account of £40. During 19-7 he paid telephone charges amounting to £250. At 31 December 19-7 he carried forward a debit balance of £90. The amount transferred to profit and loss account for the 19-7 was:
(a) £300
(b) £120
(c) £200
(d) £380

2 John Brown prepared a draft profit and loss account for 19-7 and it showed a net profit of £10,000. He then discovered that:
(i) He had forgotten to make an entry for accrued rent payable £150.

(ii) He had overlooked a stock of stationery at the year end of £230.

The net profit for 19–7 should have been:
(a) £9,620
(b) £9,770
(c) £10,080
(d) £10,380

3   (i) Explain the following entries in J. Davies' Advertising account:

Advertising Account

1983		£	1983		£
May 20 Bank		200	Apr 1	Balance b/f	160
			May 30 Bank		40
1984			1984		
Feb 16 Bank		500	Mar 31	Profit and Loss account	450
			Mar 31	Balance c/f	50
		700			700

(ii) Briefly explain how expenses accrued and expenses paid in advance are dealt with in the ledger for the purpose of closing the books at the end of the financial year of a business. (Welsh Joint Education Committee 'O' level 1984)

4   (i) L. George rents his premises at an annual rental of £1,200. On 1 June 1983 George had paid his rent up to the end of July, and during the year ended 31 May 1984 he made the following payments for rent, by cheque:

August 1	£300
November 5	£300
February 1	£300
June 1	£400

(ii) George sub-lets part of these premises to S. Broke at a rent of £480 per annum, and on 1 June 1983 Broke's rent was one month in arrears. During the year ended 31 May 1984 George received the following amounts in cash from Broke:

July 25	£40
August 18	£120
December 4	£150
April 9	£60

(iii) On 1 June 1983 George owed the Electricity Board £74 for electricity supplies up to that date, during the year he made the following payments by cheque:

June 1	£74
September 10	£82
December 5	£104
April 7	£81

On 31 May 1984 there was a balance outstanding on the electricity account of £96.

You are required:

(a) To write up George's rent payable account, rent receivable account, and electricity account for the year ended 31 May 1984 showing clearly the amounts to be transferred to the Profit and Loss account in each case.

(b) To show how the balances brought down would appear in the Balance Sheet on 31 May 1984.

(RSA Stage 1 1984)

5 (a) Mr A. Breviate has the following account in his ledger:

Advertising Account

1983		£	1982		£
Mar 31	Cash—Rent	9,600	Apr 1	Balance b/f	2,200
	Rates	2,400	1983		
	Balance c/f	1,200	Mar 31	Cash from	
				sub-tenant	800
				P & L A/c	10,200
		13,200			13,200

Upon enquiry you find that at the beginning of the year Breviate owed £2,400 in respect of the previous quarter, had prepaid rates to the extent of £600 and had received £400 in advance from a sub-tenant.

At the end of his financial year Breviate owed £2,400 for rent and had paid rates in advance amounting to £800. The sub-tenant owed £400 in respect of the previous quarter. During the year Breviate paid £9,600 in respect of rent and £2,400 in respect of rates.

You are required to prepare separate accounts for rent payable, rent receivable and rates showing clearly the opening and closing balances and the transfers to Profit and Loss account.

(b) At the beginning of his financial year Mr Breviate had a stock of stationery valued at £2,200, and at the end of the year £1,670. At the beginning of the year he owed £600 for stationery, paid £6,100 to suppliers of stationery during the year, and owed £520 at the end of the year.

You are required to prepare Mr Breviate's Stationery account for the year. (AAT 1983)

6   George Price is the proprietor of a small business. He keeps his financial records on double-entry principles and extracted the following trial balance on 31 May 1983:

	£		£
Stock 1 June 1982	7,000	Capital 1 June 1982	85,000
Cash at bank	8,000	Creditors	3,700
Furniture and fittings	7,500	Sales	40,000
Premises	65,000		
Rates	1,600		
Purchases	30,000		
Heating and lighting	1,500		
Cleaning	1,700		
Packing materials	1,400		
Drawings	5,000		
	128,700		128,700

You are required to take the following into consideration on 31 May 1983:

	£
(i) Stock on hand	9,500
(ii) Rates paid in advance	400
(iii) Stock of packing material	300

and prepare a Trading and Profit and Loss account for the year ended 31 May 1983 and a Balance Sheet at that date. (RSA Stage 1 1983)

Chapter 12
Adjustments to the Trial Balance
II: Bad and Doubtful Debts and the Provisions for Discounts

12.1 What Topics are Covered in this Chapter?

After dealing with the treatment of bad debts, we learn how to provide for doubtful debts and consider whether or not we should also provide for discounts allowed and discounts received.

12.2 Bad Debts

Most businesses find sooner or later that some of their customers either cannot or will not pay their debts even if legal action is taken against them; in which case, the debt is said to be bad.

Debts must be taken out of the Sales ledger as soon as they are known to be bad because they no longer represent assets of the business. The book-keeping entries to transfer the bad debts from the debtor's account to a Bad Debts account are:

Dr Bad Debts a/c; Cr Debtors a/c

with the amount of the debt to be written off.

The journal and ledger entries are illustrated in Fig. 12.1. (See page 124.)

Point to Note

The balance on the Bad Debts account at the year end is transferred to Profit and Loss account, so reducing the profit for the year by the losses sustained on the bad debts.

Fig. 12.1

Journal and Ledger entries to write off Bad Debts

On 1 September, B. White learns that V. Black, who owes him £100, has been made bankrupt. There is no likelihood that any of this debt will be paid.

On 6 September B. White learns that another customer, Q. Grey, has also been made bankrupt. Q. Grey owes White £400 on which White receives a dividend of 15p in the £.

B. White's Books:

Journal

		Dr. £	Cr. £
Sept 1	Bad Debts Account	100	
	V. Black		100
	Debt due from V. Black, adjudged bankrupt on — —; no dividend receivable		
Sept 6	Bad Debts Account	340	
	Q. Grey		340
	Debt due from Q. Grey, adjudged bankrupt on — —; after receipt of dividend of 15p in £ on £400		

Sales Ledger

V. Black

			£				£
Sept 1	Sundries		100	Sept 1	Bad Debts A/c	J	100

Q. Grey

			£				£
Sept 1	Sundries		400	Sept 6	Bank	CB	60
					Bad Debts A/c	J	340
			400				400

Nominal Ledger

Bad Debts Account

			£			£
Sept 1	V. Black	J	100	Dec 31	Profit and	
6	Q. Grey	J	340		Loss A/c	440
			440			440

12.3 Bad Debts Recovered in a Later Period

A debt which has been written off in one period may be recovered in a later period. In that event it is desirable that the debtor's account in the Sales ledger should record all the facts, the ultimate payment as well as the original bad debt. The debt must therefore be reinstated in the debtor's account, the corresponding credit entry being recorded in a Bad Debts Recovered account. At the year-end, the credit balance on the Bad Debts Recovered account will either be transferred direct to the credit of Profit and Loss account; or it may be transferred to the credit of Bad Debts account. Either way, the effect upon net profit is the same.

12.4 Specific and General Provisions for Doubtful Debts

As bad debts are written off in the manner described above as they arise, a trial balance includes Sales ledger balances which are still considered to be 'good', or 'collectable'. Nevertheless, some of these 'good' balances may prove to be 'bad' in the next period. Unless some action is taken to provide for that possibility in the present period, the next period may have to bear the cost of writing off those debts against its profits.

At this point, it is necessary to consider two very important accounting principles. The first is the matching concept already encountered in Chapter 11. The second is *the concept of prudence* which requires that profits should not be anticipated before they have been realised, but provision should always be made for anticipated losses.

Remember

Concept of prudence—do not anticipate profits; provide for all anticipated losses

---

To be consistent with these principles, an attempt must be made to ensure that each period benefiting from trading activities should also provide for the possibility that some of its customers may become 'bad debts' in a later period.

The term *provision* has a special meaning in accounting. It describes an amount which is put by or set aside out of profits for some particular purpose, but the amount required for that purpose is not known or cannot be estimated with a reasonable degree of accuracy. There is a much more complete definition of provision, but this will suffice for our purpose at present.

A provision for doubtful debts is an amount set aside to cover the possibility that some debtors in the Sales ledger now will prove to be 'bad' later. The expression provision for bad debts is sometimes used in place of provision for doubtful debts.

There are two ways of calculating a provision for doubtful debts:

(i) Examination of Sales ledger accounts. Doubtful debts could be those that are old, or where the debtor is making round-sum payments on account indicating that he is unable to pay complete invoices as they fall due. A provision calculated in this way is called a *specific provision*.

(ii) Calculation of the provision as a percentage of all outstanding debts. The percentage chosen will vary from firm to firm, from trade to trade, according to experience. It may also vary from year to year depending upon economic conditions. The percentages chosen may vary with the ages of the debts. Fig. 12.2 illustrates this method. Provisions calculated by the percentage method are called *general provisions*.

Fig. 12.2

Calculation of General Provision for Doubtful Debts

Age of debt	Total amount of debts outstanding in range £	Percentage of provision	Amount of provision £
Up to 1 month	100,000	1	1,000
Over 1 month but less than 2 months	80,000	3	2,400
Over 2 months but less than 3 months	65,000	5	3,250
Over 3 months	35,000	10	3,500
	280,000		10,150

12.5   Ledger Entries for Doubtful Debt Provisions

Regardless of whether a provision is specified or general, there are two methods of recording it in ledger accounts:

(a) Using a Provision for Doubtful Debts account:

> Dr Profit and Loss A/c;
> Cr Provisions for Doubtful Debts account

with the amount of the provision.

Fig. 12.3 (using data shown in Figs. 12.1 and 12.2)

Alternative ledger entries for Doubtful Debt Provisions

Method (i)
Separate accounts for Bad Debts and Provision for Doubtful Debts.

Bad Debts

			£				£
Sept 1	V. Black	J	100	Dec 31	Profit and,		
6	Q. Grey	J	340		Loss A/c	J	440
			440				440

Provision for Doubtful Debts

			£				£
Dec 31	Balance	c/d	10,150	Dec 31	Profit and		
					Loss A/c	J	10,150
				Jan 1	Balance	b/d	10,150

Profit and Loss Account (extract)

	£				
Bad debts written off	440				
Provision for Doubtful Debts	10,150				

Method (ii)
Combined Bad Debts and Provision for Doubtful Debts Account.

Bad Debts

			£				£
Sept 1	V. Black	J	100	Dec 31	Profit and		
6	Q. Grey	J	340		Loss A/c	J	10,590
Dec 31	Provision	c/d	10,150				
			10,590				10,590
				Jan 1	Balance	b/d	10,150

Profit and Loss Account (extract)

	£	£
Bad Debts Account	10,590	

Whichever method is used, the balance sheet extract will be as follows:

	£	£
Trade Debtors	280,000	
less Provision for Doubtful Debts	10,150	269,850

(b) Using the Bad Debts account only: Debit the amount of the provision to the Bad Debts account and carry it down as a credit balance. The transfer from Bad Debts account will be the total of the bad debts written off and the increase or decrease in the amount of the provision. (See Section **12.6**.)

Points to Note

(i) In method (a) a balance is carried forward on the Provision account but not on the Bad Debts account whereas in method (b) the balance is carried forward on the Bad Debts account.

(ii) The net effect upon the Profit and Loss account is the same whichever method is used.

12.6   Adjustments of Previous Year's Provision for the Current Year

As the amount required for the provision varies from year to year, the balance brought forward from the previous year will need to be

Fig. 12.4

Adjustments to Doubtful Debts Provision

Data as in Fig 12.3 for Year 1 with the following additional information: Year 2, Sales Ledger balances £425,000, Provision £16,000; Year 3, Sales Ledger balances £251,000, Provision £10,200.

Provision for Doubtful Debts

Year 1			£	Year 1			£
Dec 31	Balance	J	10,150	Dec 31	Profit and Loss A/c	c/d	10,150
Year 2				Year 2			
Dec 31	Balance	c/d	16,000	Jan 1	Balance	b/d	10,150
				Dec 31	Profit and Loss A/c	J	5,850
			16,000				16,000
Year 3				Year 3			
Dec 31	Profit and Loss A/c	J	5,800	Jan 1	Balance	b/d	16,000
	Balance	c/d	10,200				
			16,000				16,000
				Year 4			
				Jan 1	Balance	b/d	10,200

Profit and Loss Account (extracts)

		£				£
Year 1	Provision for Doubtful Debts	10,150				
Year 2	Provision for Doubtful Debts	5,850				
				Year 3	Provision for Doubtful Debts	5,800

adjusted each year. If a separate Provision account is used, credit any increase to that account and debit Profit and Loss account, or debit a decrease to the Provision account and credit Profit and Loss account. If only a Bad Debts account is used, the adjustment is made automatically by carrying down the amount required as the balance.

12.7 The Doubtful Debts Provision in the Balance Sheet

As the provision is a credit balance in the ledger, it should be deducted from debtors in the balance sheet to show the estimated amount expected to be received from debtors in the next period.

Fig. 12.5

Balance Sheet extracts to show Provision for Doubtful Debts

Balance Sheets (extracts – Asset Side only)

		£	£
Year 1	Trade debtors	280,000	
	less Provision for doubtful debts	10,150	269,850
Year 2	Trade debtors	425,000	
	less Provision for doubtful debts	16,000	409,000
Year 3	Trade debtors	251,000	
	less Provision for doubtful debts	10,200	240,800

Remember

Deduct the provision for doubtful debts from debtors in the balance sheet

12.8   Provisions for Discounts Allowable to Debtors

If a business allows cash discounts to customers, the cash receivable from debtors may be overstated in the balance sheet unless provision is made for the discounts. The provision is calculated as a percentage of the total debtors less the amount of the Provision for Doubtful Debts. Obviously, discounts will not be allowed on debts which will not be collected.

Fig. 12.6

Provision for Discounts

Data as in Fig. 12.5. A cash discount of 2 ½ % is allowed to debtors for prompt payment.

Provision for Discounts Allowed

Year 1			£	Year 1			£
Dec 31	Balance	c/d	6,746	Dec 31	Profit and Loss A/c	c/d	6,746
Year 2				Year 2			
Dec 31	Balance	c/d	10,225	Jan 1	Balance	b/d	6,746
				Dec 31	Profit and Loss A/c	J	3,479
			10,225				10,225
Year 3				Year 3			
Dec 31	Profit and Loss A/c	J	4,205	Jan 1	Balance	b/d	10,225
	Balance	c/d	6,020				
			10,225				10,225
				Year 4			
				Jan 1	Balance	b/d	6,020

Profit and Loss Account (extracts)

		£			£
Year 1	Provision for Discounts	6,746			
Year 2	Provision for Discounts	3,479			
			Year 3	Provision for Discounts	4,205

Balance Sheets (extracts — Asset Side only)

		£	£	£
Year 1	Trade Debtors		280,000	
	less Provision for doubtful			
	debts	10,150		
	Provision for discounts	6,746	16,896	263,104
Year 2	Trade Debtors		425,000	
	less Provision for doubtful			
	debts	16,000		
	Provision for discounts	10,225	26,225	398,775
Year 3	Trade Debtors		251,000	
	less Provision for doubtful			
	debts	10,200		
	Provision for discounts	6,020	16,220	234,780

Workings

	Debtors per Sales Ledger	Doubtful Debt Provision	$a - b$	Discount Provision at 2½% on[c]	$a - (b + d)$
	£[a]	£[b]	£[c]	£[d]	£[e]
Year 1	280,000	10,150	269,850	6,746	263,104
Year 2	425,000	16,000	409,000	10,225	398,775
Year 3	251,000	10,200	240,800	6,020	234,780

12.9 Discounts Receivable

If provision is made for discounts allowable to debtors, it might seem logical to take account of discounts receivable from creditors. It might be argued that this would be consistent with the principle of matching revenue and expenditure but it would also be inconsistent with the concept of prudence. Prudence is considered to be the more important principle in this case and it is generally agreed that discounts receivable should be ignored in showing creditors in a balance sheet.

12.10 Examination Hints

(i) Read examination questions based on this topic very carefully as they may state the method to be used in recording bad debt provisions, i.e. Bad Debt account only, or a separate Provision account. Make sure you can manage both methods.

(ii) Make sure you are able to adjust a previous year's provision for the current year's requirements. You only need adjust for the difference.

(iii) Make sure you know how to show provisions for doubtful debts and discounts in the balance sheet.

(iv) Be careful to calculate a provision for discounts on net debtors only, i.e. after deduction of Provision for Doubtful Debts.

(v) Be prepared to discuss the reasons for and against adjusting creditors by discounts receivable in the Balance Sheet.

12.11 What Should I Have Learned in this Chapter?

(i) It is prudent to show debtors in the balance sheet at the amount which may be expected to be received from them after allowing for possible bad debts and cash discounts.

(ii) Treating doubtful debts and cash discounts as deductions from profit in the Profit and Loss account complies with the matching principle.

(iii) A provision is an amount set aside out of profits for some particular purpose when the amount is not known or cannot be estimated with a reasonable degree of accuracy.

Exercises

In all the multiple-choice questions the student is required to select the correct answer from the lettered alternatives.

1 A provision for bad debts will be shown on a Balance Sheet as:
   (a) Added to creditors
   (b) Deducted from creditors
   (c) Deducted from debtors
   (d) As a current liability.

2 The balance on Tong's Provision for Doubtful Debts account at 1 January was £800. During the year to 31 December he wrote off debts totalling £245 and he wished to carry forward to the following year a provision equal to 10% of his debtors which totalled £10,000. The total amount to be debited in the Profit and Loss account for the year was:
   (a) £1,000
   (b) £1,245
   (c) £1,045
   (d) £445

3 (i) Give two reasons for the creation of a 'Provision for Doubtful Debts'.

(ii) On 31 May 1984 the Provision for Doubtful Debts account had a credit balance of £175 which represented 1% of the debtors at that date. On 31 May 1985 it was decided to increase the provision to £250 which would represent 2% of the debtors at that date.

   (a) Calculate the value of debtors which would appear in the balance sheet on 31 May 1984 and 31 May 1985.

   (b) Write up the Provision for Doubtful Debts account for the year ended 31 May 1985.

   (c) Suggest a reason for increasing the percentage of total debtors to be used as a provision. (London 'O' level 1985)

4 D. Harry had an exporting business which adjusted its provision for doubtful debts at the end of the year at a given percentage of the total sundry debtors. The percentage varied each year, depending on the national and international economic situation. Irrecoverable debts were written off during the year to a Bad Debts account, as and when they were known.

	Bad Debts written off during year to Bad Debts account £	Total debtors at year end £	Percentage for provision of Doubtful Debts
31 December 1979	750	14,000	5%
31 December 1980	4,085	10,000	10%
31 December 1981	2,900	15,000	5%

From the above information you are required to show:

(a) The Bad Debts account as affected by the closing entries at the end of the financial years 31 December 1979, 1980 and 1981.

(b) The Provision for Doubtful Debts account for the same years showing the provision brought forward for each year; the balance on this account on 1 January 1979 was £500.

(c) The Journal entries for transactions to both the above named accounts.

(d) An extract from the balance sheets showing how the provision would affect the sundry debtors, as at 31 December 1979, 1980 and 1981 (JMB 'O' level 1982)

5 A firm's accountant decided in 1981 to keep a Provision for Bad Debts account based upon a provision for bad debts of 5%

of debtors outstanding at the year-end. You are required to prepare the Provision for Bad Debts accounts for the years 1981, 1982 and 1983 from the following particulars:

Debtors' Balances at 31 December 1981   £4,100

,,   ,,   ,, 31 December 1982   £4,580

,,   ,,   ,, 31 December 1983   £4,060

(Cambridge 'O' level 1984)

6   Docks Limited, a window replacement company, offers fairly generous credit terms to its high-risk customers. Provision is made for bad debts at a varying percentage based on the level of outstanding trade debtors, and an assessment of general economic circumstances, resulting in the following data for the last three accounting periods:

Year to 31 March	1980	1981	1982
	£	£	£
Trade Debtors at the year end (before allowing for any bad debts)	186,680	141,200	206,200
Estimated Bad Debts (companies in liquidation)	1,680	1,200	6,200
Provision for Bad Debts	10%	12.5%	15%

The Provision for Bad Debts at 1 April 1979 amounted to £13,000.

You are required to:

(a) prepare the Provision for Bad Debts account for each of the three years to 31 March 1980, 1981 and 1982 respectively, showing how the balances would appear on the balance sheets as at these dates; and

(b) assuming that a debt of £1,000 written off as bad in 1980 was subsequently recovered in cash in 1981, state briefly how this would have affected the profit for the year to 31 March 1980, and also how it would be treated in the accounts for the year to 31 March 1981. (AAT level 2 1982)

Chapter 13

Depreciation of Fixed Assets

13.1 What Topics are Covered in this Chapter?

The nature and causes of depreciation of fixed assets; two methods of recording depreciation in the accounts; the calculation and treatment of profits and losses arising in the disposal of fixed assets.

13.2 The Nature and Causes of Depreciation

Fixed assets used in businesses will, in normal circumstances, decrease in value until they are eventually sold or discarded as scrap. The difference between the original cost of an asset and its value on disposal is called *depreciation*. For example, a motor van purchased for £8,000 and sold for £1,000 five years later has depreciated by £7,000 over the period of five years (£8,000 – £1,000).

The usual *causes of depreciation* of fixed assets are:
  (i) Wear and Tear   An asset becomes worn out as it is used to earn profits.
 (ii) Obsolescence   An asset becomes inadequate for its purpose or is replaced by an improved version.
(iii) Passage of time   Leases diminish in value as their life expires.
 (iv) Exhaustion or wastage   Mines, oil wells and quarries are examples. The resources of these assets are exhausted as they are extracted. Assets of this type are usually described as wasting assets.

Depreciation is thus a cost of carrying on a business; it is the cost to the business of the use of its fixed assets. The only asset which is recognised as not depreciating in value is freehold land as the value of this usually increases (appreciates) with time. Freehold buildings, on the other hand, depreciate and should be treated in the accounts accordingly along with the other depreciating assets

135

(e.g. plant and machinery, motor vehicles, fixtures and fittings, office furniture, goodwill, patents, trade marks, leases, etc.).

The accounting treatment of depreciation must result in a depreciation charge against the profit of the period and a deduction from the cost of the asset in the balance sheet. Before we can see how to do this, we must first look at the methods of calculating the annual charge for depreciation.

13.3   Methods of Calculating Depreciation

Three basic pieces of information are necessary for the calculation of annual depreciation charges:

(i) Cost price (a fact).
(ii) Expected life of the asset (an estimate).
(iii) The realisable, scrap or residual value (an estimate).

The cost price should be readily verifiable by reference to an invoice, contract, correspondence, etc. The expected life or residual value can only be estimated from past experience or by expert opinion. An accountant must generally rely upon a professional valuer or other technical expert for this information. The total depreciation to be provided over the life of the asset can then be calculated as in the following example.

Fig. 13.1

Calculation of Depreciation

Motor van purchased at cost of £10,000
Expected life: 4 years
Estimated residual value after 4 years: £2,000
Depreciation to be provided over 4 years: £(10,000 − 2,000) = £8,000

Two methods of calculating the annual depreciation charge are:
(i) Straight line (or fixed instalment).
(ii) Reducing balance.

13.4   Straight Line

This method uses a fixed percentage of the original cost of the asset as the annual depreciation charge. Thus the annual charge for depreciation of the motor van in Fig. 13.1 under this method is:

$$\frac{\text{Total depreciation}}{\text{Expected life}} = \frac{£8,000}{4}$$
$$= £2,000 \text{ per annum or } 25\% \text{ of cost}$$

13.5 Reducing Balance

The annual depreciation charge under this method is a fixed percentage of the written down value of the asset at the beginning of each year. The *written down value* is the original cost less depreciation provided to date. Because the percentage selected is applied each year to a reducing balance, the percentage must be considerably higher than under the straight line method.

Fig. 13.2

Comparison of Straight Line and Reducing Balance Methods

Facts as in Fig. 13.1.

		Straight Line £		Reducing Balance £
Motor van at cost		10,000		10,000
Depreciation	20% on cost		33 ½ % on reducing balance	
Year 1		2,000		3,333
Written down value (wdv)		8,000		6,667
Year 2		2,000		2,222
wdv		6,000		4,445
Year 3		2,000		1,482
wdv		4,000		2,963
Year 4		2,000		988
Residual value		£2,000		£1,975

13.6 Straight Line and Reducing Balance Methods Compared

The straight line method makes an equal charge to the business for depreciation each year. The earlier years do not have to bear a heavier charge than the later years for the use of an asset. On the other hand, it is argued that as an asset gets older and has had more use, the cost of maintaining and repairing the asset increases. It is claimed that such increasing cost is offset by the reducing charge for depreciation under the reducing balance method and that the combined charges are evened out over the life of the asset. The claim is correct in theory but rarely works out like that in practice. The straight line method is generally regarded as being most suitable in the majority of cases. Study Fig. 13.2.

13.7   Bookkeeping Entries for Depreciation

Method 1   There are two methods for recording depreciation in accounts. The one about to be described leaves the asset in its account at cost and uses a Provision for Depreciation account to record the depreciation. This is the preferred method since it readily displays the information required to be shown in the

Fig. 13.3

Using a Provision for Depreciation Account

On 1 January 19-1 Mr Jones purchased a motor van costing £10,000. He decided to depreciate the van by 20% of cost each year, using a Provision for Depreciation account. The relevant accounts for the years 19-1, 19-2 and 19-3 are as follows: —

Motor Vans

19-1			£	19-1			£
Jan 1	Bank	CB	10,000	Dec 31	Balance	c/d	10,000
19-2				19-2			
Jan 1	Balance	b/d	10,000	Dec 31	Balance	c/d	10,000
19-3				19-3			
Jan 1	Balance	b/d	10,000	Dec 31	Balance	c/d	10,000
19-4							
Jan 1	Balance	b/d	10,000				

Provision for Depreciation of Motor Vans

19-1			£	19-1			£
Dec 31	Balance	c/d	2,000	Dec 31	Profit and Loss A/c	J	2,000
19-2							
Dec 31	Balance	c/d	4,000	19-2			
				Jan 1	Balance	b/d	2,000
				Dec 31	Profit and Loss A/c	J	2,000
			4,000				4,000
19-3				19-3			
Dec 31	Balance	c/d	6,000	Jan 1	Balance	b/d	4,000
				Dec 31	Profit and Loss A/c	J	2,000
			6,000				6,000
				19-4			
				Jan 1	Balance	b/d	6,000

Profit and Loss Account (extracts)

	£
Year to 31 December 19-1	
Provision for depreciation of motor vans	2,000
Year to 31 December 19-2	
Provision for depreciation of motor vans	2,000
Year to 31 December 19-3	
Provision for depreciation of motor vans	2,000

Balance Sheet (extracts — Asset Side only)

	£
As at 31 December 19-1	
Motor vans at cost	10,000
less depreciation to date	2,000
	8,000
As at 31 December 19-2	
Motor vans at cost	10,000
less depreciation to date	4,000
	6,000
As at 31 December 19-3	
Motor vans at cost	10,000
less depreciation to date	6,000
	4,000

balance sheet, i.e. the original cost of the asset and the depreciation provided to date.

The bookkeeping entries are as follows:

Dr Profit and Loss A/c; Cr Provision for Depreciation A/c
with the annual amount of depreciation.

13.8 Bookkeeping Entries for Depreciation

Method 2 The second method does not use a Provision for Depreciation account. The annual depreciation charge is credited to the asset account and debited to Depreciation account. The balance of Depreciation account is transferred to the Profit and Loss account.

This method is illustrated in Fig. 13.4 (see page 140).

13.9 Disposal of Fixed Assets

(When depreciation has been credited to a Provision for Depreciation account.)

When an asset is sold or otherwise disposed of, the fact that it is no longer owned by the business means that it must be taken out of the relevant asset account.

Fig. 13.4

Crediting Depreciation to the Asset Account

Data as in Fig. 13.3, but Mr White has decided not to use a Provision for Depreciation Account, and to provide for depreciation at 30% pa on the reducing balance.

Motor Van

19–1			£	19–1				£
Jan 1	Bank	CB	10,000	Dec 31	Depreciation	J		3,000
					Balance	c/d		7,000
			10,000					10,000
19–2				19–2				
Jan 1	Balance	b/d	7,000	Dec 31	Depreciation	J		2,100
					Balance	c/d		4,900
			7,000					7,000
19–3				19–3				
Jan 1	Balance	b/d	4,900	Dec 31	Depreciation	J		1,470
					Balance	c/d		3,430
			4,900					4,900
19–4								
Jan 1	Balance	b/d	3,430					

Depreciation

19–1			£	19–1			£
Dec 31	Motor Van	J	3,000	Dec 31	Profit and		
					Loss A/c	J	3,000
19–2				19–2			
Dec 31	Motor Van	J	2,100	Dec 31	Profit and		
					Loss A/c	J	2,100
19–3				19–3			
Dec 31	Motor Van	J	1,470	Dec 31	Profit and		
					Loss A/c	J	1,470

As it was debited to the asset account at cost when acquired, it must now be credited to the asset account at that original cost. To complete the double-entry, the cost is debited to an account called Disposals of Fixed Assets. If depreciation has been provided in respect of the asset since it was acquired, the balance on the Provision for Depreciation account will include the amount so provided. The Provision for Depreciation account must therefore be debited with the depreciation provided on the asset to date; the double-entry is completed by a credit entry, in the Disposals of Fixed Assets account.

Cash received from the sale of the assets will be debited in the cash book and credited to the Disposals account. Any balance remaining on the Disposals account represents a profit, if a credit

Fig. 13.5

Disposal of Fixed Asset

Data as in Fig. 13.3; Mr Jones sold the van for £2,750 on 5th May 19–4.

Motor Vans

19–4			£	19–4			£
Jan 1	Balance	b/d	10,000	May 5	Disposals A/c	J	10,000

Provision for Depreciation of Motor Vans

19–4			£	19–4			£
May 5	Disposals A/c	J	6,000	Jan 1	Balance	b/d	6,000

Disposals of Fixed Assets

19–4			£	19–4			£
May 5	Motor Vans	J	10,000	May 5	Provision for depreci- ation	J	6,000
					Bank	CB	2,750
					Profit and Loss A/c —loss on disposal	J	1,250
			10,000				10,000

balance (or a loss if a debit balance) on the sale of the asset. The balance will be transferred to the Profit and Loss account at the end of the year as a profit or a loss on the sale of fixed assets.

13.10 Examination Hints

(i) Read questions carefully to ascertain whether depreciation is to be calculated for a full year in the year in which an asset is acquired, or for part of the year only. If a question does not give a specific instruction on this matter, but shows the dates on which assets are purchased, you should only provide depreciation in proportion to the part of the year for which the asset is owned.

(ii) Where appropriate, attach your depreciation calculations to your answer.

(iii) In the case of assets which are sold, be careful to calculate the correct amount of depreciation provided on the assets. Some candidates calculate depreciation on the straight line basis for more years than the estimated life of the asset so that the depreciation exceeds the original cost!

(iv) If there are two or more disposals in a year, do not balance off the Disposals account after each sale, but only at the end of the year. In this way only one balance is transferred to the Profit and Loss account.

13.11 What Should I Have Learned in this Chapter?

(i) Depreciation is an estimate of the cost of using fixed assets to earn profits and must be matched against the revenue earned.

(ii) The two principal methods of calculating depreciation are the fixed instalment or straight line, and reducing balance.

(iii) There are two methods of recording depreciation in the ledger:
(a) credit depreciation to a Provision for Depreciation account
(b) credit depreciation to the fixed asset account.

(iv) On the disposal of a fixed asset, debit the cost of the asset to a Disposals account. Credit depreciation provided to date and cash proceeds to the Disposals account. Transfer the balance, profit or loss, to the Profit and Loss account.

Exercises

1 A motor car costs £8,000 and has an expected life of four years, at the end of which time, it is estimated that the residual value will be £1,600. If it is going to be depreciated on the straight line method, the annual rate of depreciation on cost should be:
   (a) 33⅓%
   (b) 25%
   (c) 20%
   (d) 15%

2 Ms Daly purchases a motor car for use in her business at a cost of £8,000. The car is estimated to have a life of three years at the end of which time its residual value is estimated to be £2,700. If the car is depreciated on the reducing balance method at 30% per annum, at the end of three years, its net book value will be:
   (a) £2,744
   (b) £2,800
   (c) £2,700
   (d) None of these

3 Explain:
   (i) What is meant by depreciation.
   (ii) The reasons for making provision for depreciation.
   (iii) How you would calculate the provision for depreciation for a machine that cost £1,000 with a life of ten years and a saleable value at the end of its life of £100.
   (Welsh JEC 'O' level 1983)

4 (a) Depreciation is a process of allocation not of valuation. Explain.
   (b) The diminishing balance method of depreciation reflects the cost of using an asset more accurately than does the straight line method. Explain.
   (AAT level 1 June 1984)

5 The financial year end of Hodgson (Builders Merchants) Ltd is 31 December. The company's policy is to depreciate its motor vans at 20% per annum, using the straight line method, and to calculate a full year's depreciation on the assets in existence at the end of the financial year, regardless of when

they were purchased or sold. The company's vans were purchased and sold as follows:

			£
1 January 1979	Purchased	AB 101 T	2,500
1 July 1980	Purchased	CD 202 V	3,000
31 March 1981	Purchased	EF 303 W	2,000
31 March 1981	Sold	AB 101 T	1,000
1 April 1982	Purchased	GH 404 X	3,500
31 August 1982	Sold	CD 202 V	2,000

You are required to draw up the for years 1979, 1980, 1981 and 1982:

(a)   (i) the motor van account

      (ii) the provision for depreciation of motor vans account

      (iii) the disposal of motor vans account

(b) extracts of the Profit and Loss accounts

(c) extracts of the balance sheets.

(JMB 'O' level 1983)

6

Motor Vans Account

1981		£
1 Jan	T. Weldon	30,000

Provision for depreciation

	31 Dec	£
	1981 Profit and Loss	3,000
	1982 Profit and Loss	2,700
	1983 Profit and Loss	2,430
	1984 Profit and Loss	2,187

The above accounts refer to motor vans purchased. Study the accounts and answer the following questions.

(i) Were the vans paid for immediately or were they bought on credit?

(ii) What method of calculation is being used for the depreciation?

(iii) Give the figure of percentage being used for depreciation.

(iv) What is the value of the motor vans shown in the balance sheet dated 31 December 1983?

Rewrite the account for the years 1981 and 1982 in the alternative form in which the depreciation appears in the same account as the motor vans. Balance the account at the end of each year. (London 'O' level 1984)

7   Since he commenced business on 1 January 1979, Mr I. Makeit has purchased three machines for his various manufacturing activities, viz.:

Machine	Date of Purchase	Cost
A	20 January 1979	£3,200
B	18 April 1980	£6,000
C	11 June 1981	£4,200

Each machine was bought for cash.

Mr Makeit's policy is to charge a full year's depreciation in the year of purchase irrespective of the date of purchase. He uses the diminishing balance method for calculating depreciation and the rates applicable to the three machines are as follows:

Machine	% rate
A	25
B	30
C	40

You are required to prepare:

(a) a schedule showing the cost, each year's depreciation and the written down value of each machine at the end of each of the three years 1979, 1980 and 1981;

(b) the Machinery account and its related Depreciation Provision account for the said three years.

(AAT level 1 June 1982)

Chapter 14
Final Accounts
in Vertical Form

14.1 What Topics are Covered in this Chapter?

This chapter deals with the presentation of Trading and Profit and Loss accounts and balance sheets in vertical form.

14.2 Vertical Presentation of Accounts

People with some accounting training usually manage to understand final accounts which have been prepared in horizontal, or two-sided form, with reasonable ease. On the other hand, many people including owners of businesses find accounts produced in that way difficult to understand. They prefer final accounts in statement form which can be read 'down the page' in the same way as they read other material. This is known as the vertical form of accounts and is much the preferred way of producing final accounts in real life as well as in examinations.

In general the vertical forms of Trading and Profit and Loss account and Balance Sheet are:

Fig. 14.1

Final Accounts in vertical form

**Trading and Profit and Loss Account
for the Year Ended ....**

	£
Sales	x
less cost of sales	x
Gross profit	x
add other income, gains, profits	x
	x
less overheads	x
Net profit	x

Balance Sheet as at ....

	£	£
Fixed assets		x
Current assets	x	
less current liabilities	x	
(*working capital)		x
Total net assets		x
less long-term liabilities		x
(*net worth)		x
Represented by:		
Capital at beginning of year		x
Add: capital introduced in year	x	
Add: profit for year	x	
	x	
Less: drawings	x	
		x
		x

Points to Note

(i) *These words are not actually shown on a balance sheet but are included here by way of explanation.

(ii) The individual expenses that make up Overheads will be shown separately in the Profit and Loss account.

(iii) If a loss is made then it will be added to drawings and the total deducted from Capital in the Balance Sheet.

> **Remember**
>
> The balance sheet shows the working capital. It also shows that the net worth is represented by capital

Fig. 14.2 shows the final accounts of J. Box in vertical form (see page 148).

14.3   Examination Hints

(i) Master the preparation of final accounts in vertical form; most examining bodies prefer it.

(ii) Tick all adjustments in a question as you make them and ensure that all adjustments have been ticked on the question paper to avoid missing any.

Fig. 14.2

Final Accounts in vertical form

J. Box: Trading and Profit and Loss Account
for the Year Ended 31 December 19-7

		£	£
Sales			18,000
less cost of sales:			
Stock at 1.1.-6		2,000	
Purchases		12,850	
		14,850	
less stock at 31.12.-7		3,400	
			11,450
Gross profit			6,550
add rent receivable			560
			7,110
less:			
Salaries and wages		2,400	
Rent and rates		1,220	
Stationery and postage		395	
Sundry expenses		10	
Depreciation:			
Fixtures and fittings	500		
Motor Vans	300		
		800	
Provision for doubtful debts		34	
Loan interest		200	5,059
Net profit carried to capital account			2,051

J. Box: Balance Sheet as at 31 December 19-7

	Cost	Depreci-ation	Net Book Value
FIXED ASSETS	£	£	£
Fixtures and fittings	5,000	500	4,500
Motor Vans	3,000	300	2,700
	8,000	800	7,200
CURRENT ASSETS			
Stock		3,400	
Debtors	1,700		
less provision	34	1,666	
Prepayments		50	
Cash at bank		616	
		5,732	
less CURRENT LIABILITIES			
Trade creditors	932		
Accrued expenses	255	1,187	
WORKING CAPITAL			4,545
			11,745
less Loan – B. Cox			2,000
			9,745
Represented by:			
Capital:			
Balance at 1.1.19-7			12,000
add Profit for year			2,051
			14,051
less Drawings			4,306
			£9,745

14.4   What Should I Have Learned in this Chapter?

(i) Final accounts in vertical form are often easier for most people to understand than horizontal accounts.

(ii) A Trading and Profit and Loss account in vertical form is just as much a part of the double-entry system as one prepared in horizontal form.

Exercises

1   The following Trial Balance was extracted from the books of David Jones at the close of business on 31 December 1981.

	£	£
Capital account 1 January 1981		4,104
Drawings	3,000	
Fixtures and fittings	800	
Insurance	405	
Rent and rates	1,240	
Wages and salaries	1,900	
Discounts allowed and received	440	210
Bad debts	304	
Trade debtors	1,251	
Trade creditors		1,254
Stock—1 January 1981	1,508	
Purchases	9,040	
Sales		16,170
Cash in hand	210	
Cash at bank	1,090	
Purchase returns		320
Sales returns	505	
Postage and stationery	260	
Carriage outwards	105	
	22,058	22,058

From this Trial Balance, and from the notes given below, you are required to prepare the Trading and Profit and Loss account of David Jones for the year ended 31 December 1981, and a Balance Sheet as at that date.

(i) Stock 31 December 1981, £1,610

(ii) Wages and Salaries accrued, due at 31 December 1981, £65

(iii) Rates are prepaid on 31 December 1981, £115

(iv) A further £60 Bad Debts are to be written off.

(v) There is a stock of stamps to the value of £14 at 31 December 1981.

(Adapted from RSA 1982)

2   Louis Bartram is the owner of a warehouse. He commenced business on 1 October 1985. The following balances were extracted from his books on 31 March 1986:

		£	£
Purchases		32,650	
Salaries and wages	3840 / 5760	9,600	
Premises		22,000	
Carriage inwards		1,186	
Sales			61,480
Returns outwards			250
Carriage on sales		320	
Sales returns		128	
Rent of office and showroom		1,200	600 piep.
Capital 1st October 1985			38,612
Postage and telephone		694	
General expenses		8,467	
Cash at bank and in hand		9,630	
Drawings		512 + 650	
Motor vehicles		12,000	
Debtors and creditors		3,976	2,830
Motor vehicle expenses		898	
Discounts allowed and received		162	251
		103,423	103,423

The following information should be taken into consideration:

(a) Stock on 31 March 1986 was valued at £5,820.

(b) Two fifths of salaries and wages had been incurred in putting the goods into a saleable condition.

(c) Rent of £1,200 shown above was in respect of the 12 months ended 30 September 1986.

(d) The proprietor had taken goods worth £650 at cost for his own use but no entry had been made in the books.

Required:

    (i) Prepare a Trading and Profit and Loss account for the six months ended 31 March 1986, showing clearly net purchases, cost of stock sold, cost of sales and net turnover.

    (ii) Write up the Capital account of Louis Bartram for the six months to 31 March 1986.

Note: A Balance Sheet is *not* required.

(RSA April 1986)

3 The following Trial Balance was extracted from the books of
William Watson, a sole trader, at the close of business on 31
October 1984:

	Dr	Cr
	£	£
Debtors and creditors	4,110	2,070
Discounts	530	290
Capital account 1 November 1983		5,200
Drawings	2,760	
Bank overdraft		1,090
Bills receivable and payable	550	380
Purchases and sales	9,840	17,630
Sales and purchases returns	720	360
Wages and salaries	3,250	
Office furniture	800	
Delivery van	960	
Van running expenses	420	
Rent and rates	710	
Cash	90	
Stock 1 November 1983	1,970	
Bad debts written off	270	
Sundry expenses	260	
Provision for bad and doubtful debts		220
	27,240	27,240

Notes:
(1) Stock 31 October 1984—£3,040.
(2) Increase the Provision for Bad and Doubtful Debts by £40
    to £260.
(3) Wages accrued 31 October 1984—£70.
(4) Rates prepaid 31 October 1984—£60.
(5) Provide for depreciation:
       Office furniture—£80
       Delivery van—£120.

Required:
Prepare the Trading and Profit and Loss accounts for the year
ended 31 October 1984 together with a Balance Sheet as at that
date.
(LCCI 1984)

4 D. Younger owns a retail shop. His Trial Balance on 31 May 1984 was as follows:

	Debit £	Credit £
Capital		28,000
Stock—1 June 1983	4,900	
Debtors and creditors	2,300	2,000
Insurance	350	
Sales		42,300
Wages and salaries	5,800	
Drawings	600	
Shop equipment (cost £10,000)	8,000	
Buildings at cost	24,000	
Purchases	22,240	
Heating and lighting	790	
Sales returns	140	
Discount allowed and received	20	70
Car expenses	140	
Carriage on purchases	200	
Rent received from sub-letting		150
Cash and bank balance	3,200	
Bad debts	140	
Bad Debt provision		300
	72,820	72,820

You are asked to prepare:

Trading account, Profit and Loss account for the year ended 31 May 1984 and Balance Sheet as at that date.

The following notes are to be taken into consideration:

(i) The closing stock is valued at £5,750.

(ii) A credit purchase of £700 was entered twice in the books.

(iii) Insurance is prepaid by £80 on 31 May 1984.

(iv) The Bad Debt provision is to be reduced to £200.

(v) During the year Younger had taken his car into the business but failed to record it in the books. The car was valued at £4,000 when taken in.

(vi) You are to charge depreciation of 10% on the original cost of the shop equipment and 20% depreciation on the valuation of the motor-car.

(Northern Ireland 'O' level 1984)

Chapter 15
Control and Valuation of Stock-in-Trade

15.1 What Topics are Covered in this Chapter?

This chapter explains the need for a proper system of controlling stock and outlines a typical, simple system. We then compare some methods of valuing stock.

15.2 Stock-in-Trade

Most businesses with which we will be at all familiar exist to earn profit by making or buying goods and then selling them. We call the goods *stock-in-trade*. Stock is therefore at the heart of activities of such businesses and great care must be exercised in controlling it and valuing it. Control is essential to avoid loss of stock by theft or carelessness. Proper valuation of stocks at the year-end is necessary to ensure that profits are neither over- nor under-stated. You will recall that gross profit depends upon turnover and cost of sales. Cost of sales, in turn, depends partly upon the value of closing stock.

Basically, good stock control involves keeping adequate records and comparing those records regularly with the stock actually on hand. The records consist of Goods Received Notes (GRNs—Fig.15.1), Stores Requisitions (SRs—Fig. 15.2), Bin Cards (Fig. 15.3) and Stores Ledger (Fig. 15.4). The stores ledger is distinct from the nominal ledger which is part of the financial accounts system. The stores ledger contains detailed accounts for all the items which go to make up the Stock account in the General ledger. (See pages 155–156.)

15.3 Stock Control System

Businesses differ in their nature and in the way they are organised so that no one stock control system will suit all businesses. The

Fig. 15.1

Goods Received Note

The A.B. Manufacturing Co plc **Goods Received Note**		
GRN No... SUPPLIER... DATE GOODS RECEIVED....................................... ORDER No..		
DESCRIPTION OF GOODS:	QUANTITY:	No. OF PACKAGES
RECEIVED BY	DATE	
REMARKS:		
INSPECTED BY	DATE	
REMARKS:		

Fig. 15.2

Stores Requisition

The A.B. Manufacturing Co plc SR No. **Stores Requisition**				
Dept. .... Job No..............				
MATERIAL	CODE No.	QTY.	UNIT PRICE	£
REQUISITION BY......... APPROVED BY........ DATE...............				

system now described is very basic and oversimplified but it contains the essential features of every satisfactory system.

A gatekeeper should be stationed at the entrance to a firm's delivery bay. He should enter all goods delivered to the firm on a GRN which he will complete in triplicate. One copy of the GRN

Fig. 15.3

Bin Card

DATE	RECEIVED		ISSUED		BALANCE	
	GRN No.	Quantity	SR No.	Quantity	Quantity	Check

The A.B. Manufacturing Co plc
Bin Card

DESCRIPTION OF STOCK..................... CODE No...............
BIN No.......................... RE-ORDER LEVEL........................

Fig. 15.4

Stores Ledger Card

The A.B. Manufacturing Co plc
Stores Ledger Card

DESCRIPTION OF STORES.................... CODE No...............

MAXIMUM STOCK			MINIMUM STOCK			RE-ORDER LEVEL	
RECEIPTS			ISSUES			BALANCE	
Date	Ref	Quantity	Date	Ref	Quantity	Quantity	Price £

will go to the storekeeper, the second will go to the accounts department and the gatekeeper will retain the third copy.

The storekeeper will check the goods received against his copy of the GRN and then place the goods into store. Each rack, bin or floor space in which goods are stored will have a Bin Card and the receipt of goods will be recorded on it. The accounts department will update the Stores ledger from their copy of the GRN, which they will also use to check invoices before payment.

The storekeeper will issue goods from store on receipt of a properly authorised SR which will be used as the basis for recording the items on the Bin Card before it is passed to the accounts department for the appropriate entry to be made in the Stores ledger. At regular intervals, the actual stocks on hand should be checked and compared with the Bin Cards, and the Bin Cards compared with the Stores ledger.

Stock-taking is an essential step to be taken before the preparation of final accounts at the year end. A description of each item of stock will be entered on the stock sheets with the quantity that has been physically counted. The unit prices will be entered, multiplied by the quantities, and the amount for each type of stock entered into a total column on the stock sheet. The total column will be added to arrive at the total stock in hand.

15.4   Prudence and Cost and Net Realisable Value

Profit must not be overstated or anticipated before it is realised. Stock must not be valued higher than cost, and if net realisable value is lower, then that must be used. Cost, as we already know from Chapter 9 may include a proper proportion of 'carriage inwards'. It may also include a proportion of any charges incurred in putting the stock into saleable condition, e.g. packaging. Net realisable value is the price at which goods can be sold, less any further costs of putting it into a saleable condition. For example, stock which cost £100 and which can be sold for £110 providing a further £15 is spent in making it saleable has a net realisable value of £(110 – 15) = £95 and as this is less than cost (£100), the stock should be valued at £95.

Remember

Stocks should be valued at the lower of cost and net realisable value (prudence concept)

15.5   FIFO, LIFO and AVCO

A problem may arise when deciding what is the cost price of stock. If stock can be identified with particular invoices, the cost price is known. The cost of operating a system to identify stock with invoices in that way will usually be more than any benefits to be obtained from the system. Stock is usually valued, therefore, in one of three ways:

(i) First in, first out (FIFO). The stock is deemed to be used or sold in rotation, i.e. earliest purchases used first.

(ii) Last in, first out (LIFO). The most recent purchases of stock are assumed to be used before earlier purchases.

(iii) Average cost (AVCO). Each receipt of stock entails a fresh calculation of the average cost of stock in hand.

Fig. 15.5

Methods of Pricing Stock

FIFO							
	Receipts and Issues				Balance		
Date	Units Received	Units Issued	Unit Price	£	Units	Price	£
			£			£	
April 1	200		10	2,000	200	10	2,000
4		100	10	1,000	100	10	1,000
6	150		12	1,800	100	10	
					150	12	2,800
8		120	(100) 10	1,000			
			(20) 12	240			
				1,240	130	12	1,560

LIFO							
	Receipts and Issues				Balance		
Date	Units Received	Units Issued	Unit Price	£	Units	Price	£
			£			£	
April 1	200		10	2,000	200	10	2,000
4		100	10	1,000	100	10	1,000
6	150		12	1,800	100	10	
					150	12	2,800
8		120	12	1,440	100	10	
					30	12	1,360

	Receipts and Issues				Balance		
AVERAGE PRICE							
Date	Units Received	Units Issued	Unit Price	£	Units	Average Price £	£
April 1	200		£ 10	2,000		£	2,000
4		100	10	1,000	100	10.00	1,000
6	150		12	1,800	1,000 = 100 × 10 1,800 = 150 × 12		
					2,800 ÷ 250 = 11.20		
					250	11.20	2,800
8		120	11.20	1,344	130	11.20	1,456

Note that the words *deemed* and *assumed* are used in describing FIFO and LIFO. Stock is not necessarily issued in that order; it is merely a convention for calculating stock values.

Each of the three methods is illustrated in Fig. 15.5.

Points to Note

(i) Each method places a different value on stock.

(ii) FIFO is the method usually preferred as it is the most simple and, in times of rising prices, produces a higher stock valuation figure, hence more profit.

(iii) LIFO produces lower closing stock figures in times of rising prices therefore lower profits. This is not very acceptable to the owners of a business, especially as it assumes a poor method of stock control, i.e. stock is not issued in rotation and is not acceptable at all by income tax officials whose job it is to tax people on realistic profits.

(iv) AVCO has the disadvantage of requiring a new average to be calculated with every delivery of stock.

15.6 Effect of Stock Valuation on Profits

The basis upon which stocks are valued affect the profit for the year. The closing stock of one year, however, is the opening stock of the next year. Therefore, any distortion of profit in one year tends to be evened out in the next year. In fact, over the whole life of a business, the total profits will be the same whichever method of valuing stock is used. (See Fig. 15.6 on page 160.)

Fig. 15.6

Effect of Stock Valuation on Profits

Business started in Year 1 and closed in Year 4

Stock valued	Year	1	2	3
		£	£	£
FIFO		1,000	2,000	3,000
LIFO		500	1,000	2,500

Annual sales: £10,000; Annual purchases: £5,000.

a. FIFO	Year	1		2		3		4	Total
			£		£		£	£	£
Sales			10,000		10,000		10,000	10,000	
Opening stock			1,000		2,000		3,000		
Purchases		5,000	5,000		5,000		5,000		
		5,000	6,000		7,000		8,000		
Closing stock		1,000	2,000		3,000				
Cost of sales			4,000		4,000		4,000	8,000	
Gross profit			6,000		6,000		6,000	2,000	20,000

b. LIFO	Year	1		2		3		4	Total
			£		£		£	£	£
Sales			10,000		10,000		10,000	10,000	
Opening stock			500		1,000		2,500		
Purchases		5,000	5,000		5,000		5,000		
		5,000	5,500		6,000		7,500		
Closing stock		500	1,000		2,500		—		
Cost of sales			4,500		4,500		3,500	7,500	
Gross profit			5,500		5,500		6,500	2,500	20,000

In order to avoid artificial fluctuations in profits from year to year, which would amount to manipulation of profit if done intentionally, whichever method of valuing stock is selected should be applied consistently from year to year unless a change is required by a change in circumstances. This introduces another basic accounting principle known as *the consistency concept* which applies to the accounting treatment of all items recorded in the accounts.

> **Remember**
>
> Concept of consistency: all items should be treated consistently in accounts from one year to another

15.7 Examination Hints

 (i) Be prepared to explain FIFO, LIFO and AVCO, giving examples and to compute stock values from given data.
 (ii) Be prepared to explain the effect of FIFO, LIFO and AVCO on gross and net profit and its relevance in the Balance Sheet.
(iii) Make sure you understand and are able to explain the concept of consistency.

15.8 What Should I Have Learned in this Chapter?

  (i) Stock is an important item in most businesses and must be controlled and valued with care.
 (ii) Three methods of valuing stock are FIFO, LIFO and AVCO.
(iii) The method of valuing stock is important in the calculation of annual profits, but has no effect upon the total profits over the whole life of a business.
(iv) The concept of consistency must be applied to the valuation of stock as well as to all other items in the accounts.

Exercises

1 On 1 April Brown purchased 200 bodgetts for £1 each. He purchased another 50 bodgetts on 10 April for £1.20 each and a further 100 on 28 April at £1.40 each. He sold 150 bodgetts on 12 April and a further 80 on 20 April. His closing stock on 30 April, valued on FIFO basis will be valued at:
  (a) £120
  (b) £164
  (c) £168
  (d) £144.

2   At 31 December 19-7 Patel undervalued his closing stock by
£300. This under valuation would have the following effect
upon his gross profit for the year ended 31 December 19-7:
(a) to increase it by £300
(b) to decrease it by £300
(c) to increase it by £600
(d) to decrease it by £600.

3   (a) Explain the meaning of the following terms, used in
connection with stock valuation:
  (i) first in first out (FIFO)
  (ii) last in first out (LIFO).
(b) Use an example to show which of the two methods (FIFO
or LIFO) will produce a higher figure of stock valuation in
times of rising prices.
(c) Explain the effect on a firm's gross profit of overvaluing
closing stock.
(AEB June 1983)

4   At 1 January 1981 Brian Jenkins had 1,500 articles in stock
which had cost him £2 each. During the month of January, he
purchased 2,000 more articles at the same price. He sold 2,500
at £3.00 each and 100 at £2.50 each.
  You are required to:
  (i) Draw up a simple stock record to show the number of
  items in stock at the end of the month.
  (ii) Prepare his Trading account for the month of January
  to show clearly the cost of sales and gross profit.
(RSA Stage 1 1982)

5   Edward Greenwood is a sole trader whose year-end is 31
January each year. Owing to pressure of business, he is unable
to value his stock-in-trade at the close of business on 31
January 1984 but he does so on 7 February 1984 when the
value, at cost price, is calculated at £2,830.
  For the period 1-7 February his purchases were £296 of
which goods costing £54 were in transit at the time of
stocktaking.
  Sales for the period 1-7 February amounted to £460, all of
which had left the warehouse at the time of stocktaking.
Greenwood's gross profit is 20% of sales.
  Also during the period 1-7 February, Greenwood took
goods costing £38 for his personal use.
  Included in the valuation figure of £2,830 given above were

goods which cost £120, but which had a market price of £97 only at the date of the year-end, i.e. 31 January 1984.

Required:
Calculate the figure which should be shown as 'Stock at 31 January 1984' in Greenwood's Trading account for the year ended 31 January 1984.

Note: Calculations must be shown.
(LCCI 1984)

6   (a) Explain the meaning of the statement 'cost or net realisable value, whichever is the lower', which is frequently used in connection with stock valuation.
   (b) State how an undervalued closing stock would affect the calculation of:
      (i) the gross and net profits at the end of the year in which the incorrect valuation occurred
      (ii) the net profit of the following year.
   (c) Give two reasons why closing stock may be valued at less than cost price.
   (d) Explain why, whether closing stock is over or undervalued (assuming this is the only mistake), the balance sheet totals will still agree.
   (AEB 'O' level June 1985)

7   The following figures are taken from the annual accounts of Trumpington Brothers. The accounting year of the firm ends on 31 December.

	Stock at 31 December £	Net Profit for year £
1979	31,000	7,000
1980	24,300	14,900
1981	42,800	23,100
1982	32,700	11,400

An examination of the Partnership's record shows that whilst the stock at 31 December 1982 was correctly valued at £32,700, there were errors in the valuation of the stock at the end of the three previous years. The stock at 31 December 1978 had been valued correctly.

The stock at 31 December 1979 was undervalued by £4,000.
The stock at 31 December 1980 was undervalued by £2,700.
The stock at 31 December 1981 was overvalued by £5,200.

You are required:
(a) to redraft the above table, setting out all the items at the amounts at which they would have appeared in the annual accounts if stock had been correctly valued at all relevant dates, and
(b) to point out, very briefly, why these changes in the amounts of each year's net profits are important for the owners when studying the progress of the business. Discussion is not required on the principles of stock valuation.

Show all workings adjacent to your answer.
(Cambridge 'O' level 1983)

Chapter 16

Partnership Accounts

16.1 What Topics are Covered in this Chapter?

This chapter explains what a partnership is and why some people choose to carry on business in partnership. We then consider partnership agreements and some provisions of the Partnership Act 1890 before looking at the special requirements of accounting for partnerships, goodwill and partnership changes.

16.2 Partnerships

Two or more people may carry on business together with the intention of earning profits. Such an arrangement is called a *partnership*. Except for certain professional people like solicitors and accountants no firm may have more than 20 partners. People usually enter into partnerships because they are unable individually to raise sufficient capital. Perhaps somebody is good at making things but he needs a partner who is better than he at selling them to ensure the business is successful. These are but two of many reasons why people enter into partnerships.

16.3 Partnership Agreements and the Partnership Act 1890

Partners need to agree on certain basic matters affecting their rights as partners, such as the amount of capital each is to contribute, and how profits or losses are to be shared. If they do not contribute capital equally, they may agree that they are to be paid interest on their capital to give an extra share of profit to those who contribute most.

On the other hand, to discourage partners from withdrawing their shares of profit from the partnership too readily, they may agree to charge interest on drawings. If a partner makes a loan to the firm over and above his agreed amount of capital, there must be agreement as to the amount of interest he will receive on his loan. A partner's services to the firm may be recognised by payment to him of a salary, but you must remember that this is simply another method of dividing the profits.

All the foregoing matters should be covered by a partnership agreement which need not be in writing, but should be and usually is. In the absence of agreement on any point, the rights and duties of partners are decided by the *Partnership Act 1890*. This states that all partners may contribute equally to the capital of the firm and that profits and losses shall be shared equally. Interest on partners' loans shall be paid at the rate of 5% per annum, but the partners shall not be entitled to interest on capital nor required to pay interest on drawings. Partners are not entitled to salaries.

Remember

Partnership Act 1890.
Unless agreed otherwise:
Equal capital and shares of profits/losses.
Interest on loans 5% p.a.
No interest on capital or drawings.
No salaries.

Every partner is jointly liable with the other partners for the firm's debts and may take part in conducting the firm's business, unless special steps have been taken to limit his liability for the debts.

16.4   Partnership Accounts

Interest on partners' loans to the firm is an expense of the firm and is debited in the Profit and Loss account; it is a charge to be taken into account in arriving at the net profit of the firm. All other amounts paid or due to the partners, including their salaries, are shares, or appropriations, of profit and are shown in a Profit and Loss Appropriation account placed immediately following the Profit and Loss account. It is not usual to give the Appropriation account a separate heading.

Remember

Debit interest on partners' loans to Profit and Loss account

Debit partners' salaries to Profit and Loss Appropriation account

---

There must be separate Capital and Drawings accounts for each partner. It is usual to treat the partners' capitals as fixed amounts, not increased by profits nor reduced by drawings or losses. Profit shares, salaries and interest on capital, if any, are credited to Partners' Current accounts, which are also debited with their shares of losses and the balances on their Drawings accounts at the year end, and any interest on drawings. In an examination show the Capital, Drawings and Current accounts in columnar form.

Fig. 16.1

Appropriation, Capital and Current Accounts with Balance Sheet extract

Black and Brown are in partnership sharing profits equally. The following data is available for the year to 31st December 19-7: Capitals at 1.1.-7: Black, £5,000; Brown, £3,000; drawings for year to 31.12.-7: Black £1,200, Brown £1,000; Loan to firm: Black £2,000 with interest at 8% p.a.; salary: Brown £800 p.a. Interest on capital and drawings, 5% p.a. Profit for year to 31.12.-7 after interest: £10,000.

Black and Brown: Profit and Loss and Appropriation Accounts (Extract)
for the year to 31.12.-7

	£	£
(Net profit before interest)		10,160
Interest on loan — Black		160
Net profit		10,000
Add: Interest on drawings: Black	60	
Brown	50	
		110
		10,110
Deduct: Salary: Brown	800	
Interest on capital: Black	250	
Brown	150	400	1,200
		8,910
Shares of profit: Black (½)	4,455	
Brown (½)	4,455	8,910

Capital Accounts

	Black £	Brown £			Black £	Brown £
			19-7 Jan 1	Balances b/d	5,000	5,000

Current Accounts

19-7 Dec 31		Black £	Brown £	19-7 Dec 31		Black £	Brown £
	Drawings	1,200	1,000		P & L A/c— interest on loan	160	
	P & L— Approp. A/c— interest on drawings	60	50		P & L A/c: Salary		800
	Balances c/d	3,605	4,355		interest on capital	250	150
					Profit	4,455	4,455
		4,865	5,405			4,865	5,405
				19-8 Jan 1	Balances b/d	3,605	4,355

Black and White: Balance Sheet as at 31 December 19-7 (extract)

Capital	Capital Accounts £	Current Accounts £	£
Black	5,000	3,605	8,605
Brown	3,000	4,355	7,355
	8,000	7,960	15,960
Long term liability: Black, loan account			2,000

16.5   Sale of a Business and Goodwill

When a business is sold the buyer may acquire the fixed assets and stock, leaving the vendor to collect the book debts and pay the creditors. Alternatively, he may take over the book debts and creditors as well. He will not, of course, buy the cash at bank and in hand. The price will rarely reflect the amounts at which these items appear in the balance sheet but will be fixed by what the buyer is prepared to pay and what the seller is prepared to accept. The seller is therefore likely to make a profit or loss on the deal.

The book-keeping entries to record the sale of a business require a Realisation account in the books of the seller and a Purchase of Business account in the books of the buyer.

In the books of the seller, the book values of the assets and liabilities involved in the sale must be transferred to the

Realisation account which will also be credited with the sale price. A credit balance on the Realisation account represents a profit on sale, a debit balance represents a loss. In either case, the balance must be transferred to Capital account. In the case of a partnership, the profit or loss will be divided in profit-sharing ratio. When the sale proceeds have been debited in the cash book, the cash balance will be sufficient to pay first any remaining creditors and then to repay the vendors' capital account.

Fig. 16.2

Sale of partnership business

Bigg and Cropper are in partnership sharing profits equally. Their summarised balance sheet at 31 March 19–7 was: Capital: Bigg £8,000, Cropper £5,000; Creditors: £1,400; Fixed assets £11,000; Stock £1,300; Debtors £1,200: cash £900. They agree to sell the business to Wilson and Morris for £16,000, made up as follows: Fixed assets £12,000; Stock £1,000; Debtors £1,000 and Goodwill £2,000. Creditors will not be taken over by Wilson and Morris, who will each contribute £10,000 to the capital of their business.

In the books of Bigg and Cropper:

Realisation Account

Mar 31	Fixed			19–7			£
	assets	J	11,000	Mar 1	Wilson		
	Stock	J	1,300		and		
	Debtors	J	1,200		Morris	CB	16,000
	Bal. Biggs						
	(½)1,250						
	Cropper						
	(½)1,250		2,500				
			16,000				16,000

Cash

19–7			£	19–7			£
Mar 31	Balance	b/d	900	Mar 31	Creditors		1,400
	Wilson and				Capital		
	Morris		16,000		A/cs:		
					Bigg		9,250
					Cropper		6,250
			16,900				16,900

Capital Accounts

19-7		Bigg £	Cropper £	19-7		Bigg £	Cropper £
Mar 31	Cash	9,250	6,250	Mar 31	Balance b/f	8,000	5,000
					Realisation A/c	1,250	1,250
		9,250	6,250			9,250	6,250

In the books of Wilson and Morris:

Purchase of Business

19-7			£	19-7			£
Mar 31	Vendors A/c	J	16,000	Mar 31	Fixed assets	J	12,000
					Stock	J	1,000
					Debtors	J	1,000
					Goodwill	J	2,000
			16,000				16,000

Bank

19-7			£	19-7			£
Mar 31	Capital A/cs			Mar 31	Vendors A/c		16,000
	Wilson		10,000		Balance	c/d	4,000
	Morris		10,000				
			20,000				20,000
19-7							
Apr 1	Balance	b/d	4,000				

Points to Note

(i) To save space in this example, fixed assets have been shown as a single item, but in practice they would be shown separately.

(ii) The assets are shown in Wilson and Morris's books at the price they paid for them, not necessarily at the amounts at which they were shown in Bigg and Cropper's books.

(iii) It is generally accepted that goodwill should not be retained in the books because of the near impossibility of valuing it realistically, and even the uncertainty that it exists at all in many cases. It is usually written off as soon as possible against profits.

16.6 Retirement of Partners

When a partner retires, he is entitled to have his interest in the firm, represented by the balance on his Capital and Current accounts, repaid to him by the remaining partners. Alternatively, he may leave the money in the business as a loan to the firm, and the balance on his Capital account is transferred to a loan account. Either way, the calculation of his interest in the firm entails a correct valuation of the net assets of the business, including goodwill which may not appear in the books. This entails the use of a Revaluation account. The difference beween this and a Realisation account is that only increases or decreases in asset and liability values are recorded in the Revaluation account. Increases and decreases in the values of assets and liabilities, including goodwill, are transferred to the Revaluation account. Any balance on the Revaluation account is transferred to the Partners' Capital accounts in profit-sharing ratios. The remaining partners may not wish to show goodwill in the books, in which case the goodwill will be redebited to their Capital accounts in their new profit-sharing ratios.

Point to Note

A similar revaluation of assets including goodwill is necessary when profit-sharing ratios are altered without a change in partners.

Fig. 16.3

Retirement of partner

Black, Brown and White are in partnership sharing profits in the proportion 3:2:1. At 31 December 19-7 White decided to retire, at which date the summarised balance sheet was: Fixed assets £18,000; stock £2,000; debtors £2,300; cash £5,700; creditors £4,000; capitals: Black £12,000, Brown £8,000, White £4,000. Fixed assets were estimated to be worth £21,000 and stock £1,000. Goodwill was valued at £4,000. Black and Brown repaid White's capital and decided not to retain goodwill in the books. They will share profits in future equally.

Revaluation Account

		£			£
Stock	J	1,000	Fixed assets	J	3,000
Capitals:			Goodwill	J	4,000
Black (3/6)	J	3,000			
Brown (2/6)	J	2,000			
White (1/6)	J	1,000			
		7,000			7,000

Capital Accounts

	Black £	Brown £	White £		Black £	Brown £	White £
Cash			5,000	Balance b/f	12,000	8,000	4,000
Goodwill	2,000	2,000		Revaluation A/c	3,000	2,000	1,000
Balances c/d	13,000	8,000					
	15,000	10,000	5,000		15,000	10,000	5,000
				Balances b/d	13,000	8,000	

Goodwill

		£		£
Revaluation A/c	J	4,000	Capital A/cs: Black	2,000
			Brown	2,000
		4,000		4,000

Fig. 16.4

Admission of new partner

Margaret and Mary are in partnership sharing profits equally; each has contributed £7,000 to the firm's capital. On 1 January 19-7 they admit Lorraine as a partner and the profits will continue to be shared equally. Lorraine pays £6,000 into the firm of which £2,000 represents her payment for her share of goodwill. It was decided not to retain goodwill in the books.

Capital Accounts

	Margaret £	Mary £	Lorraine £		Margaret £	Mary £	Lorraine £
Goodwill	2,000	2,000	2,000	Balances b/d	7,000	7,000	
Balances c/d	8,000	8,000	4,000	Goodwill	3,000	3,000	
				Bank			6,000
	10,000	10,000	6,000		10,000	10,000	6,000
				Balances b/d	8,000	8,000	4,000

Goodwill

	£		£
Capital A/cs:		Capital A/cs:	
Margaret (½)	3,000	Margaret (⅓)	2,000
Mary (½)	3,000	Mary (⅓)	2,000
		Lorraine (⅓)	2,000
	6,000		6,000

Points to Note

(i) Lorraine paid £2,000 for one third share of goodwill. Therefore goodwill must be worth £6,000.

(ii) The net effect has been to increase Margaret's and Mary's capital by £1,000 each, Lorraine has really bought her share of the goodwill from them in the ratio in which they shared profits.

(iii) The Goodwill account has been shown only as an aid to following the book-keeping entries. The same result would have been achieved by crediting goodwill to the old Partners' Capital accounts in their original profit-sharing ratio and debiting it to the new partnership Capital accounts in their new profit-sharing ratio without opening a Goodwill account.

16.7   Admission of New Partner

On the admission of a new partner, the Capital accounts of the original partners must be adjusted to reflect their respective interests in the firm immediately before the new partner is admitted. A Revaluation account will be used and the existing Partners' Capital account will be adjusted in their old profit-sharing ratios.

Where an adjustment for goodwill is required, Goodwill account will be debited and the original Partners' Capital accounts credited in their old profit-sharing ratios. If they decide that goodwill is not to remain in the books of the new partnership, Goodwill account will be closed by a credit entry and the Capital accounts of all partners in the new partnership will be debited in their new profit-sharing ratios.

16.8   Examination Hints

(i) Read partnership questions carefully and give effect to the terms of the partnership agreement; in the absence of such terms, apply the Partnership Act 1890 provisions.

(ii) Some questions require the entries in Partners' Current accounts to be shown in the Balance Sheet.

(iii) Note whether or not goodwill is to remain in the books.

16.9   What Should I Have Learned in this Chapter?

(i) The rights of partners should be defined in an agreement which should be in writing. The Partnerships Act 1890 applies where there is no agreement.

(ii) Interest on partners' loans is debited in the Profit and Loss account. All other amounts paid or credited to the partners are appropriations of profit and are shown in a Profit and Loss Appropriation account.

(iii) Partnership changes usually require a revaluation of assets and any profit or loss on the Revaluation account should be transferred to the Partners' Capital accounts in the ratio in which they hitherto showed profits and losses.

(iv) Goodwill should be valued on a partnership change and treated in the same way as a revaluation of assets. Prudence requires that goodwill should not be retained in the books and should be written back to the partners' Capital accounts in the new profit-sharing ratio.

Exercises

1   Adams, Brown and Carter are in partnership, sharing profits and losses on the basis of 2 : 1 : 1. Their Net Profit for the year ended 29 February 1984 is £9,530 before taking into consideration the following matters:

The Capital accounts of the partners have been fixed for the past year at the following figures:

Adams	£10,000
Brown	£6,000
Carter	£4,000

The partners are entitled to interest on their Capital accounts at the rate of 8% per annum. In addition, partnership salaries are due as follows:

Brown   £1,500; Carter   £1,100.

The partners' total drawings for the year ended 29 February 1984 have been as follows:

Adams	£2,000
Brown	£1,800
Carter	£1,600

Since the drawings have been made at various times during the year, it is agreed that the partners should be charged interest at the fixed rate of 5% on their total drawings.

Required:

Prepare the Appropriation account of the partnership for the year ended 29 February 1984.

(LCCI Elementary 1984)

2 (a) What is the purpose of the Appropriation account when compiling the final accounts of a partnership?
   (b) Black, White and Grey are in partnership and share profits and losses in the ratio of 3 : 2 : 1 respectively. From the following information prepare:
      (i) the Appropriation account for the partnership,
      (ii) the partners' Current accounts as they appear in the ledger.

	£	£
Net profit for year		24,000
Capital		
Black	12,000	
White	6,000	
Grey	10,000	28,000
Loan account		
Grey		10,000
Current accounts		
Black		4,000 (Dr)
White		3,000 (Cr)
Grey		5,000 (Cr)
Partnership salaries		
Black	8,000	
White	10,000	18,000
Drawings		
Black	5,000	
White	10,000	15,000
Interest on drawings		
Black	600	
White	900	1,500

   Interest on partners' capital is allowed at 10% per annum.
   Interest on Grey's loan is at 20% per annum.
(Joint Matriculation Board 1983)

3 Arthur and George enter into partnership to take over the business of Harry from 1 January 1985. They are to share profits and losses equally, and the purchase is to be on the basis of the final balance sheet of Harry, shown overleaf:

Balance Sheet

Liabilities	£	Assets	£
Capital	21,300	Plant and machinery	12,000
Sundry creditors	2,000	Furniture and fittings	1,500
		Sundry debtors	3,800
		Stock	5,200
		Cash at bank	800
	23,300		23,300

Arthur and George each contributed £13,500 in cash as capital and the money was paid into a bank account in the partnership's name.

The purchase price was agreed at £26,000 which includes goodwill, and a cheque for that amount was paid over to Harry.

All the assets and liabilities were taken over with the exception of the cash balance. The partners decided to revalue the furniture and fittings at £1,000 and to open an account for the Goodwill.

You are required to prepare:
(a) the Journal entries, including brief narration, relating to the above transactions
(b) the opening Balance Sheet for the partnership.

(Cambridge 'O' level 1985)

4   Thomas Hampton and George French, two sole traders, decide to form a partnership as from 1 February 1984. Their respective Balance Sheets as at the close of business on 31 January 1984 were as follows:

Hampton

	£		£
Capital	4,210	Fixtures and fittings	1,960
Creditors	970	Stock	1,780
Bank overdraft	460	Debtors	1,830
		Cash	70
	5,640		5,640

French

	£		£
Capital	4,900	Delivery van	960
Creditors	1,080	Stock	2,120
		Debtors	2,270
		Bank	630
	5,980		5,980

The partnership takes over all the assets and creditors of Hampton *except* the cash. The overdraft is *not* taken over.

For the purpose of the partnership, the assets of Hampton are valued as follows:

Stock £1,780
Fixtures and fittings £1,750
Goodwill £500

Of the debtors to be taken over, £90 are written of as bad.

With regard to the business of French, all the assets and liabilities are taken over with the following revised valuations:

Van £900
Stock £1,950

Goodwill is valued at £700 and there are no bad debts.

Required:

(i) Calculate the opening capital of each of the partners.

Note: Calculations must be shown.

(ii) Draw up the opening Balance Sheet of the partnership.
(LCCI 1984)

5 Day and Week are in partnership sharing profits and losses in the ratio 3 : 2. The following Trial Balance has been extracted from the books of account as at 31 October 1982:

	Dr £	Cr £
Creditors		3,000
Office equipment, at cost	50,000	
Debtors	10,000	
Cash at bank	9,200	
Partners' Capital accounts (at 1 November 1981)		
Day		20,000
Week		10,000
Partners' Current accounts		
Day		2,000
Week	800	
Net profit for the year to 31 October 1982		35,000
	70,000	70,000

Notes:

(1) No appropriations of profit for the year have yet been made.

(2 Week is entitled to a salary of £5,000 per annum.

(3)' Interest on the partners' capital accounts is allowed at a rate of 10% per annum.

(4) Day decides to retire on 31 October 1982, and Month will join Week in partnership as from 1 November 1982. Profits and losses will be shared equally.

(5) The goodwill of the old partnership is estimated to be worth £10,000; Month is to introduce £20,000 in cash as his capital into the new partnership, but no goodwill account is to be opened.

(6) The amount owing to Day on his retirement is to be retained as a loan to the new partnership, except for £16,200 which will be withdrawn in cash. At the same time, Week will also withdraw £10,000 in cash.

(7) All adjustments necessary to close the old partnership and open the new one are to be made in the partners' Current accounts.

You are required to:

(a) prepare Day and Week's profit and loss Appropriation account for the year to 31 October 1982.

(b) prepare the old and new partnership accounts necessary to record the above transactions.

(c) compile the balance sheet of Week and Month as at 1 November 1982.

(AAT 1982)

Chapter 17
The Accounts of Limited Companies

17.1 What Topics are Covered in this Chapter?

The chapter first describes the nature and purpose of limited companies. It compares shareholders with sole traders and partners, then deals with share capital and dividends, debentures and debenture interest. The chapter concludes with the final accounts of limited companies and the purchase of a business by a limited company.

17.2 Limited Companies

Sole traders and partners are personally liable for the whole of the debts of their businesses. If their business assets are insufficient to pay the creditors, their non business assets, including their houses and other possessions may have to be sold to pay the creditors. Their liability can, however, be limited if the business has previously been formed into a limited liability company. The persons who provide the capital of the company are called members or shareholders, and their liability for the debts of the company is limited to the amount they have agreed to subscribe as capital. There must be at least two shareholders. Shareholders as such are not allowed to take part in managing a company; they appoint directors for this purpose.

Shareholders may control the activities of directors by voting for or against resolutions in general meetings of the shareholders.

A company is regarded for all legal purposes as a separate person from the shareholders. When a company is formed, it is registered with the *Registrar of Companies* in accordance with the *Companies Act 1985*, the provisions of which govern limited companies. The registration documents must state the maximum amount of capital the company will have; this is called its *authorised capital*. A company need not issue all its authorised capital at once.

It may issue part of it only and that is known as its *issued capital*. The capital may be divided into different kinds of shares, the most usual of which are ordinary shares and preference shares. Each share represents a fixed amount of capital (eg, £1, 50p or 10p) known as its nominal value.

A company may require shareholders to pay only part of the nominal value of their shares, leaving the remainder to be paid if and when required. The part which has been paid is known as the *called capital*, and the unpaid part is *uncalled capital*.

Fig. 17.1

Share Capital

When the Bowler Hat Co Ltd was registered, it was allowed to raise up to £100,000 capital in ordinary shares of £1 each. It issued 80,000 shares and required the shareholders to pay only 75p for each share purchased at that stage, the other 25p being payable at a later date.

The Bowler Hat Co Ltd has:

Authorised capital of 100,000 ordinary shares of
£1 each: £100,000

Issued share capital of 80,000 ordinary shares of
£1 each: £80,000

Called up share capital of 80,000 ordinary shares of
£1 each, 75p per share paid: £60,000

Uncalled capital of 80,000 ordinary shares of £1
each 25p per share uncalled: £20,000

17.3   Share Premium

It may be thought that a company will always issue its shares *at par*, that is, at their nominal value so that a £1 share will cost the shareholder £1. Sometimes, shares in a company are expected to be particularly attractive to investors and are offered at more than their *par value*. A £1 share, for instance, may be offered at £1.25; the 25p is a premium which investors will be prepared to pay to acquire each £1 share. In this way, the company makes a profit on issuing its shares but this profit may not be used to pay dividends as it has not been earned in the course of normal trading. It is a capital profit and not a revenue profit and may only be used in certain limited ways as prescribed by the Companies Act 1985. It must be shown in the Balance Sheet as a *capital reserve* which is an amount set aside instead of being distributed to shareholders.

A reserve which is not a capital reserve is a *revenue reserve*. Companies may not issue shares at a discount, i.e. at less than their nominal value.

17.4   Types of Share Capital

Preference shares give their holders certain preferential rights over other shareholders, such as the right to receive repayment of their capital in priority to ordinary shareholders when the company is 'wound up', which is the term to describe the end of a company's existence. The preference shareholders may therefore be in a better position than ordinary shareholders if the net assets of the company are insufficient to repay all shareholders.

Preference shareholders are also entitled to receive their dividends in priority to ordinary shareholders and may therefore have an advantage when profits are low. The annual rate of dividend to which preferential shareholders are entitled forms part of the description of the shares, e.g. 8% preference shares entitle the holder to a dividend equal to 8% of the nominal value of the shares each year. If, in any year, profits are insufficient to cover the preference dividend, holders of simple preference shares lose their right to any unpaid dividend for that year.

Cumulative preference shares (often known as Cum. Pref. shares) entitle the holders to arrears of preference dividends in following years if sufficient profits become available. Preference shares may also be described either as *participating* or *non-participating*. The former description means that their holders may receive a further share of profits if sufficient remain after the ordinary shareholders have received their dividend. Non-participating shares do not carry this right.

Because of their preferential position, preference shareholders do not normally have the right to vote at company meetings.

Ordinary shares confer on their holders the right to vote at meetings of the members. They also carry the right to share the profits remaining after the preference shareholders have been paid their dividends. On a winding-up of a company, the ordinary shareholders share the proceeds of the assets remaining after all prior claims have been paid. They may do well or badly as a result. The ordinary share capital of a company is known as the *equity*.

17.5   Revenue Reserves

The directors of a company may decide to set some profits aside instead of distributing them all to shareholders as dividends. Perhaps they intend a big expansion of the business in the future or to invest heavily in the latest technology. They have incurred no liability for these schemes yet but decide it would be prudent to reserve some of the profits in anticipation of future requirements. These amounts, which are set aside out of revenue, are called *revenue reserves* and, unlike capital reserves such as the share premium account, may be distributed as dividends if the directors decide later that they are no longer required for their original purpose. Like the share premium account, these reserves must be shown separately on the balance sheet immediately following the capital.

17.6   Dividends

A shareholder's share of profits is called a *dividend*. At the end of each financial year, the directors propose the amount of dividend to be paid in the form of a resolution to be voted on by the shareholders at their annual general meeting when they consider the annual accounts of the company. If they vote in favour of the resolution, as they usually do, the dividend is *declared* and may then be paid. It follows that at the date of the balance sheet, the dividend has been proposed but not declared or paid, and must therefore be shown as a current liability.

Before directors recommend payment of a dividend, they must consider the profit available, taxation, if any, to be paid out of the profit, the need to transfer any of the profit to reserve and the amount, if any, of preference dividend. The remaining profit will then be available for the ordinary shareholders. If, for example, the profit available for dividend is £10,000 and the issued share capital is 100,000 shares of £1 each, i.e. £100,000, the dividend could be expressed as a percentage of the nominal value of the shares, i.e. 10%; or in pence per share, i.e. 10 pence per share. Notice that it is the *nominal* value of the share which matters. Somebody who receives a 10% dividend on a £1 share for which he has paid £1.25 receives 10p, not 12½p.

Remember

Calculate dividends on nominal value of issued share capital

It is unlikely that the proposed dividend will exactly equal the amount of profit available for distribution, so that there will usually be a balance to be carried forward as a reserve to the following year.

17.7   Debentures and Debenture Interest

A loan made to a company is acknowledged by the company in a document called a *debenture* which contains all the terms of the loan including any security given to the lenders and the rate of interest payable. Debentures are similar in some respects to shares but there are some important differences. Debenture holders are creditors of the company, not members of it. They have no right to vote in company meetings. The company pays interest, not dividends, on debentures, and it is payable whether or not the company has made a profit. *Debenture interest* is therefore debited in the Profit and Loss account, while dividends being appropriations of profit, are debited in the Appropriation account.

Remember

Debenture interest is debited in Profit and Loss account

17.8   Accounts of Limited Companies

The Companies Act 1985 contains a very large number of complex rules governing the accounts of limited companies. Most of them are outside the scope of this book which covers all those you need to know at this stage.

As we have already mentioned, the allocation of profit is shown in an Appropriation account and any unallocated balance is shown in the Balance Sheet as a reserve; it will be carried forward and credited in the next year's Appropriation account.

The balance sheet must show full details of the authorised capital and the issue capital together with details of reserves. Debentures will be shown as long term liabilities unless they are to be *redeemed*, or repaid, within the next 12 months. Dividends proposed but not paid must be shown as current liabilities.

Another important requirement is that fixed assets must be shown at gross book value (normally cost), less depreciation provisions to date, giving the net book values. (See Fig. 17.2 on pages 184–185.)

Points to Note (See Fig. **17.2**)

(i) The balance sheet clearly shows fixed assets, current assets, current liabilities and working capital.

(ii) The debenture loan may be shown in the 'Financed by' section of the Balance Sheet as an addition to share capital and reserves instead of being deducted from the net assets.

17.9   Conversion of a Business into a Limited Company by a Sole Trader or Partnership

This is really the sale of an existing business to a limited company which may have been formed for the purpose. In this case, the

Fig. 17.2

The Final Accounts of a limited company

The following information is available for The Bowler Hat Co Ltd for the year to 31 December 19-6:

Authorised capital: 100,000 ordinary shares of £1 each and 20,000 6% preference shares of £1 each. Issued capital: 80,000 shares of £1 each at £1.20 fully paid; 20,000 preference shares of £1 each fully paid; 8% Debentures: £10,000; profit for the year to 31.12.-6: £12,500 (after interest); undistributed profit brought forward from 31.12.-5: £300.

The directors recommend a transfer to general reserve of £2,000 and an ordinary dividend of 10%. (Taxation is ignored.)

The Bowler Hat Co Ltd
Profit and Loss Account
for the year to 31 December 19-6 (extract)

		£
Net profit before interest		13,300
Interest on 8% Debentures		800
Net profit for year		12,500
Add balance brought forward		300
		12,800
Less transfer to general reserve		2,000
		10,800
Proposed dividends: Preference (6%)	1,200	
Ordinary (10%)	8,000	
		9,200
Balance carried forward		£1,600

(To illustrate the balance sheet, some figures not given above have been assumed for the sake of completeness.)

The Bowler Hat Co Ltd
Balance Sheet as at 31 December 19-6

	Cost	Depreciation to date	Net Book Value
FIXED ASSETS	£	£	£
Freehold premises	80,000	20,000	60,000
Plant and machinery	55,000	28,000	27,000
Motor vehicles	21,000	8,000	13,000
	156,000	56,000	100,000
CURRENT ASSETS			
Stock		24,000	
Debtors and prepayments		17,400	
Cash at bank and in hand		2,500	
		43,900	
Less CURRENT LIABILITIES			
Proposed dividends: Preference	1,200		
Ordinary	8,000		
Creditors and accrued expenses	5,100	14,300	
WORKING CAPITAL			29,600
			129,600
Less LONG TERM LIABILITY: Debenture loan			10,000
			119,600
Financed by:			
Share capital:			
Authorised—100,000 Ordinary shares of £1 each			100,000
20,000 6% Preference shares of £1 each			20,000
Issued—80,000 Ordinary shares of £1 each fully paid			80,000
20,000 6% Preference shares of £1 each fully paid			20,000
			100,000
Reserves:			
Share premium account		16,000	
General reserve		2,000	
Profit and Loss account		1,600	
			19,600
			119,600

consideration for the sale consists of shares in the company. In the vendor's books, the shares will be credited to the company's account and debited to the vendor's capital account. If the company is an existing one which has previously been trading, the issued capital will be increased by the shares forming the purchase consideration and will be balanced by the addition of the assets and liabilities acquired to its own assets and liabilities.

17.10   Examination Hints

(i) Make sure you can prepare a company Balance Sheet in proper form as shown in Fig. 17.2.
(ii) Remember that debenture interest must be paid even if the company makes a loss, and debit it in the Profit and Loss account.
(iii) Calculate dividends on the nominal value of the issued share capital.

17.11   What Should I Have Learned in this Chapter?

(i) A limited liability company limits the liability of shareholders for the debts of the company to the amount they have agreed to subscribe for shares.
(ii) Shares are of various kinds, the main ones being preference and ordinary. Only cumulative preference shares entitle their holders to arrears of dividend.
(iii) 'Proposed' dividends must appear as current liabilities in the Balance Sheet.

Exercises

1   A company's Balance Sheet shows the following information:
   Authorised capital:
      100,000 ordinary shares of £1 each, of which 70,000 were issued
      25,000 6% preference shares of £1 each, of which 20,000 were issued
      Share premium account £14,000
      General reserves £45,000
      9% debentures of £1 each, £30,000.
   What is the issued capital of the company?
   (a) £120,000
   (b) £90,000
   (c) £84,000
   (d) £115,000.

2 In a company's balance sheet, debentures will be found under which of the following headings?
(a) Share capital
(b) Reserves
(c) Long term liabilities
(d) Current assets.

3 A limited company has an issued share capital of £10,000 ordinary shares of £1 each which it has issued at a premium of 10%. At present these shares are worth £1.25 each. The shares will be shown in the company's Balance Sheet as
(a) £11,000
(b) £12,500
(c) £10,000
(d) £9,000

4 The following financial statement was prepared by a person with little training and knowledge of accounting. By coincidence the statement balanced.

B. Simber Ltd
Statement of the financial position of the Company at 31 May 1984

	£		£
Machinery (at cost)	15,000	Authorised and issued	
Depreciation on		share capital	
machinery (to date)	3,500	100,000 £1 ordinary	
General reserve	10,000	shares (50p paid)	100,000
Profit and Loss account		Loan to the company (10	
(credit balance 31 May		years—10%)	20,000
1984)	8,000	Debtors	18,000
Premises (at cost)	40,000	Cash	300
Provision for doubtful			
debts	1,800		
Bank overdraft	4,000		
Stock 1 June 1983	16,000		
Stock 31 May 1984	12,000		
Proposed dividends	5,000		
Goodwill	20,000		
Creditors	3,000		
	138,300		138,300

You are required to use the relevant information in the statement and prepare a balance sheet in *vertical* form, indicating the total capital employed and the working capital. (JMB 'O' level June 1984)

5   The Green Meadow Cleaning Company is registered with an authorised capital of £25,000,000 divided into 5,000,000 10% preference shares of £1 each and 20,000,000 ordinary shares of £1 each.

The following Trial Balance was extracted from the company's books on 31 December 1983.

		£000s			£000s
Premises	B/S	20,000	Preference capital	B/S	5,000
Machinery	B/S	4,000	Ordinary capital	B/S	15,000
Motor vans	B/S	100	Profit and loss		10
Electric power	P&L	10,300	12% debentures	B/S	1,000
Wages	P&L	26,000	Provision for		
Heat and light	P&L	1,500	depreciation:		
Cleaning materials	P&L	400	Machinery	B/S	600
Rates	P&L	700	Vans	B/S	20
Van expenses	P&L	50	Creditors	B/S	15
Bank	B/S	902	Receipts for cleaning	P&L	42,318
Cash	B/S	11			
		63,963			63,963

Prepare an account to show the cleaning company's profit or loss for the year ended 31 December 1983, and a Balance Sheet on that date before the Appropriation account is prepared and dividends declared or paid.

Take into consideration the following:

	£000s
(i) Rates paid in advance	140
(ii) Heat and light account unpaid	7
(iii) Provision for depreciation of machinery to be increased to	900
(iv) Provision for depreciation of motor vans to be increased to	70
(v) Provision for the debenture interest	120

(London 'O' level 1984)

6   The following balances, at 1 January 1984, were taken from the books of Sunderland Limited, which had an authorised capital of 100,000 ordinary shares of £1 each. Issued share capital £60,000 in ordinary shares of £1 each, fully paid; premises £52,000; fittings and equipment £16,200; debtors £9,005; creditors £6,323; stock £4,263; balance at bank £646; profit and loss account, credit balance £8,291; proposed dividend for 1983 £7,500.

During the month of January 1984, some of the company's transactions were:
(1) sold an item of equipment, book value £5,320, for £4,000 by cheque
(2) sold goods on credit £4,000, which had been marked up by 25% on cost
(3) paid the share dividend for 1983, in full.

Required:
(a) The balance sheet of Sunderland Limited at 31 January 1984, assuming there were no other transactions in January, in a form which shows clearly the shareholders' funds and the working capital. Your balance sheet must include the three transactions occurring in January. Where a balance sheet figure has changed as a result of these transactions, you are advised to indicate the direction and amount of the change in brackets, next to the item concerned, within the Balance Sheet.
(b) (i) A definition of ordinary shareholders' funds;
    (ii) An explanation of the meaning of the term 'limited liability'.
(c) An explanation of the main purpose to a company of its Profit and Loss Appropriation account.
(AEB 'O' level 1984)

Chapter 18
The Accounts of Non-Commercial Organisations

18.1 What Topics are Covered in this Chapter?

We now consider the accounting needs of organisations which are not carried on for profit. We study three financial statements produced for such bodies: Receipts and Payments accounts, Income and Expenditure accounts and Balance Sheets.

18.2 Non-Commercial organisations

These include clubs and societies of all kinds, churches, charities and any activity carried on to promote an interest other than the making of profit. In all these cases, the financial affairs of the organisation are usually in the hands of one person, or perhaps of a small committee, who must account to the members for their stewardship. Usually the person entrusted with the stewardship of

Fig. 18.1

Receipts and Payment Account

The Engate and Southfield Sports and Social Club

Receipts and Payments Account for the Year to 31 December 19-7

	£		£
Balance at 1.1.-7	142	Rent of sports ground	500
Subscriptions	1,120	Groundsman's wages	400
Bar receipts	616	Bar stocks	320
Raffle tickets	40	Bartender's wages	150
Dance tickets	75	Prizes	12
		Electricity	160
		New lawn mower	200
		Sports equipment	122
		Balance at 31.12.-7	129
	£1,993		£1,993

club funds is unskilled as a book-keeper apart from being a very busy member of the community, but is pressed into service as honorary (i.e. unpaid) treasurer of the club. Hopefully he or she will keep some record of the club's finances, and that should be a cash book. Many treasurers are quite good at the job and perform a thankless task efficiently.

For the sake of convenience, we will refer to 'clubs' for the remainder of this chapter as the principles are much the same for these as for other non commercial organisations.

18.3   Receipts and Payments Account

This is the simplest form of financial statement which may be produced for a club.

Points to Note (See Fig. 18.1 on page 190.)

   (i) The account is simply a summarised version of the cash book, including the bala⁻ces of cash at the beginning and end of the year.
  (ii) If the cash book contains accounts for cash at bank and cash in hand the summaries of both will have to be combined for the Receipts and Payments account.
 (iii) Many of the items are totals of payments made at intervals during the year, e.g. rent, wages and electricity. A cash book with analysis columns on the same principle as an analysed petty cash book greatly assists the preparation of the Receipts and Payments account especially if it has analysis columns on the receipts side as well.
  (iv) The account includes capital expenditure (mower and equipment) as well as running expenses.
   (v) A Receipts and Payments account is compiled on a cash basis. It ignores the fact that some of the items may relate to an earlier or later period or that some amounts relating to the year in question will not have been entered in the cash book during the year.
  (vi) For many small clubs, a Receipts and Payments account is all that is required.

Remember

A Receipts and Payments account is a cash book summary

Fig. 18.2

Income and Expenditure Account

The data for the Engate and Southfield Sports and Social Club is as in Fig. 18.1 plus the following further information:

	At 31.12.-6	At 31.12.-7
	£	£
Subscriptions owing	90	100
Subscriptions in advance	10	35
Creditors for bar stocks	120	95
Rent paid in advance	80	90
Electricity owing	40	50
Bar stocks	140	100

Bar Trading Account

		£		£
Bar stocks at 1.1.-7		140	Bar receipts	616
Purchases	320			
Add creditors at 31.12.-7	95			
	415			
Less creditors at 31.12.-6	120			
		295		
		435		
less stock at 31.12.-7		100		
		335		
Bartender's wages		150		
		485		
Profit carried to I & E A/c		131		
		616		616

The Engate and Southfield Sports and Social Club

Income and Expenditure Account for the Year to 31 December 19-7

	£	£
Subscriptions $(1,120 - 90 - 35 + 10 + 100)$		1,105
Profit on bar		131
Raffle tickets	40	
less prizes	12	28
Dance tickets		75
		1,339
Less Rent of ground $(500 + 80 - 90)$	490	
Groundsman's wages	400	
Electricity $(160 - 40 + 50)$	170	1,060
Excess of income over expenditure		279

Points to Note

(i) The Income and Expenditure account does not include capital items shown in the Receipts and Payments account.

(ii) The Income and Expenditure account has been adjusted by opening and closing accruals and prepayments.

(iii) The surplus is described as 'surplus of income over expenditure', not as 'profit'. A 'loss' is described as an 'excess of expenditure over income'.

(iv) In practice, arrears of subscription may be written off as bad debts in the following year as the club is unlikely to take any effective action to enforce payment.

Remember

An Income and Expenditure account contains only revenue items on an 'accruals and prepaid' basis

---

18.4 Income and Expenditure Account

As a Receipts and Payments account contains a mixture of capital and revenue items and ignores the principles of matching expenditure to revenue, another form of annual financial statement may be required to fulfil the purpose that a Profit and Loss account has in a commercial undertaking; such a statement is an Income and Expenditure account.

A club may augment its funds by various subsidiary activities such as a bar which is akin to a trading activity. In that event, a trading account is usually produced for that activity and the profit from that account is transferred to the Income and Expenditure account.

Income from other fund-raising activities such as raffles and dances will be shown in the Income and Expenditure account less any relevant expenses to disclose the net proceeds from such activities.

18.5 Balance Sheet

The main point to remember is that a club does not have a capital account. The net assets are represented, or financed, by an

Accumulated Fund which is increased by surpluses of income over expenditure and reduced by excesses of expenditure over income.

Fig. 18.3

Balance Sheet

The summarised balance sheet of the Engate and Southfield Sports and Social Club at 31 December 19-6 was as follows: motor mower £400; equipment £50; subscriptions owing £90; subscriptions in advance £10; creditors £160; prepayments £80; bar stocks £140; cash in hand £142; Accumulated Fund £732. Other information is taken from Figs. 18.1 and 18.2.

The Engate and Southfield Sports and Social Club

Balance Sheet as at 31 December 19-7

	£	£
Fixed assets: Motor mowers (400 + 200)	600	
Equipment (50 + 122)	172	772
Current assets: Bar stocks	100	
Subscriptions owing	100	
Rent prepaid	90	
Cash in hand	129	
	419	
less Current liabilities:		
Subscriptions in advance	35	
Creditors for bar stocks	95	
Electricity	50	180	239
		£1,011
Financed by: Accumulated Fund:		
Balance at 1.1.-7		732
add Excess of income over expenditure		279
		£1,011

18.6   Examination Hints

(i) Read questions carefully and make sure you give effect to all requirements, e.g. depreciation of fixed assets. Only write off arrears of subscriptions if instructed by the question.

(ii) These questions usually require only a few adjustments for accruals and prepayments which may be shown in brackets, as in Fig. 18.3.

18.7 What Should I Have Learned in this Chapter?

(i) Non-commercial organisations prepare either Receipts and Payments accounts or Income and Expenditure accounts, or both.

(ii) Receipts and Payments accounts are prepared on a cash basis, Income and Expenditure accounts are prepared on an accruals basis.

(iii) Non-commercial organisations use an Accumulated Fund account instead of a Capital account.

Exercises

1 The following information relates to the affairs of the Clydeville Social Club which ended its financial year on 31 December 1983:

1983		£
1 January	Subscriptions for 1982 in arrear	120
During 1983	Subscriptions for current year received	4,710
	Arrears for 1982 received	90
	Subscriptions paid in advance for 1984	27
31 December	Subscriptions for 1983 not received	84
1 January	Rates in arrears	200
8 January	Rates due in November 1982 paid	400
8 May 1983	Rates due and paid	450
7 November 1983	Rates due and paid	450

Rates due in November each year covers the period from 1 October that year to 31 March in the following year.

Calculate for the year ended 31 December 1983 the amount for (i) subscriptions and (ii) rates which should be shown in the

(a) Receipts and Payments account

(b) Income and Expenditure account

(c) Balance Sheet at 31 December 1983, as an asset or liability.

(London 'O' level 1984)

2   The Shockers Cricket Club was formed on 1 April 1980. From their Receipts and Payments account shown below, you are required to prepare:
   (i) an Income and Expenditure account for the year ended 31 March 1981
   (ii) a balance sheet as at that date.

Receipts and Payments Account (year ended 31 March 1981)

	£		£
Loans from members @		Bar refreshments	
8% per annum	450	purchased	203
Bar takings	246	Purchase of lockers for	
Subscriptions from		players	180
members	540	Travelling expenses	96
Match receipts	114	Printing	48
		Stationery and postage	28
		Rent	225
		Cricket league fees	69
		Rates and insurance	150
		Purchase of sporting	
		equipment	152
		Balance c/d	199
	1,350		1,350

Notes at 31 March 1981:
   (i) A stationery bill of £6 is outstanding.
   (ii) There were bar stocks valued at £48.
   (iii) The interest on loans from members was due for the full year ended 31 March 1981.
   (iv) Rent was prepaid into the forthcoming year £25.
   (v) £80 is to be paid to the Club Treasurer for his services.
(RSA 1982)

3   The following were the assets and liabilities of the Fitorama Sports Club on 1 July 1983:

	£
Assets	
Premises at cost	28,000
Fittings and equipment	4,200
Deposit in building society	2,700
Cash and bank balance	2,027
Liabilities	
Electricity bill outstanding	168

The club's cash book for the year to 30 June 1984 showed the following:

Receipts	£	Payments	£
Balance b/fwd	2,027	Rates	1,250
Subscriptions for year	4,870	Groundsman	2,200
Competition entry fees	2,700	Purchase of sports	
Sale of dance tickets	450	equipment	1,650
		League entry fee	20
		Dance expenses	300
		Prizes for competitions	3,050
		Electricity	740
		Balance c/fwd	837
	10,047		10,047

You are required to:
(a) Calculate the accumulated fund at 1 July 1983.
(b) Prepare the club's Income and Expenditure account for the year ended 30 June 1984, and a Balance Sheet on that date after taking into account the following points:
    (1) An electricity account of £194 was outstanding at the end of the year.
    (2) The amount paid for rates included £200 paid in advance.
    (3) During the year interest of £107 has been received from the building society. This interest has been reinvested in the Society. (RSA 1984)

4   You were appointed Treasurer of the Alpha Debating Society, a new club formed on 1 March 1983.

    Using the information given below you are to prepare for the first Annual Meeting on 29 February 1984:
      (i) The Receipts and Payments account.
     (ii) The Tea-Bar Trading account.
    (iii) The Income and Expenditure account.
    (iv) The Balance Sheet as at 29 February 1984.
Information:
(a) The annual subscription is £5. Forty-eight members joined and all have paid their subscriptions. Three members have also paid the second year's subscription.
(b) The annual hire of rooms cost £60; the club has paid £40.
(c) Furniture costing £150 has been bought and paid for.
(d) Tea, biscuits, etc costing £118 has been bought. £18 of this has not been paid.
(e) The Secretary's expenses amounted to £14. They have been paid.
(f) £58 fees to visiting speakers have been paid.

(g) The takings of the tea-bar were £194.

(h) The closing stock of tea, biscuits, etc on 29 February was £16.

(i) You are to charge 10% depreciation on the furniture.

(Northern Ireland 1984)

5   Crete High School has a camp in Wales for two weeks on a yearly basis to enable its pupils to qualify for the Duke of Edinburgh's Award. The following balances remained on 1 August 1982, immediately after the 1982 camp: tents £400; cash at bank £132; pots and pans £94; debtors £36.

Details of the 1983 camp were: 300 pupils attended, paying fees of £11 each. The pupils were divided into groups of five and each group paid £2 for a map of Snowdonia which became their property. School fund provided a subsidy of £2 per pupil. The following payments were made: hire of coaches £1,350; site fees £287; purchase of additional tents £250; purchase of food and drink £1,855; mountain rescue fees £28; ambulance fees £12; staff travelling expenses £86; maps of Snowdonia £100.

On 31 July 1983, site fees £32 were still outstanding, stock of tinned food was valued at £80 and there was £184 at the bank. Debtors remaining after the 1982 camp were written off as irrecoverable. Total fixed assets were to be depreciated by £78.   (AEB 'O' level 1984)

Required:

(a) For Crete High School
    (i) the income and expenditure account for the year ended 31 July 1983
    (ii) the balance sheet as at 31 July 1983.

(b) An explanation as to what the accumulated fund comprised at 1 August 1982.

During the first few days of August 1983 the stock of tinned food was sold to staff and parents at an average mark up of 15% on cost and the outstanding site fees account was settled. Before school closed for the summer, it was decided to buy five tents at £15 each and twenty compasses at £1.50 each.

Required:

(c) A statement showing whether sufficient funds existed to make the necessary purchases (tents and compasses). If insufficient funds are available, how much will be required from school funds?

Chapter 19

Incomplete Records

19.1　What Topics are Covered in this Chapter?

This chapter shows how Trading and Profit and Loss accounts and Balance Sheets may be produced for businesses for which proper double-entry accounting records have not been kept.

19.2　Incomplete Records

Many small businesses are run by people who may be excellent in their chosen trade but who know practically nothing about book-keeping and accounts. Such people, if they are wise, will seek the services of a skilled book-keeper or accountant to maintain their business records in good order. Otherwise, it is usual to find that no proper records have been kept and, of course, no annual accounts have been produced. The trader gets into difficulty with the local Inspector of Taxes whose job it is to see that people are assessed to income tax on their earnings or profits. Whatever the reason, the time arrives sooner or later when accounts are required for the business.

Such records as have been kept may consist of any one or more of the following: cash book, bank statements, cheque counterfoils, copies of bank paying-in slips, invoices and statements and, perhaps, copies of receipts given to customers. There may even be till rolls.

19.3　Statement of Affairs

The most elementary technique for calculating the profit or loss of a business over a period of time is to use the accounting equation in one of its forms: capital = assets − liabilities, and to apply the principle that profits increase capital and losses decrease capital. If we can calculate capitals at the beginning and end of a period, the difference beween the two capitals will indicate the profit or loss for the period, subject to adjustments for any new capital introduced and any withdrawn.

> **Remember**
>
> Adjust closing capital by additions to it and drawings
> during the period covered

To calculate capital at any time, we need to know the assets and liabilities existing at that time. While it may be easy to list these as they exist now, it may be more difficult to list them as they existed a year ago. We can probably rely on memory as far as fixed assets are concerned, but debtors and creditors a year ago can only be ascertained by looking at the copies of invoices. Cash can be arrived at by adding the usual amount of cash kept in hand to the balance on the bank statements. Stock will probably have to be estimated from memory. With this information, we can calculate the capital at the beginning and end of the period.

Fig. 19.1

Calculation of Profits from Statement of Affairs

Gupta runs a one-man business as a builder/decorator. From such records as are available, otherwise from memory, he is able to provide the following information for 19-7: Plant and loose tools at 1.1.-7: £1,000 (31.12.-7: £1,150); stock of materials at 1.1.-7: £200 (31.12.-7: £140); debtors at 1.1.-7: £300 (31.12.-7: £650); creditors at 1.1.-7: £40 (31.12.-7: £180); cash at 1.1.-7: £120 (31.12.-7: £400).

During the year he has drawn £20 a week as living expenses.

Statement of affairs

	At 1.1.-7 £	At 31.12.-7 £
Assets:		
Plant and loose tools	1,000	1,150
Stocks of materials	200	140
Debtors	300	650
Cash	120	400
	1,620	2,340
Less liabilities — creditors	40	180
	op. Cap 1,580	2,160
Add drawings during year (52 × £20)		1,040
		3,200
Deduct opening capital		1,580
Increase in capital = profit for year		£1,620

Points to Note

(i) Statements of affairs are often prepared in the form of a horizontal (two-sided) statement; we have used the vertical form as it is easier to follow.

(ii) The statements resemble Balance Sheets but are not called that because Balance Sheets contain balances extracted from books of account, which cannot be the case when the records are incomplete.

(iii) Gupta's drawings are added to the capital at 31 December 19-7 because, had he not drawn any money out of the business, the assets would have been greater by that amount.

(iv) A disadvantage of calculating profit in this manner from statements of affairs is the absence of details which would be available had a Trading and Profit and Loss account been prepared.

19.4   Trading and Profit and Loss Accounts and Balance Sheets

If a cash book has been kept, it should be possible to use the details of receipts and payments to produce final accounts. Even if a cash book has not been kept, it may be possible to prepare one from whatever other information is available, such as bank statements, paying-in slips, cheque counterfoils or copy receipts.

The steps are:

(i) prepare opening statement of affairs,

(ii) write up and analyse cash book, comparing it with bank statements, if possible,

(iii) adjust cash book summary for accruals and prepayments,

(iv) prepare final accounts.

(See Fig. 19.2 on pages 202-203).

Points to Note

(i) To arrive at the sales it was first necessary to calculate cost of sales. Sales were

$$£2,055 \times \frac{140}{100} = £2,877$$

(ii) Cash payments made out of takings (creditors £400, sundry expenses £115) must be added to the cheque payments.

Fig. 19.2

Final Accounts from incomplete records

Ms Pretty has been in business for a few years selling fancy goods. A cash book is the only record she has kept in which she has recorded all amounts banked, and all cheques drawn. The following is a summary of the cash book for the year to 31 December 19–7:

	£		£
Balance at 1.1.–7	500	Creditors for goods	1,215
Paid into bank	2,000	Rent	300
Loan from father	200	Electricity	160
		Postage and stationery	40
		Purchase of shop fittings	120
		Cheques drawn for personal	
		expenses	700
		Balance c/d	165
	£2,700		£2,700

Ms Pretty banked her takings after paying the following in cash: creditors £400; sundry expenses £115.

At 31.12.–6 Ms Pretty estimated her assets and liabilities to be: shop fittings £600; stock £980; debtors £120; rent prepaid £40; creditors for goods £210; electricity owing £30.

At 31.12.–7 the following data is available: stock £520; debtors £80; rent prepaid £50; creditors for goods £190; electricity owing £25. Ms Pretty sells her goods at 40% above cost price.

Statement of affairs at 1.1.19–7

	£	£
Assets: Shopfittings		600
Stock		980
Debtors		120
Rent prepaid		40
Cash		500
		2,240
Less liabilities: Creditors for goods	210	
Electricity owing	30	
		240
Capital at 1.1.19–7		£2,000

Ms Pretty
Trading and Profit and Loss Account
for the year to 31 December 19-7

	£	£
Sales (cost of sales plus 40%) (see note i)		2,877
Stock at 1.1.-7	980	
Purchases (1, 215 – 210 + 190 + 400) (see note ii)	1,595	
	2,575	
Less stock at 31.12.-7	520	
Cost of sales		2,055
Gross profit		822
Less Rent (300 + 40 – 50)	290	
Electricity (160 – 30 + 25)	155	
Postage and stationery	40	
Sundry expenses (see note ii)	115	
		600
Net profit		£222

Ms Pretty
Balance Sheet as at 31 December 19-7

	£	£	£
Fixed assets: Shop fittings (600 + 120)			720
Current assets: Stock		520	
Debtors		80	
Rent prepaid		50	
Cash		165	
		815	
Less Current liabilities: Creditors	190		
Electricity owing	25		
		215	
Working capital			600
			£1,320
Financed by Capital: Balance at 1.1.-7		2,000	
Net profit for year		222	
		2,222	
Less drawings (700 + 402) (see note iv)		1,102	
			1,120
Loan			200
			£1,320

(iii) Shop fittings purchased during the year £120, is capital expenditure and must be added to the assets at 1 January 19-7.

(iv) Summarised cash receipts and payments:

		£
Sales		2,877
Less debtors at 31 December 19-7		80
		2,797
Add debtors at 1 January 19-7		120
Cash received in year		2,917
Payments: Banked	2,000	
Creditors	400	
Sundry expenses	115	
		2,515
Cash not accounted for—treated as drawings		402

19.5   Stock Lost by Fire or Theft

The sales figure in Fig. 19.2 was a 'missing' figure; we had to calculate it from the cost of sales. Similar techniques must sometimes be used to calculate the value of stock lost by theft or fire for the purposes of making an insurance claim. If the stock records have been kept accurately and up to date at the time of the loss, there should be no problem provided the records have survived the fire or theft. However, all too often, such records have not been kept and it is necessary to obtain whatever information is available to calculate the loss of stock. The method involves the preparation of a trading account as at the date of the loss, with the closing stock as a balancing figure to complete the account. We look first at a simple example.

Fig. 19.3

Calculation of missing stock

Sobers's balance sheet at 31 December 19-6 showed his stock on that date at £3,000. On 31 March 19-7, his premises were burgled and all the stock was taken. His records showed that from 1 January 19-7 to 31 March 19-7 his purchases amounted to £4,000 and his sales were £7,500. Sobers adds 50% to cost price to arrive at his selling price. Calculate the value of stock which was stolen.

Trading Account for the Period 1 January to 31 March 19-7

	£		£
Stock at 1.1.-7	3,000	Sales	7,500
Purchases	4,000		
	7,000		
Stock at 31.3.-7	?		
Cost of sales	?		
Gross profit	?		
	7,500		7,500

Gross profit:
50% is added to cost of goods sold to arrive at sales price. The addition to cost is called *mark-up*. The mark-up is ½ of the cost. To express this as a fraction of sales, add the numerator of the fraction to the denominator:

$$\frac{1}{2+1} = \frac{1}{3}$$

The difference between cost price and selling price is therefore ½ of cost price or ⅓ of selling price (see note below). Therefore, on sales of £7,500, the gross profit, or margin, is £7,500 × ⅓ = £2,500.

Cost of sales:
If the gross profit is £2,500, cost of sales is £(7,500 − 2,500) = £5,000.

Stock at 31.3.-7
Opening stock plus purchases = £7,000 and cost of sales = £5,000. Therefore closing stock is £(7,000 − 5,000) = £2,000.

The value of the stolen stock was therefore £2,000.

Point to Note

Mark-up and margin are very important topics in accounting. *Mark-up* is gross profit expressed as a fraction or percentage of cost of sales; *margin* is gross profit expressed as a fraction or percentage of sales. To calculate margin from mark-up, convert percentage, if necessary, to a fraction and add the numerator of the fraction to the denominator.

e.g. mark-up = 25% or ¼ ; margin = 1/4 + 1 = ⅕

To calculate the mark-up from the margin, take the fraction of the margin and deduct the numerator from the denominator.

e.g. margin = 20% or ⅕; mark-up = 1/5 − 1 = ¼

Example: Cost price = £10. Mark-up = 50% or ½ = £5; Selling price is £15. Margin = 1/2 + 1 (or ⅓) of £15 = £5.

In a more complicated question it may be necessary also to calculate the purchases and sales.

Fig. 19.4

Calculation of stock destroyed by fire

Richards lost the whole of his stock in a fire on 30 June 19-7 together with his records of sales and purchases. His last balance sheet, at 31 March 19-7, showed stock at £4,200, debtors £2,500 and creditors £1,750.

Records salvaged from the fire showed that between 1 April and 30 June he had received £3,800 from debtors and paid £1,600 to creditors; and that at 30 June he was owed £1,900 and owed creditors £1,130.

Richards expected to sell his goods at a margin of 25%.

Calculation of stock lost:

Debtors Summary

	£		£
Debtors at 31.3.-7	2,500	Cash received	3,800
Sales (balancing figure)	3,200	Debtors at 30.6.-7	1,900
	5,700		5,700

Creditors Summary

	£		£
Cash paid	1,600	Creditors at 31.3.-7	1,750
Balances at 30.6.-7	1,130	Purchases (balancing	
		figure)	980
	2,730		2,730

Trading Account for the Period 1 April to 30 June 19-7

	£		£
Stock at 1.4.-7	4,200	Sales	3,200
Purchases	980		
	5,180		
Stock at 30.6.-7	?		
Cost of sales	?		
Gross profit			
(¼ of £3,200)	800		
	3,200		3,200

Cost of sales = Sales *less* gross profit £(3,200 − 800) = £2,400

Stock at 30.6.-7 = Opening stock and purchases − cost of sales = £(5,180 − 2,400) = £2,780

Value of stock destroyed by fire = £2,780

Points to Note

(i) The missing figures for purchases and sales are calculated by finding the amounts necessary to make the opening balances of creditors and debtors, respectively, after adjusting for cash paid and received, come to the closing creditors and debtors.

(ii) The margin is 25% or ¼; therefore the mark-up is $1/4 - 1 = \frac{1}{3}$. Mark-up = cost of sales £2,400 × ⅓ = £800.

19.6 Examination Hints

(i) This chapter should be mastered thoroughly as it covers topics found in many examinations.

(ii) The calculation of profits and preparation of final accounts from incomplete records should present no difficulty if the earlier chapters have been mastered. Difficulty with this topic indicates a necessity to revise topics covered earlier in this book.

19.7 What Should I Have Learned in this Chapter?

(i) Profit for a period may be calculated by a comparison of the opening and closing capitals for the period as shown by statements of affairs.

(ii) If a record of cash receipts and payments has been kept, final accounts may be produced.

(iii) Stock losses may be calculated notwithstanding the lack of stock records.

Exercises

1   Frank Emery is a sole trader who does not operate the double-entry system of book-keeping. His records are accurate, however, and from them the following information has been obtained:

	31 May 1984 £	31 May 1985 £
Stock	1,970	2,140
Debtors	2,330	2,790
Delivery van (*estimated value*)	900	800
Creditors	1,660	1,720
Cash at bank		740
Bank overdraft	390	

During the year ended 31 May 1985 his drawings have been: Cash £1,250, Goods at cost price £110.

Required:
(i) Showing your calculations in each case:
    (a) Calculate Emery's capital at 31 May 1984 and 31 May 1985.
    (b) Calculate Emery's net profit for the year ended 31 May 1985.
(ii) Draw up Emery's Capital account for the year ended 31 May 1985 as it would appear under the double-entry system.

(LCCI Elementary 1985)

2   The following items were taken from the books of Mr S. Thompson, trading as a newsagent, who did not keep proper books of accounts during 1981.

	1 January 1981 £	31 December 1981 £
Stock	860	1,300
Equipment	1,600	2,400
Building	5,000	8,000
Cash at home	20	140
Cash in bank	100	700
Debtors	140	720
Creditors	600	850

Each week Mr Thompson withdraws £30 from the business for his own use.

Prepare a statement of Profit or Loss for the year.

(Northern Ireland 1982)

3   J. Smith and R. Brown are in business but have not kept any books of account. Records give the following information:

	1 March 1982 £	28 February 1983 £
Premises at valuation	53,000	56,000
Stock	7,000	8,400
Debtors	3,700	2,900
Cash in hand and at bank	1,010	870
Creditors	420	610
Drawings during year: J. Smith	5,000	5,000
R. Brown	5,000	5,000

They commenced business with equal contributions of capital, agreed to equal shares of profit and have always taken equal drawings.

(a) Set out the Balance Sheet on 1 March 1982.

(b) Set out the Balance Sheet on 28 February 1983, showing the profit for the year divided between the partners. No additional capital has been brought in during the year.

(c) No additions have been made to the premises, the increase in value being entirely due to inflation. What effect, if any, should this have on the drawings which may be made by the partners?

(London 'O' level 1984)

4   A. Muddle, a trader, did not keep his books on the double-entry system, but his valuation of the assets and liabilities on the dates named were as follows:

	30 June 1982 £	30 June 1983 £
Stock	4,936	4,690
Bank overdraft	454	92
Delivery van	960	960
Debtors	1,128	1,506
Cash in hand	30	70
Fixtures and fittings	2,450	2,450
Creditors	738	514
Expenses owing	80	—

You are required to prepare a Statement of Affairs (Balance Sheet) as at 30 June 1983, showing the net profit and as much detail as possible, taking into account the following additional information obtained from A. Muddle on 30 June 1983:

(a) Muddle had withdrawn £2,450 from the bank during the year for private purposes.

(b) Muddle had also taken £200 of goods from the business for his own private use.

(c) £40 of the outstanding debts were deemed to be irrecoverable.

(d) It was agreed that 15% depreciation should be written off the value of the delivery van on 30 June 1983.

(e) Muddle had paid £200 for delivery van repairs from his private bank account in order to keep down the business bank overdraft at 30 June 1983.

(Cambridge 'O' level 1983)

5 William Wallace started business on 1 January 1981 with capital consisting entirely of cash, £35,000. He has never kept double-entry records but has drawn up statements of affairs at each year's end. These show the following:

	1981	1982	1983
	£	£	£
Premises at valuation	30,000	30,000	35,000
Motor vans	7,000	5,000	13,000
Stock	4,500	5,400	2,900
Cash at bank	1,300	1,800	1,200
Creditors	2,400	2,600	2,900
New capital introduced			10,000
Drawings	5,000	5,000	7,000

(a) Calculate William Wallace's profit or loss for each year from 1981 to 1983.

(b) Comment on the apparent figure of profit or loss for the year ended 31 December 1983. You are informed that the increase in the value of the premises is entirely due to revaluation. No additional premises have been acquired or sold during the three years.

(London 'O' level 1985)

6 On 14 April 1985 the warehouse of Joseph Shipley caught fire and the whole of his stock in trade was destroyed apart from goods with a cost price value of £285. Fortunately Shipley's books and records were kept in a fireproof safe and the following information is available:

(1) Stock in trade at 31 December 1984 was £1,344 at cost price.

(2) Purchases from 1 January 1985 to the date of the fire amounted to £1,960. Of these, goods to the cost price of £70 were still in transit at the time of the fire.

(3) Sales from 1 January 1985 to the date of the fire amounted to £2,775 and all these goods had been despatched before the fire took place.

(4) Shipley's gross profit is 20% of Sales.

Required:
Calculate the value—at cost price—of the goods destroyed in the fire.

Note: Calculations must be shown.
(LCCI 1985)

Chapter 20

Departmental Accounts

20.1 What Topics are Covered in this Chapter?

We learn how to produce accounts in a form which reveals separate departmental results for a business having two or more departments. We see how analysed books of prime entry are used to provide the details required for Departmental accounts.

20.2 Departmental Trading and Profit and Loss Accounts

The owners and managers of a business with more than one department should not be satisfied with a form of accounts which produces only one overall figure for the profit or loss of the business as a whole. They need to know how much profit or loss each department has made.

We are familiar with columnar accounts from our studies of two and three column cash books and Partnership capital, Current and Drawings accounts. We now apply the same principle to Departmental accounts. If we have separate departmental figures for stocks, purchases and sales, Departmental Trading accounts present no problem. It may be a little more difficult, however, to prepare Departmental Profit and Loss accounts because of the nature of some of the expenses. Some expenses can easily be allocated to departments; for instance departmental salaries can be ascertained from a pay-roll analysis whilst the cost of repairing and repolishing furniture will apply to the Furniture Department, and servicing of refrigeration equipment would be allocated to the restaurant. Otherwise, overheads must be apportioned over the departments on some reasonable basis. Some suggested bases are:

(i) Rent, rates, electricity and property insurance, general maintenance and cleaning: in proportion to floor space occupied.

(ii) Insurance of plant, machinery, stock: in proportion to the book values of these items in individual departments.

(iii) Commissions, delivery expenses, discounts allowed: in proportion to sales.

(iv) Discounts received: in proportion to purchases.

(v) General office salaries, accountancy and other general office expenses: in proportion to sales.

Remember

Overheads should be apportioned according to their nature

One very important point to remember in connection with the apportionment of expenses is that it is not an exact science, being based upon estimates or guesswork. The basis should always be a convenient one because even if an exact one could be found, it could cost more in time and labour than it is worth. The costs of obtaining information must always be weighed against the benefits likely to result from it. Therefore, undue accuracy should never be attributed to financial statements such as Departmental accounts.

Fig. 20.1

Departmental Trading and Profit and Loss Accounts

Engate and Southfield & Co. is a wellknown store with three departments: Furniture, Clothing and Sports Equipment. The following information is available for the year ended 31 December 19-7:

	Furniture £	Clothing £	Sports Equipment £
Sales	50,000	30,000	20,000
Purchases	30,000	20,000	10,000
Stock at 1.1.-7	3,200	4,000	2,700
Stock at 31.12.-7	4,300	5,000	3,100
Sales staff salaries	6,000	5,500	3,200

Floor area occupied: Furniture 8,000 sq. ft., Clothing 7,000 sq. ft., Sports Equipment 5,000 sq. ft.

Overheads for the year were: office wages £10,000; rent and rates £9,000; electricity £2,400; cleaning £2,000; advertising £1,000; discounts received £1,200; discounts allowed £1,500.

Overheads are to be apportioned as follows:

In proportion to sales: office wages, advertising.

In proportion to floor area: rent and rates, electricity, cleaning.

Discounts received: 2% of purchases.

Discounts allowed: 1½% of sales.

Engate and Southfield & Co.

**Trading and Profit and Loss Account
for the Year ended 31 December 19-7**

	Furniture £	£	Clothing £	£	Sports £	£
Sales		50,000		30,000		20,000
Stock at 1.1.-7	3,200		4,000		2,700	
Purchases	30,000		20,000		10,000	
	33,200		24,000		12,700	
less stock at 31.12.-7	4,300		5,000		3,100	
Cost of sales		28,900		19,000		9,600
Gross profit		21,100		11,000		10,400
add Discounts received		600		400		200
		21,700		11,400		10,600
Less: Sales staff salaries	6,000		5,500		3,200	
Office wages	5,000		3,000		2,000	
Rent and rates	3,600		3,150		2,250	
Electricity	960		840		600	
Cleaning	800		700		500	
Advertising	500		300		200	
Discounts received	750		450		300	
		17,610		13,940		9,050
Net profit (loss)		4,090		(2,540)		1,550

In view of the remarks in 20.2, it is quite common for businesses to produce departmental trading accounts which can be prepared with a high degree of accuracy, but to carry the combined departmental gross profits down to a general Profit and Loss account to produce one figure of net profit for the business as a whole.

20.3 Analysed Books of Prime Entry

Obviously it is necessary to have separate Sales and Purchases accounts in the nominal ledger for each department if we are to prepare Departmental accounts. This suggests that sales and purchases must be analysed over the departments when they are entered in the books of prime entry. This could be done by keeping separate books for each department but, apart from being cumbersome, difficulties would be created when invoices contain items for more than one department. The best method is to use analysed books of prime entry. We have already encountered these in Chapter 2. The ruling should be adapted to provide columns for the departments.

Fig. 20.2

Analysed Departmental Purchase Day Book

				A	B	C	D	E
Date Feb 1	Supplier O'Donnell &	Inv. No.	Fo	Total	VAT	Furniture	Clothing	Sports
	Co.	1,001	31	432	56	376		
	I. Patel Ltd.	1,002	45	610	80		405	125
	Tong & Co. Ltd.	1,003	53	376		49	327	
				1,418	136	425	732	125
					NL19	NL7	NL11	NL14

Points to Note

(i) The amount of each invoice entered in the total column, A, is posted to the credit of the suppliers' personal account.

(ii) The total of the VAT column, B, is posted to the debit of VAT account.

(iii) The totals of columns C, D and E are posted to the debit of separate Sales accounts for the Furniture, Clothing and Sports Departments.

(iv) The total of column A must equal the total of columns B to E.

(v) The Sales Day Book and the Returns Books will be analysed in a similar manner, and separate Sales and Returns accounts maintained for each department.

20.4   Examination Hint

No student who has mastered the preparation of Trading and Profit and Loss accounts in an acceptable form should experience difficulty in preparing Departmental accounts but it is essential to read the question carefully for instructions on the apportionment of overheads and to perform the calculations accurately.

20.5   What Should I Have Learned in this Chapter?

(i) It is important to have separate financial information for each department of a departmental business to aid management decision-making.

(ii) Departmental accounts cannot be more accurate than the bases used to apportion expenses over the department.

(iii) The cost of trying to obtain an absolutely accurate system of apportionment of overheads over departments must be weighed against the benefit expected to be obtained from it. Absolute accuracy is virtually impossible to achieve anyway.

(iv) Financial accounts by themselves cannot contain all the information management needs to make business decisions.

Exercise

John Armstrong has a store which is divided into three departments: hardware, electrical and gardening. He wishes to apportion the following expenses to the departments.

	£	Basis of Apportionment
Selling expenses	480	Departmental Sales
Delivery expenses	2,400	Departmental Sales
Administrative expenses	2,000	Departmental Wages
Heating and lighting	300	Departmental Floor Area
Rent and rates	1,500	Departmental Floor Area

The trading profits for the departments were:

Hardware—£16,000;   Electrical—£20,000;   Gardening—£12,000.

Given the following information, prepare a statement of profit and loss for John Armstrong's business in columnar form, showing expenses and net profit for each department.

Departments	Hardware	Electrical	Gardening
Sales	£50,000	£40,000	£30,000
Wages	£10,000	£10,000	£5,000
Floor area (sq ft)	1,000	1,500	500

(Northern Ireland 1982)

Chapter 21

Control Accounts

21.1 What Topics are Covered in this Chapter?

The previous chapters have dealt with the recording of all aspects of purchases and sales by way of posting to a Supplier or Customer account, details already entered in the various Day Books or Cash Book. This chapter deals with the situation when many Supplier or Customer accounts are in use and an arithmetical check, other than a Trial Balance, is required to test the accuracy of the ledgers.

21.2 The Ledgers Involved

Because many businesses will grow rapidly in size, it will soon become apparent that the main system of books must be subdivided in order to collect together all accounts of a similar nature, e.g. Suppliers accounts, Customer accounts and Nominal accounts (expenses, assets, liabilities, etc). This chapter deals specifically with Suppliers accounts and Customer accounts. These, as you can see, will be kept in the *Purchases ledger* and *Sales ledger* respectively.

21.3 Other Names Given to the Control Accounts

It must be obvious that the Control account concerned with the Purchases ledger is called the *Purchases ledger control* and that concerned with the Sales ledger the *Sales ledger control*.

You will know that the Purchases ledger contains details of creditors, while the Sales ledger contains details of debtors. Therefore, sometimes the accounts are called *Creditors Control* and *Debtors Control*.

21.4 How is a Control Account Constructed?

In order to understand how the Control account is constructed, it is first necessary to understand that it is nothing more than a condensed version of the ledger concerned with all the accounts, superimposed one on top of the other.

This being the case, it should be easy to see that rather than the individual amounts posted to each account being entered into the Control account, it is the totals of all the transactions that are involved. Because totals are dealt with in this way, a further name for this type of account is a *Total account*.

Taking a very simple case, if the opening balance of a Supplier account was known and other information concerning purchases and payments for goods was available, then the closing balance can be calculated.

If this line of thought was applied to the whole Purchases ledger, and remembering the superimposed accounts already explained, then if all opening balances were known, together with the total credit purchases and payments against these invoices, then a figure could be calculated to represent the total of the credit balances to carry forward. (See Fig. 21.1.)

It can be seen that the actual construction of the account is the same as that for the individual, except that totals are used instead of individual transaction details.

21.5 Checking the Accuracy of the Ledger

(From the Control account balance and by listing individual balances.)

Once the Control account has been prepared and balanced, the simple task of ascertaining its accuracy remains.

This job is easily done by making a list of all the balances in the ledger and comparing the total of this list with the arithmetical balance obtained from the Control accounts. Remembering the superimposed accounts, the balance on the Control account must equal that of the listing.

If the totals agree, there is no problem. If they do not agree, then an error has been discovered and must be investigated. The main advantage is that the error has been isolated to one particular ledger.

Remember

The arithmetical balance on the control account must be equal to the total of all individual balances in the ledger being controlled

---

21.6   When Goods have been Returned or a Cheque has been Returned by the Bank

It has already been explained that if goods have been returned then a credit note will have been issued and this will have been entered in either the Purchases or Sales Returns Book.

Just as the total of the Purchases or Sales Day Book was taken to its Control account, so is the total of the Returns Book, except of course that it will appear on the opposite side of either the purchases or sales.

Likewise, if a cheque is returned by the bank after a customer has paid for his goods, then this will be entered as a credit in the Cash Book (to cancel the original debit) and the total of all returned cheques will be posted to the Control account.

By now, it should seem clear that the Control account follows the same format as an individual account within either the Purchases or Sales ledger.

21.7   The Control Account and Double-entry

Consider the following example:

Fig. 21.1

Sales Ledger

A. Brown

Jan 2	Inv. 001	SD1	100	Jan 5	Bank	CB1	150
3	Inv. 003	SD1	50	31	Balance	c/d	75
25	Inv. 009	SD1	75				
			225				225
Feb 1	Balance	b/d	75				

P. Green

Jan 2	Inv. 002	SD1	200	Jan 10	Bank	CB1	340
4	Inv. 005	SD1	150		Discount		
15	Inv. 008	SD1	100		Allowed	CB1	10
				31	Balance	c/d	100
			450				450
Feb 1	Balance	b/d	100				

F. Adams

Jan 4	Inv. 004	SD1	500	Jan 6	Bank	CB1	500
10	Inv. 007	SD1	400	31	Balance	c/d	400
			900				900
Feb 1	Balance	b/d	400				

R. Black

Jan 5	Inv. 006	SD1	120	Jan 31	Balance	c/d	420
28	Inv. 010	SD1	300				
			420				420
Feb 1	Balance	b/d	420				

Debtors Listing 31 January

A. Brown	75
P. Green	100
F. Adams	400
R. Black	420
	995

Sales Ledger Control Account

Jan 31	Total invoices to Sales A/c	S1	1,995	Jan 31	Total received per Bank		990
					Discount Allowed	D1	10
					Balances per List	c/d	995
			1,995				1,995
Feb 1	Balances per List	b/d	995				

Point to Note
Remember that the figures used in the Control Account are taken from the total columns of the Day Books and Cash Book (books of prime entry).

It is easy to see that the Control account is merely a carbon copy of the total of all other accounts within the ledger and this may give rise to some confusion and thoughts of *double debits* and *double credits*.

It should be remembered that the Control account is not actually part of double-entry but simply a summary of what should have gone in the respective ledgers. It serves the function of an arithmetical check and can be likened to a Trial Balance for a particular ledger.

Fig. 21.2

Error occurring in the Sales ledger

Consider the same facts as in Fig. 21.1 but suppose that the discount allowed to P. Green had been omitted in the posting to his Ledger Account (but not in the Control Account).

P. Green's account would be as follows:

P. Green

Jan 2	Inv. 002	SD1	200	Jan 10	Bank	CB1	340
4	Inv. 005	SD1	150	31	Balance	c/d	110
15	Inv. 008	SD1	100				
			450				450
Feb 1	Balance	b/d	110				

The list of balances would be:

A. Brown	75
P. Green	110
F. Adams	400
R. Black	420
	1,005

Point to Note

Clearly this would not agree with the Control Account and subsequent investigation would locate the error.

21.8 Using the Balance on the Control Account in the Main Trial Balance

Having regard to the text in **Section 21.7,** it may seem wrong to include the balances of the Control account as part of the main Trial Balance, but consider some of the main facts already mentioned.

If the Control account balance is the sum total of all the balances in the Purchases or Sales ledger, then surely instead of listing each individual balance in the Trial Balance (and each ledger may contain upwards of 100 accounts), it must be easier and make more sense to include the one figure which represents the sum total of all the balances in a particular ledger.

It is quite common to find the ledger of a business divided into three parts, namely the Purchases ledger, Sales ledger and General ledger, with the Purchases and Sales ledger controls appearing in the General ledger, thus the main Trial Balance will only include the balance on the Control accounts.

In this way, the separate Supplier and Customer accounts and not the Control accounts become Memorandum accounts.

If the principles of double-entry have been understood, then the above should not only make sense but seem perfectly logical.

21.9   Entering discounts

The question of discounts received and given will have been fully discussed in Chapter 4 and it should be known that the discount (or allowance) is nothing more than a reduction for prompt payment and follows cash in the Supplier or Customer account with the corresponding credit and debit entry posted to discounts received or discounts allowed.

Knowing the format of the Control account, it should not be too difficult to realise where the discount belongs or to see that the total will arise from the various discount columns of the Cash Book (not part of double-entry but merely memorandum as in a Day Book).

21.10   Customers who are also Suppliers

It may happen that a supplier is also a customer and, in this case, there will be an entry in the Sales ledger (Debtors ledger) for goods supplied by us on credit and an entry in the Purchases ledger (Creditors ledger) for goods purchased on credit. Rather than actually paying for each other's goods, a decision may be taken to set the two accounts off against each other and for one person to pay the difference.

This can be done quite simply, once the decision has been made, by entering the details in both the Sales and Purchases ledgers in the relevant named account. If we had bought £2,000 of goods from Mr A and sold him £1,500 of goods, being both credit transactions, then Mr A's account in the Sales ledger would have a debit balance of £1,500 while his account in the Purchases ledger would have a credit balance of £2,000.

By setting one amount against the other, Mr A's account in the Sales ledger would be credited with £1,500, so closing off this account, and his account in the Purchases ledger would be debited with £1,500, thus leaving a balance of £500 to be cleared by cash or cheque.

The posting reference would be between the Sales ledger and Purchases ledger and double-entry is maintained. If these types of entries occur frequently, then a special transfer journal would be used in order to keep track of events and to reduce the risk of errors. This type of transaction between ledgers is known as a *contra* transaction and is commonly referenced by the sign ₵ (a crossed c) followed by the account reference, e.g. ₵A (contra entry to Mr A's account whose reference happens to be A).

How does this affect the control accounts?

Just as you have seen that the total of all payments for goods purchased on credit are posted to the debit of the Purchases ledger control, the same applies to the total of amounts transferred by way of contra entries described above. The opposite is of course true for contra entries to the Sales ledger control.

Fig. 21.3

Contra Postings between Ledgers and Control Accounts

Suppose R. Black is also a supplier of goods and it is decided to contra payments with his firm. The position in February could be as follows:

Sales Ledger

R. Black

Feb 1	Balance	b/d	420	Feb 28	R. Black– Purchase Ledger	R1₵	300
				28	Bank	CB1	120
			420				420

Purchases Ledger

R. Black

| Feb 28 | R. Black– Sales Ledger | R1₵ | 300 | Feb 10 | Goods | DB1 | 300 |

Points to Note

(i) The Journal entry for the contra will be:

		Dr.	Cr.
Feb 28	Purchase Ledger—R. Black	300	
	Sales Ledger—R. Black		300
	Being contra entry to R. Black		

(ii) The contra will appear in both Control Accounts in place of the normal cash or bank entries.

21.11   Bad Debts

Bad debts will only occur within the Sales ledger and the subject was explained in Chapter 12.

The Debtor's account will have been credited with the amount of the bad debt while the Bad Debt account will have been debited.

The Control accounts will be affected because a balance (the amount of the bad debt) will have been written off. The correct procedure will be to credit the Control account with the total amount of the bad debts during the period under review.

21.12   Opening Balances—Debits and Credits

Balances on Control accounts are normally either a debit (representing assets such as debtors) or a credit (representing for example the liability to creditors). However, in practice, a ledger account may have a balance which is opposite to the one normally expected. A customer who buys from us on credit, then pays the amount due, and is then credited with the value of the goods when he returns them to us, will have a credit balance on his account in the Sales ledger. Normally such an account would have a debit balance.

A listing of the Sales ledger account balances would show the total debit balances and the total credit balances. The Control account could show either the opening balances (both debit and credit) or one balance being the net figure.

21.13   What if the Ledgers are very Large and Cumbersome?

The answer is easy and would involve subdividing the Sales or Purchases ledger normally on an alphabetical basis, e.g. A—M and N—Z, thus subdividing the work load and further controlling a smaller part of the ledger. Each subdivision of the ledger would need its own Control account.

21.14   The Advantages of Control Accounts

The main advantages have been discussed in this chapter but may be enumerated as follows:
   (i) They enable a periodic check to be made on the Sales and Purchases ledgers without the necessity of extracting a full Trial Balance.

(ii) If errors have occurred, they enable them to be narrowed down to specific parts of the system, thereby making the job of location easier.

(iii) Normally the person writing up the Sales or Purchases ledger will not be the same person who prepares the Control account. The advantage here is that an independent check now exists within the system which will, hopefully, pinpoint errors as two people are unlikely to make the same mistake and should also reduce the risk of fraud caused by 'manipulating' the books.

(iv) It enables Management figures to be extracted on a regular basis by using the arithmetical balance produced by constructing a Control account in the Trial Balance without having to extract all of the individual balances in the separate Sales and Purchases ledgers.

21.15   Examination Hints

(i) When faced with a difference on a Control account, remember that, if items are totally outside the Debtors and Creditors ledger, they should be ignored for Control account purposes.

(ii) If the error will affect the Control account, it may be easier to correct the other account first. This will enable the correct double-entry to be made to the Control account.

(iii) Many questions ask for Journal entries. It is a help to construct working accounts in order to follow the double-entry, and hence produce the correct Journal entry.

21.16   What Should I Have Learned in this Chapter?

(i) The Control account is necessary to prove the accuracy of the Debtors or Creditors ledger.

(ii) Control accounts and Total accounts are the same.

(iii) Either the Control account or the separate Ledger accounts are part of double-entry but not both; i.e. one or other will serve the purpose of Memorandum accounts.

(iv) That Cash Books and Day Books are totalled periodically and the totals are posted to the Control accounts.

(v) At suitable intervals, the balances on the Personal accounts are extracted from the ledgers, listed and totalled and the total of the outstanding balances can then be reconciled to the balance on the appropriate Control account and any errors located and corrected.

(vi) In certain circumstances, i.e. when a customer is also a supplier, a direct transfer may be made between the Debtors and Creditors ledgers.

Exercises

1 (a) What are the advantages of preparing Sales and Purchases Ledger Control accounts?
   (b) Give the sources from which you could obtain the information to prepare these Control accounts.
   (c) From the following information prepare a Sales Ledger Control account for the month of April 1986.

		£
Sales ledger balances as at 1 April	Dr	14,730
	Cr	315
Discount allowed		208
Cash received from debtors		28,318
Returns inwards		417
Sales		31,618
Bad debts		150
Interest charged on overdue Sales ledger account		35
Customers cheques dishonoured		23
Debit balance in Sales ledger transferred to Purchases ledger		198
Credit balance in the Sales ledger as at 30 April 1986		214

2 J. Smith keeps Control accounts for his Sales ledger and his Purchases ledgers. The following details for 1986 were extracted from his books:

	£
Debit balance in Sales Ledger Control account on 1 January 1986	5,984
Sales per Sales Day Book	85,155
Discounts allowed per Cash Book	1,841
Amounts received from trade debtors	74,317
Debit balances in Sales ledger set off against credit balances in Purchases ledger	518
Bad debts written off	724
Dishonoured cheque, re-presented and paid, included twice in amounts received from debtors figures	180

A list of balances was extracted from the Sales ledger at 31 December 1986. The total of this list, £13,746, did not agree with the final balance, on the Draft Control account and the following errors were found:

(i) A debtors balance for £185 was included twice on the list of balances.

(ii) The Sales Day Book was overcast by £200.

(iii) A sales invoice for £98 was entered in the Day Book but not posted to the customer's account in the Sales ledger.

(iv) A sales invoice for £125 had been entered twice in the Day Book and posted twice to the customer's account.

(v) An allowance to a customer for £60 had been credited to his Personal account, but no entry had been made elsewhere.

You are required to prepare:

(a) a Sales Ledger Control account for 1986 as it would appear after all these matters have been corrected

(b) a statement showing the amended total of debtors.

3   Mainway Dealers Limited maintains a Debtors' (Sales) ledger and a Creditors' (Purchases) ledger.

The monthly accounts of the company for May 1986 are now being prepared and the following information is now available:

		£
Debtors' ledger as at 1 May 1986	Debit balances	16,720
	Credit balances	1,146
Creditors' ledger as at 1 May 1986	Debit balances	280
	Credit balances	7,470
Credit sales May 1986		19,380
Credit purchases May 1986		6,700
Cash and cheques received May 1986	Debtors' ledger	15,497
	Creditors' ledger	130
Cheques paid May 1986	Debtors' ledger	470
	Creditors' ledger	6,320
Credit notes issued May 1986 for goods returned by customers		1,198
Credit notes received from suppliers May 1986 for goods returned by Mainway Dealers Limited		240
*Cheques received and subsequently dishonoured May 1986	Debtors' ledger	320
Discounts allowed May 1986		430
Discounts received May 1986		338
Bad debts written off May 1986		131

		£
*Bad debt written off in December 1985 but recovered in May 1986 (R. Bell)		142

*Included in cash and cheques received May 1986 £15,497.

Debtors' ledger as at 31 May 1986	Debit balances	to be determined
	Credit balances	670
Creditors' ledger as at 31 May 1986	Debit balances	365
	Credit balances	to be determined

It has been decided to set off a debt due from a customer, L. Green, of £300 against a debt due to L. Green of £1,200 in the Creditors' ledger.

The company has decided to create a provision for doubtful debts of 2.5% of the amount due to Mainway Dealers Limited on 31 May 1986 according to the Debtors' Ledger Control account.

Required:

(a) Prepare the Debtors' Ledger Control account and the Creditors' Ledger Control account for May 1986 in the books of Mainway Dealers Limited. (20 marks)

(b) An extract of the balance sheet as at 31 May 1986 of Mainway Dealers Limited relating to the company's trade debtors and trade creditors. (5 marks)

(AAT June 1986) (Total 25 marks)

Chapter 22
Suspense Accounts and the Correction of Errors

22.1 What Topics are Covered in this Chapter?

The correction of those errors that are discovered is explained; the correction also of the profit if necessary.

22.2 The Effect of Errors

When an error is made in the ledger, it may or may not affect the double-entry; therefore a Trial Balance which agrees is not always a sign that the ledger is free of errors.

22.3 Errors Which Do Not Affect the Trial Balance

The errors that can be made are listed in Chapter 7 and for revision purposes are noted here:
(a) Errors of omission
(b) Errors of commission
(c) Errors of principle
(d) Errors of original entry
(e) Complete reversal of entries
(f) Compensating errors.

22.4 Correcting Errors

The above errors do not affect double-entry and, when discovered, can be corrected by a Journal transferring the amount into the correct account or else originating the posting for an error of omission.

When the error is such that double-entry has been affected, the Trial Balance will not agree. If the error cannot be located immediately, an amount equal to the difference may be inserted into the Trial Balance in order to make it balance and to enable final accounts to be prepared. The difference can then be found at a later stage when time permits.

When this is done, the difference is placed to a suspense account and the Trial Balance appears thus:

	Dr £	Cr £
Original balances	1,000	990
Suspense account		10
	1,000	1,000

Indicating a credit difference of £10.

As the various errors are located, those which do not affect double-entry but are due to mispostings to incorrect accounts are reversed or adjusted simply by Journal entries.

22.5   Errors Affecting Double-entry

These must be corrected through the Suspense account. When the error is located, a Journal entry noting the transfer between the incorrect account and the Suspense account should be made before actually making the transfer.

In order to reduce confusion, it is easier to locate the account with the error and then decide whether that account requires a debit or credit entry to correct it. Remembering the rule of double-entry that 'every debit has a credit', it must follow that the Suspense account receives the opposite side of the correcting transaction.

Example

The Trial Balance disagrees by £90 as a shortage on the debit side and a Suspense account is opened. It is discovered that £100 for motor expenses is correctly credited in the Cash Book but has been debited to motor expenses as £10.

Suspense Account

Jan 1	TB Difference	90					

Motor Expenses

Dec 1	Cash Book	10	Dec 31	Profit & Loss a/c	10

To correct the above, first decide which is incorrect and then decide how to correct it. In this case, the Motor Expenses account needs a debit of £90. This being the case, the only account that can be credited is the Suspense account.

The following Journal is required:

		Dr	Cr

Jan 31	Motor Expenses
	    Suspense account
	    Being correction of £100 cash expenses
	        posted as £10
		90	90

The accounts are as follows:

Suspense Account

Jan 1	TB Difference	90	Jan 31	Motor expenses— per journal	90

Motor Expenses

Dec 1	Cash Book	10	Dec 31	Profit & Loss	10
Jan 31	Suspense a/c— per journal	90	Jan 31	Profit & Loss	90

The Suspense account is now clear and the Trial Balance will agree. The credit for the £100 now in motor expenses has always been correctly located in the Cash account.

22.6   Effect on Profits

Apart from clearing the Suspense account once the errors have been located, it may be necessary to consider whether any of the errors would have had an effect on the reported profit.

Consider the previous example when motor expenses were stated in the account at £10 instead of £100. This would have the effect of overstating profit by £90 (or understating losses by the same amount). The corrected profit figure is obtained by drawing up a simple statement as follows:

		£
Reported profit		1,000
Adjustments	+	−
Misposting to motor expenses		90
	−	90
Net adjustment		− 90
Restated profit		910

Remember

Errors are corrected by making additional entries

22.7 Examination Hints

(i) Remember to analyse the error when it is explained and, if it affects double-entry, then it will affect the Suspense account.

(ii) Once the error has been located, it may be easier to correct the other account first and thus be able to make the correct double-entry posting to the Suspense account.

(iii) Many questions will ask for Journal entries. It is a help to construct working accounts in order to follow the double-entry, and hence produce the correct Journal entry.

(iv) Remember that when a revised profit statement is requested, errors which do not affect the Suspense account may have an effect on the restated profit.

22.8 What Should I Have Learned in this Chapter?

(i) When a difference appears in a Trial Balance, a Suspense account may be opened to enable draft final accounts to be completed.

(ii) That the error causing a difference on the Trial Balance may be a combination of several errors which will ultimately affect not only the Profit and Loss account but also the Balance Sheet.

(iii) That only errors of double-entry will affect or create a Suspense account.

Exercises

1 Jim Brown's Trial Balance extracted on 30 June 198– did not agree. In the early part of the following month the errors discovered were:

(a) The total of the returns outwards book £62 had not been posted to the ledger.

(b) A payment for envelopes for £18 had been entered in the Stationery account as £15.

(c) The invoice received from A. F. Job in the amount of £300 had been lost. No entries for this amount had been made.

(d) The account of M. Young had a debit balance of £54; this was brought down as £45.

You are required:
   (i) To prepare Journal entries to correct the above.
   (ii) To prepare the Suspense account showing the original difference.
   (iii) To describe four types of error which do not affect the agreement of the Trial Balance and give an example of each.

2   After preparing his Trial Balance A. Brown has a debit difference of £420 and he opens a Suspense account. Further investigation shows:
   (a) £70 received from F. Indus and credited to his account has not been entered in the Bank account.
   (b) A. Brown has taken goods for his personal use valued at £138, no entries have been made.
   (c) A payment of £94 to R. Green has been credited to his account.
   (d) Discounts allowed (£396) and received (£426) have been posted to the Discount accounts as credits and debits respectively.
   (e) Rent received of £222 has not been entered in the Bank account.
   (f) £422 owed by P. Blake has been debited incorrectly to G. Blake.

You are required:
   (i) To prepare the Suspense account making the entries necessary to eliminate the debit balance therein.
   (ii) To what extent is the balancing of a Trial Balance evidence of absence of error?

3   On 31 December 1982 M. Johnson extracted a Trial Balance. The debit side of the Trial Balance totalled £18,150 and the credit side £18,436. Johnson opened a Suspense account for the difference.
   Subsequently he found the following errors:
   (a) The total of the Purchases Day Book for the month of December £6,748 had been posted to the Purchases account as £6,478.
   (b) A cash payment of £69 made by S. Brown had been entered in the cash book, but had not been posted to the Debtors account.
   (c) An entry of £50 in the Sales Journal for B. James was posted in error to the account of B. Jones.

(d) The total of discount allowed for one week had been credited to the Discount account £37.

(e) A private purchase of £65 had been included in the business purchases.

You are required to:

(i) Draw up a Suspense account as it would appear in the ledger. It is Johnson's policy not to carry a balance forward to the succeeding year.

(ii) Show, by means of Journal entries, how the foregoing items would be dealt with.

(iii) Draw up a statement of adjusted profit showing the effect the corrections would have on the company's profit for the year. Net Profit before corrections is £20,000.

4 **A** At the close of business on 31 December 1983, Albert Fox, a sole trader, extracted a Trial Balance from his books. The Trial Balance did not agree but Fox entered the difference in a Suspense account. He then prepared his Trading and Profit and Loss account for the year ended 31 December 1983 in the normal way. The Profit and Loss account so prepared showed a Net Profit amounting to £6,000.

During January 1984 Fox discovered the following errors in his books and these accounted for the entire difference in the Trial Balance.

(i) The Sales Day Book had been undercast by £240 and posted to the Sales account accordingly.

(ii) A purchase of goods from J. Bell for £74 was correctly entered in the Purchases Day Book but was posted to Bell's account as £47.

(iii) Discounts allowed for the month of June amounting to £498 had not been posted to the General ledger.

(iv) Bank charges for September of £83 were correctly entered in the Cash Book but were credited to the Bank Charges account in the General ledger.

(v) Bad Debts account had been debited with items of £60 and £37 in respect of bad debts but the Personal accounts had not been credited.

You are required to:

(a) Show by means of Journal entries how the foregoing items should be dealt with.

(b) Draw up a Suspense account and determine the opening balance thereon.

(c) Draw up a statement of adjusted Net Profit showing the correct profit figure after the above corrections have been made.

B Describe five types of errors which do not affect the agreement of the Trial Balance, and illustrate the correction of such errors with Journal entries.

5   Allan Smith, an inexperienced accounts clerk, extracted the following Trial Balance, as at 31 March 1986, from the books of John Bold, a small trader.

	£	£
Purchases	75,950	
Sales		94,650
Trade debtors	7,170	
Trade creditors		4,730
Salaries	9,310	
Light and heat	760	
Printing and stationery	376	
Stock at 1 April 1985	5,100	
Stock at 31 March 1986		9,500
Provision for doubtful debts	110	
Balance at bank	2,300	
Cash in hand	360	
Freehold premises:		
At cost	22,000	
Provision for depreciation	8,800	
Motor vehicles:		
At cost	16,000	
Provision for depreciation	12,000	
Capital at 1 April 1985		23,096
Drawings		6,500
Suspense		21,760
	160,236	160,236

In the course of preparing the final accounts for the year ended 31 March 1986, the following discoveries were made:

(1) No entries have been made in the books for the following entries in the bank statements of John Bold:

1986	Payments	£
March 26	Bank charges	16
March 31	Cheque dishonoured	25

Note: The cheque dishonoured had been received earlier in March from Peter Good, debtor.

(2) In arriving at the figure of £7,170 for trade debtors in the above Trial Balance, a trade creditor (Lionel White £70) was included as a debtor.

(3) No entries have been made in the books for a credit sale to Mary Black on 29 March 1986 of goods of £160.

(4) No entries have been made in the books for goods costing £800 withdrawn from the business by John Bold for his own use.

(5) Cash sales of £700 in June 1985 have been posted to the credit of Trade Debtors' accounts.

(6) Discounts received of £400 during the year under review have not been posted to the appropriate nominal ledger account.

(7) The remaining balance of the Suspense account is due to cash sales for January and February 1986 being posted from the Cash Book to the debit of the Purchases account.

Required:

(a) The Journal entry necessary to correct for item (7) above.
   Note: A narrative should be included.   (8 marks)

(b) Prepare a corrected Trial Balance as at 31 March 1986.

(17 marks)

(AAT 1986)   (Total 25 marks)

Chapter 23

Manufacturing Accounts

23.1 What Topics are Covered in this Chapter?

Manufacturing accounts and their preparation; why they are needed.

23.2 The Need for a Manufacturing Account

Up to date, the accounts dealt with have been for trading organisations (apart from Chapter 18 dealing with clubs and societies), who have been purchasing their trading stock from various suppliers in order to sell at a profit.

Apart from the above situation, there are many firms, whether sole trader, partnership or limited company who manufacture the final product to be sold from raw materials.

In this instance, a Manufacturing account is required in order to arrive at the final cost of manufacture. The manufacturing organisation will still need a Trading and Profit and Loss account which will be in the same form as has been studied previously. The only major difference is that, in the Trading account, the entry for *Purchases* is replaced by the *Cost of Manufacture*. The cost of manufacture is calculated using a manufacturing account.

23.3 Different Types of Cost

The costs needed to prepare a Manufacturing account can be broken down into two main categories and are known as direct and indirect costs.

The main or *direct costs* are those of raw materials and labour which together are known as the *prime cost*, although any expense which can be traced directly to any unit of production is also a direct cost. The *indirect costs* are those associated with production but cannot be traced directly to a particular production unit. These costs will include the general factory overheads such as light, heat and power, rent, rates and insurance, depreciation of production machinery, etc.

Certain labour costs, such as supervision by foremen or factory managers, will also be indirect costs because they are not traceable to a production unit but are absorbed as a general overhead.

The total of direct costs (prime cost) and indirect costs is known as the *cost of manufacture* (production cost).

23.4   The Effect of Stocks

One complication in constructing the Manufacturing account is to remember that there may be opening and closing stocks of raw materials and opening and closing values to attach to partly completed items (work in progress).

These adjustments can be seen in the pro-forma Manufacturing account which follows:

Fig. 23.1

Pro-Forma Manufacturing Account

Year ended . . . .

Opening stock of raw materials		x	Production cost of completed goods carried down to Trading Account	xxx
Purchases		x		
		xx		
Less closing stock of raw materials		x		
Cost of raw materials consumed		xx		
Direct manufacturing wages		x		
Prime Cost		xx		
Factory overheads:				
Rent and rates	x			
Light, heat and power	x			
Indirect wages	x			
Depreciation of production machinery	x			
		xx		
		xx		
Opening work in progress		x		
		xxx		
Less closing work in progress		x		
		xxx		xxx

Point to Note

The Trading Account is prepared in the normal way, but substituting the production cost of completed goods for the usual purchases figure.

Pro-Forma Trading and Profit and Loss Account

Year ended . . . .

Opening stock of finished goods	x	Sales	xxx
Production cost of completed goods b/d	x		
	x		
Closing stock of finished goods	x		
Cost of Sales	xx		
Gross Profit c/d	xx		
	xxx		xxx
Expenses:		Gross Profit b/d	xxx
Administration expenses	x	Other revenue receipts	x
Selling and distribution expenses	x		
Financial and other expenses	x		
Depreciation of office furniture and equipment	x		
Net Profit	xx		
	xxxx		xxxx

Another complication arises when there is a mix of manufactured and purchased goods, the problem being how much gross profit to attribute to the manufacturing side of the business rather than trading and how the value of mixed manufactured and purchased stock is ascertained at the year end.

23.5   Provision for Unrealised Profit

The final complication arises where there may have been a provision for unrealised profit brought forward and, in this instance, it is only necessary to adjust the brought forward provision by an amount equal to the difference between the opening provision and the closing provision as calculated. Remember, it is not the total of the new provision that is credited to the unrealised profit account but merely the difference as stated above.

This transfer can be likened to that required when increasing or decreasing a provision for doubtful debts, when it should be remembered that the adjustment is equal to the difference between the opening and closing provision required.

The provision for unrealised profit account will show a credit balance at the year end and this is shown on the Balance Sheet as a deduction from the final closing stock figure, thus in effect reducing the actual stock figure shown to cost.

It is possible that goods may be transferred from the Manufacturing account to the Trading account at market value, thus creating a manufacturing profit which is the difference between the calculated manufacturing cost and the higher transfer value.

Another problem is to identify and separate the bought in and manufactured stock at the year end and to create a provision for that part of the manufacturing profit which is not yet realised. This *provision for unrealised profit* arises because, if any manufactured stock items are left on the shelves at the year-end and they have been valued at market price, then part of that value relates to the manufacturing profit which is as yet unrealised as the goods have not been sold.

The following simple example illustrates these points:

Fig. 23.2

Manufacturing, Trading and Profit and Loss Account
B. &. D. Limited, Year ended 31 May 1983

	£	£
Manufacturing cost of completed goods (2,000 items)		50,000 a
Manufacturing profit (difference c − a)		10,000 b
To Trading Account		60,000 c
Sales		144,000
Less: Cost of sales		
Opening stock (250 bought items)	7,500	
Cost of manufacture	60,000	
Purchases (350 bought items)	10,500	
	78,000	
Closing stock (100 bought, 100 manufactured)	6,000	
		72,000
Gross Profit		72,000
Manufacturing profit	10,000	
Less Provision for unrealised profit	500	
		9,500
		81,500

Journal Entries Required

		£	£
Trading Account	.	500	
Provision for unrealised profit			500
being provision for unrealised profit on			
100 manufactured items in stock at			
year-end			

There will be times when opening stock contains items of manufactured goods shown at market price and, as explained, a provision for unrealised profit will already have been made in the previous year. The entries will have been those shown as the Journal in the previous example.

There is, therefore, a balance of £500 brought forward on the Provision for Unrealised Profit account.

If, at the end of the next year, closing stock contains 150 items of manufactured stock, the increase in provision will be for the additional 50 items and will be £250.

The account will appear as follows:

Fig. 23.3

Provision for Unrealised Profit Account

1983				1983			
May 31	Balance	c/d	500	May 31	P & L A/c— (100 @ £5)		500
				June 1	Balance	b/d	500
1984				1984			
May 31	Balance	c/d	750	May 31	P & L A/c— Increase		250
			750				750
				June 1	Balance	b/d	750

Point to Note
The amount of £750 is now shown on the Balance Sheet as a deduction against closing stock.

23.6 Examination Hints

(i) Remember to include only amounts specific to manufacture and pay special attention to instructions to apportion certain expenses between Manufacturing accounts and the Profit and Loss account.

(ii) Remember that 'wages' go to the Manufacturing account whereas, unless otherwise specified, salaries will go to the Profit and Loss account.

(iii) Remember that three types of stock may be referred to, which are:

(a) Raw materials

(b) Work in progress

(c) Finished goods

You must remember how to deal with each of these items in the Manufacturing account, Trading and Profit and Loss account and Balance Sheet.

23.7 What Should I Have Learned in this Chapter?

(i) All costs of production are collected together in the Manufacturing account to obtain the cost of manufacture which is carried down to the Trading accounts and will be an addition to purchases or else take the place of purchases.

(ii) The direct costs of manufacture are collectively known as *prime cost*.

(iii) Manufacturing accounts are a useful tool for management purposes as they highlight distinctions between the costs and profitability associated with manufacturing operations and those associated with trading operations.

Exercises

1   Nixon is the proprietor of a firm manufacturing furniture in East London. He makes up his accounts to 31 March each year. Set out below is Nixon's Trial Balance at 31 March 1984.

	£	£	
Advertising	900		
Bad debts	405		
Bad debts provision		1,500	
Bank charges	320		
Nixon Capital account 1 April		34,000	
Nixon Current account 1 April		2,623	
Nixon drawings	7,000		
Discounts		612	
Carried forward	8,625	38,735	

		£	£
	Brought forward	8,625	38,735
Factory power		4,614	
Fixtures and fittings		900	
General expenses—factory		305	
office		446	
Insurance		802	
Light and heat		482	
Plant and machinery 1 April		15,000	
Plant and machinery bought			
30 September	6 months	2,000	
Purchases		34,668	
Packing and transport		1,085	
Rent and rates		1,486	
Repairs to plant		785	
Salaries—office		3,690	
Sales			79,615
Stocks—1 April			
Raw materials		5,240	
Finished goods		7,390	
Work in progress		1,680	
Wages—factory		20,700	
Trading debtors and creditors		10,560	6,250
Cash at bank		3,966	
Cash in hand		176	
		124,600	124,600

Stocks at 31 March were:	£
Raw materials	3,640
Work in progress	1,690
Finished goods	9,650

The following liabilities are to be provided for:

	£
Factory power	560
Rent and rates	386
Light and heat	160
General expenses—factory	40
office	65

Insurance paid in advance is £190.

Five-sixths of Rent and rates, Light and heat and Insurance are to be allocated to the factory and one-sixth to the office.

Provide Depreciation at 10% per annum on Plant and machinery and 5% per annum on Fixtures and fittings.
Increase the Bad debts Provision by £600.
You are required to prepare a Manufacturing, Trading and Profit and Loss accounts for the year ended 31 March 1984.

2   During the financial year ended on 31 March 1980, the Lulworth Manufacturing Company completed 50,500 units of its standard product. From the information set out below, you are to prepare Manufacturing, Trading and Profit and Loss accounts for the year ended 31 March 1980.

Schedule of Balances as at 31 March 1980

Stocks: Raw materials	6,575
Finished goods (2,650 units)	7,650
Work in progress	5,270
Wages	46,750
Purchases	107,850
Plant and machinery (cost £85,000)	63,500
Returns outwards	1,850
Carriage inwards	2,500
Sales (50,625 units)	242,452
Advertising	2,490
Salaries	43,620
Delivery vans (cost £25,000)	18,650
Discount received	1,140
Insurance	840
Power and lighting	5,600
Office expenses	8,490
Delivery van expenses	1,076

Notes:

(i) On 31 March 1980 the following valuations were made:

	£
Raw material stock	7,560
Work in progress	7,995

The value of the stock of finished goods at this date is based on the average unit cost of production for the year.

(ii) Expenses to be apportioned as production costs are:

Salaries	10%
Insurance	75%
Power and lighting	80%

(iii) Depreciation is calculated by the diminishing balance method as follows:

Plant and machinery   20%

Delivery vans   30%

(iv) On 31 March £1,250 wages and £380 salaries were unpaid.

3   The Newgate Manufacturing Company produces one standard article. From the information given you are to prepare the Manufacturing, Trading and Profit and Loss accounts for the year ended 31 May 1981.

Balances extracted from the ledger at 31 May 1981

	£
Stocks: Raw materials	7,106
Work in progress	3,976
Finished goods	8,402
Plant and machinery at cost	80,000
Office equipment at cost	40,000
Wages	75,873
Returns inwards	597
Carriage inwards	806
Purchases	107,850
Sales	237,590
Returns outwards	880
Carriage outwards	240
Office expenses	2,476
Salaries	24,180
Advertising	1,750
Delivery vans at cost	20,000
Delivery vans expenses	5,176
Discounts received	904
Insurance	1,200
Power and lighting	1,600

Notes:

(i) On 31 May 1981 stocks were valued:

	£
Raw materials	8,107
Work in progress	4,176
Finished goods	7,500

(ii) Expenses to be apportioned to the factory are:

Salaries	10%
Insurance	75%
Power and lighting	80%

(iii) Depreciation is charged by the straight line method as follows:

Plant and machinery	15%	12000 M
Office equipment	10%	4,000 Rol.
Delivery vans	20%	4000 X
		20,000 B

Chapter 24
Interpretation and Analysis of Accounts Statements

24.1 What Topics are Covered in this Chapter?

How we analyse the results of a business; who wants information and what they want.

24.2 The Parties Interested in Analysing Accounts

Up to now, the main concern has been to record the transactions of a business with a view to using them to prepare final accounts.

It must be realised that a number of different parties may be interested in the results of a business for varying reasons and each will want to extract information in order to view the business for differing needs.

Examples of the end users of the accounts could be:

(i) Management who will want to form a comparison between either previous years or competitors or both.

(ii) Lending organisations will need to judge the credit-worthiness of the business, as will larger trade suppliers.

(iii) Investors will want to form an opinion as to whether to invest in the business in the future or maintain current investment.

In all the examples quoted, it is necessary to use comparisons, either with previous years of the same business or with competitors or both, in order to obtain a reasonable interpretation and to be able to make the required decision.

The main tools of interpretation and analysis are the use of ratios but firstly it is important to understand the various types of cost concerned.

24.3 Fixed and Variable Expenses

Fixed and variable expenses are most often discussed when considering a manufacturing organisation which will have raw material costs, heat and power, salaries, rent, etc. as main items of expense.

If the manufacturer decided to increase production, then obviously costs would increase but not all in proportion to the increase in turnover. This is because some costs are *fixed* and others *variable*. An example of a fixed cost would be rent as this would remain static despite the fact that output and hence sales had risen (assuming no further factory accommodation is required).

Other costs, such as raw material costs and production wages are variable as these will go up and down in relationship to the production and turnover being achieved.

Fixed costs will remain constant regardless of changes in production and sales, while variable costs will move up and down with changes in production and sales.

24.4 The Use of Ratios

When analysis and interpretation of accounts statements is required, the most common method is to look at various *ratios* in order to provide a guide to the final interpretation of the accounts provided.

It is important to understand that the use of ratios is only significant when comparisons can be made, either between two different accounting periods for one company or two separate companies, possibly providing the same service.

24.5 Key Ratios

There are several *key ratios* which can be used and these are listed and discussed below. The example in Fig. 24.1 shows a set of accounts with the ratio calculations. The ratios can be broken down broadly into three—profitability, liquidity and financial ratios.

Profitability

(i) *Gross Profit Margin* is the first and perhaps one of the most frequently used ratios and measures the *Gross Profit* as a percentage of *Sales*.

The calculation is:

$$\frac{\text{Gross Profit}}{\text{Sales}} \times \frac{100}{1} = \text{GP}\%$$

This measures the efficiency of a business in its main area of buying and selling. When making a comparison between one year and another, it is hoped that the Gross Profit percentage achieved is fairly constant and that the Gross Profit is sufficient to cover all overheads and provide a healthy Net Profit.

Any changes in the percentage should, of course, be investigated and reasons for the change should be identified. Various reasons for changes could be reduced selling prices, increased cost of sales or shrinkage caused by theft. This list is not meant to be exhaustive.

(ii) *Net Profit Margin* measures the Net Profit as a percentage of Sales and is found by the calculation:

$$\frac{\text{Net Profit}}{\text{Sales}} \times \frac{100}{1} = \text{NP}\%$$

The ratio should be similar from one year to the next and, therefore, any change in ratio (assuming that this is not caused by a change in the Gross Profit ratio) could probably be explained by any undue increases or decreases in overhead expenses.

An investigation of the overhead expenses would enable the increase or decrease to be located and remedied.

(iii) *Asset Turnover* indicates how well a company is utilising its assets.

The calculation for asset turnover is as follows:

$$\frac{\text{Sales}}{\text{Capital employed}} = \text{Asset turnover}$$

If the asset turnover is low, it indicates that a company is not achieving the volume of business for the assets employed.

Remember

Capital = Assets – Liabilities = net assets

Investigation may indicate that sales turnover should be increased or some of the assets should be sold in order to push up the figures for asset turnover.

(iv) *Stock Turnover* is a ratio which indicates the rates at which a company is turning over (replacing) its stock and is found by the calculation:

$$\frac{\text{Cost of goods sold}}{\text{Average stock}} = \text{Stock turnover per annum.}$$

A healthy business would expect its stock turnover to remain fairly constant or even to increase slightly. It must be borne in mind that different businesses would have a different rate of stock turnover. For example, a supermarket would expect a high stock turnover whereas a company specialising in the heavy engineering industry would expect a low stock turnover figure.

(v) *Return on Capital Employed* may be expressed as a percentage of (a) ordinary shareholders' capital or (b) long term capital and is primarily used by potential investors in a company.

The formulae used are as follows:

$$\text{(a)} \quad \frac{\text{Net Profit before tax and dividends}}{\text{Ordinary share capital + reserves}} \times \frac{100}{1} \%$$

$$\text{(b)} \quad \frac{\text{Net Profit before interest, tax and dividends}}{\text{Total issued share capital + reserves}} \times \frac{100}{1} \%$$
$$+ \text{long term loans.}$$

The formula in (a) above shows the effectiveness of the ordinary shareholders' funds and will be of interest to ordinary shareholders (or potential ordinary shareholders), while that in (b) measures the effectiveness of all the long term capital and may be of more use not only to investors but to providers of other long term capital, e.g. debenture loans.

(*Note:* There are differing views on the way that Return on Capital Employed should be calculated. Should the formulae in (a) and (b) above show Net Profit after tax and before interest and dividends or before tax? The return after tax shows the return available to owners/loan capital providers, whilst the before tax return relates directly to the profitability of the company without any adjustments for varying tax rates which are at the whim of the Chancellor of the Exchequer. For comparisons within a company from year to year the authors recommend the formula shown.)

Liquidity Ratios

(i) The *Current Ratio* is the first ratio to consider under this heading. This measures the ability of a company to pay its short term creditors (amounts due to be paid within one year) from its resources of current assets. In this way, it will indicate that the fixed assets will remain intact.

The calculation is as follows:

$$\frac{\text{Current assets}}{\text{Current liabilities}} = \text{Current Ratio expressed as x : 1}$$

where 1 = current liabilities
and where x = current assets.

It would be expected that the current assets (if not already represented by cash) would be converted to cash at roughly the same rate as the creditors fell due for payment.

It may reasonably be assumed that an average Current Ratio achieved over a broad spectrum of businesses would be 1.5 : 1 and this would be considered healthy.

There would, of course, be examples of a ratio more or less than 1.5 : 1 being acceptable, e.g. a mainly 'cash' business where no large reliance was placed on credit facilities could be expected to have a current ratio slightly less than the average, while a business that, by its very nature, relied upon credit terms may feel more at ease with a current ratio of, say, 2 : 1.

A ratio greater than 2 : 1 could indicate a surplus of cash, stock or debtors. In this case, surplus cash could be reinvested in fixed assets to promote further growth.

If there is surplus stock, this must be investigated to make sure the stock is not damaged, redundant or unsaleable for any other reason.

If the debtors are too high, then internal credit control must be tightened and the debtors made to settle their accounts in order to bring more cash into the business which may, in turn, be reinvested once the debtors' position is satisfactory.

(ii) *Liquid or Quick Ratio* (sometimes known as the acid test ratio) is similar to the Current Ratio discussed above, except that stock is not included in the calculation. This reduces the risk of relying on a ratio which may indicate slow moving or redundant stock.

The calculation is as follows:

$$\frac{\text{Current assets less stock}}{\text{Current liabilities}} = \text{Liquid Ratio expressed as x : 1}$$

where 1 = current liabilities.

This ratio may be regarded as a better indication of the immediate solvency of a company because it disregards the time taken to convert stock into either cash or debtors.

As 1.5 : 1 could be considered average for the current ratio, so may 1 : 1 be considered a reasonable average to measure the liquid ratio.

(iii) *Stocks and Net Current Assets* is a ratio that follows from the other liquidity ratios and measures the importance of stock as a percentage of working capital.

The calculation is as follows:

$$\frac{\text{Stock}}{\text{Net current assets}} \times \frac{100}{1}\%$$

If the percentage appears too high, investigation may show that the stock carried is too high for the particular company, there is bad stock control or that obsolete and redundant stocks are being held.

If the percentage is too low, investigation may show that cash balances are too high or that debtors are too high as a result of bad credit control or debt collection.

(iv) *Period of Credit Taken by Debtors* is also known as the average collection period. This measures the length of time the company takes to collect its debts.

The calculation is as follows:

$$\frac{\text{Debtors (balance sheet)}}{\text{Credit sales for year}} \times \frac{365}{1} = \text{number of days to pay}$$

If the period of credit given is, say, 30 days and the calculation shows the average time to pay is more than this, then an indication of bad credit control has been identified and can be remedied.

(v) *Period of Credit Taken from Creditors.* This calculation is similar to that above, except trade creditors are substituted for debtors and credit purchases for credit sales.

$$\frac{\text{Trade creditors (balance sheet)}}{\text{Credit purchases for year}} \times \frac{365}{1} = \frac{\text{number of days}}{\text{to pay}}$$

This measures the speed at which a company is paying its creditors.

If the company is given terms of 30 days and the calculation shows that debts are being paid within this time, then it may be prudent to delay some payments in order to increase cash flow.

If the period is in excess of that given, then possible reasons should be investigated and the possibility that the company could be experiencing difficulties should not be overlooked.

Finance Ratios

The most commonly used ratio in this section and the only one under discussion is that of *gearing* and is represented by the following formula:

$$\frac{\text{Fixed interest loans and preference capital}}{\text{Capital employed}} \times 100 = \%$$

A low geared business is where the gearing is less than 100%.
A high geared business is where the gearing is more than 100%.
A business is neutrally geared if the gearing is exactly 100%.

Lower gearing signifies that there is more equity finance in the business than fixed term loans whereas high gearing signifies the exact opposite.

The gearing ratio becomes important when a company wishes to raise extra finance. A highly geared business may experience difficulty in raising further long term finance. A provider of finance to a highly geared company may insist that the company itself provides part of the finance required by issuing further ordinary shares or retaining any future profits by way of General Reserves.

Fig. 24.1

Worked example of Ratios

Bee Gee Limited

Profit and Loss Account Year ended 31 July 198–

	£
Turnover	24,000
Operating profit	1,360
Debenture interest	296
Pre-tax profit	1,064
Corporation tax	424
	640
Preference dividend	40
Balance available for ordinary shareholders	600

Balance Sheet as at 31 July 198-

Fixed assets		10,400
Current assets		
Stock	2,400	
Debtors	3,600	
Cash at bank	400	
	6,400	
Current liabilities	3,200	
		3,200
		13,600
Long term loan (debenture)		5,600
		8,000
Represented by:		
Capital and reserves		
Ordinary shares of £1		4,000
Preference shares of £1		800
Profit and Loss Account		3,200
		8,000

Note:
Gross Profit before expenses was £12,000.

Assume all sales are credit sales.

Assume opening and closing stock is constant.

Gross Profit percentage
$$\frac{12,000}{24,000} \times \frac{100}{1} = 50\%$$

Net Profit percentage
$$\frac{1,064}{24,000} \times \frac{100}{1} = 4.43\%$$

Asset Turnover
$$\frac{24,000}{8,000} = 3$$

Stock Turnover
If gross profit is £12,000 the cost of goods sold equals £12,000.

$$\frac{12,000}{3,600} = 3.33 \text{ times per annum}$$

Return on Capital Employed

$$\frac{1,064}{4,000+3,200} \times \frac{100}{1} = 14.77\%$$

or

$$\frac{1,360}{4,000+800+3,200+5,600} = 10\%$$

Current Ratio

$$\frac{6,400}{3,200} = 2:1$$

Liquid (Quick) Ratio

$$\frac{6,400-2,400}{3,200} = 1.25:1$$

Stock to Net Current Assets

$$\frac{2,400}{3,200} \times \frac{100}{1} = 75\%$$

Period of credit taken by debtors

$$\frac{3,600}{24,000} \times \frac{365}{1} = 55 \text{ days}$$

Period of credit taken from creditors

$$\frac{3,200}{12,000} \times \frac{365}{1} = 97 \text{ days}$$

Gearing

$$\frac{5,600+800}{8,000} \times \frac{100}{1} = 80\%$$

(signifies slightly less than neutral gearing—there is still scope for further long term borrowing.)

24.6   Comparing Like with Like

Ratio analysis is a convenient method of comparing the results of different companies and measuring performance over years. This method of analysis does have limitations. In particular, comparisons should be made between like figures and values, otherwise wrong conclusions may be drawn from the results.

Several illustrations will emphasise this point.

  (i) Two similar sized companies making the same type of product—one company long established on land and buildings purchased many years ago whilst the other company has been in existence for only a short time. The older company could be showing land and buildings at original cost, which would be considerably less than the corresponding figure for the younger company.

 (ii) A sole trader business would not show in the final accounts any salary to the owner whilst a company will show directors' salaries paid to the 'management'.

(iii) One business may be paying leasehold rent for property whilst another business may own its buildings and be paying no rent.

(iv) There are a number of methods of depreciation; the use of different methods by different companies will mean that the asset values will not be comparable.

 (v) Capital structure may differ and a company may vary its use of share and loan capital from year to year.

Remember

Changes in a ratio need careful examination before drawing a conclusion

---

24.7   Examination Hints

  (i) Unless given specific instructions, use as many ratios as possible to illustrate an answer and describe *briefly* the results obtained using each ratio. Sometimes, the examiner will only be looking for a knowledge that ratio analysis exists, and *intelligent* comment on the results.

 (ii) If time is running out, it is important to state the formula to use and to show the figures taken from the accounts within that formula. Do not worry about calculating the final results. You can always make comments using an assumption, e.g. assuming the correct current ratio was 4 : 1, then etc., etc.

(iii) In an exam with 2,000 candidates, the examiner will be faced with 2,000 different answers; just make sure that your answer is based on sound principles and makes sense.

(iv) Make sure you compare like with like.

24.8   What Should I Have Learned From this Chapter?

(i) The performance of a business or company can be analysed by the use of certain key accounting ratios.

(ii) Ratio analysis measures three key areas, namely profitability, liquidity and financial performance.

(iii) To be meaningful, ratios must be used as a comparison between two or more sets of figures; either two or more years of the same company or two or more different businesses.

(iv) Ratio analysis does have limitations.

Exercises

1   Redwing Ltd is incorporated with an authorised capital of £30,000 divided into shares of £1 each.

The following information related to its trading activities during the year ended 31 May 19–9.

Summarised Balance Sheet as at 31 May	19–8		19–9	
	£	£	£	£
Equipment (less depreciation)		8,000		25,000
Stock	4,200		3,500	
Debtors	2,240		1,200	
				4,700
Bank	1,780	8,220		
		16,220		29,700
Creditors	2,450		4,750	
Overdraft			1,220	5,970
		13,770		23,730
Issued capital		12,000		20,000
Retained profits		1,770		3,730
		13,770		23,730

Cost of Goods sold during the year £46,200.

You are required:
(a) To calculate:
     (i) liquid ratio.
     (ii) current ratio.
     (iii) working capital at the beginning and end of the year.
     (iv) rate of turnover.
(b) To explain, in the light of your answers to (a), what policy
     the company has followed during the year and its possible
     effect on the shareholders' investment.

2   J. Kirk, the finance director of Enterprise Limited, prepares
    accounts for internal use at quarterly intervals. Details from
    two recent Balance Sheets are as follows:

	31 December 19–3		31 March 19–4	
	£	£	£	£
CURRENT ASSETS				
Stock		24,000		48,300
Debtors		40,000		58,800
Prepayments		5,000		6,300
Cash in hand		600		525
		69,600		113,925
CURRENT LIABILITIES				
Trade creditors	16,000		25,200	
Accrued expenses	2,000		4,200	
Bank overdraft	38,000		60,900	
		56,000		90,300
NET CURRENT ASSETS		13,600		23,625

Notes:
   (i) Total credit sales for the year ended 31 March 19–4 were
       £252,000.
   (ii) Total working days are approximately 300 per annum.
You are required to:
(a) Explain the importance of liquidity.
(b) Calculate:
       (i) the current ratio.
       (ii) the quick ratio.
       (iii) the debtors' turnover period.
     at each of the above dates.
(c) List briefly at least five points discussing the limitations of
     ratio analysis in this area, mentioning any other informa-
     tion which would be relevant to an appraisal of liquidity.

3   The following abridged information relates to the activities of
B. G. Spender Ltd.

Trading & Profit & Loss Account for the year ended 31 December

	19-0		19-1
	£		£
Sales revenue	500,000		600,000
Cost of sales	400,000		520,000
Gross profit	100,000		80,000
Expenses	40,000		50,000
Net profit	60,000		30,000

Balance Sheet as at 31 December

	19-0		19-1	
	£	£	£	£
Plant and equipment		80,000		120,000
Stock	15,000		18,000	
Debtors	8,000		7,000	
Bank	6,000		(9,000)	
	29,000		16,000	
Creditors	6,000	23,000	12,000	4,000
		103,000		124,000
Financed by				
Issued share capital		90,000		100,000
Retained profits		13,000		4,000
10% Debenture				20,000
		103,000		124,000

Note:
Figures in brackets (thus) are negative.
You are required:
(a) to set out your interpretation of the Company's performance during the year ended 31 December 19-1 supporting
your answer with any ratios or comparisons you consider
appropriate.
(b) to indicate what policy you think the Company should
adopt for the year ending 31 December 19-2.

4   Gordon Ray is currently reviewing his results for the year
ended 31 December 1985 and comparing them with those of

Smooth Dealers Limited, a company engaged in the same trade.

The chairman of Smooth Dealers Limited receives an annual salary of £12,000 for performing duties very similar to those performed by Gordon Ray in his business. The summarised final accounts for 1985 of Gordon Ray and Smooth Dealers Limited are as follows:

Trading and profit and loss accounts
for the year ended 31 December 1985

Gordon Ray £'000s		Smooth Dealers Limited £'000s
90	Turnover	150
48	*Less:* Cost of sales	80
42	Gross profit	70
12	Administrative expenses	37
15	Sales and distribution expenses	25
—	Debenture interest	3
27		65
15	Net profit	5

Balance sheets as at 31 December 1985

Gordon Ray £'000s		Smooth Dealers Limited £'000s
60	Fixed assets	50
28	Current assets: Stock	56
22	Debtors	69
6	Balance at bank	10
56		135
16	Current liabilities: Creditors	25
40	Net current assets	110
100	Net capital employed	160
100	Capital account	
	Ordinary share capital	80
	Retained earnings	50
	10% debenture stock	30
100		160

Required:

(a) Calculate five appropriate ratios comparing the results of Gordon Ray with those of Smooth Dealers Limited and briefly comment on each ratio.

(20 marks)

(b) Outline three distinct reasons why a comparison of the amount of profit earned by different businesses should be approached with great care.

(5 marks)

(AAT 1986)   (Total 25 marks)

Chapter 25
Value Added Tax and the Use of Analysed Books

25.1 What Topics are Covered in this Chapter?

Value Added Tax—its collection, recording and payment; keeping the VAT account and completing the VAT Return.

25.2 Records and Customs and Excise

Value Added Tax or VAT as it will be referred to hereafter is a tax which is levied on the supply of goods and services and is known as an *indirect* tax. It is administered by Customs and Excise and is collected by the registered traders and is normally accounted to the Customs and Excise on a quarterly basis (except in certain circumstances when monthly accounting may be beneficial to the registered trader).

A registered trader is obliged by law to keep such records that are sufficient to show all transactions concerning VAT and these records must be kept for a minimum of six years.

25.3 A Tax on the Consumer

VAT is a cumulative tax which is levied and collected at the various stages of manufacture, wholesaling and the ultimate purchases by the end consumer and may be explained simply by the following example:

	Net	VAT @ 15%	Gross
	£	£	£
Manufacturer buys raw materials for	100	15	115
Manufacturer sells to wholesaler for	160	24	184
Wholesaler sells to retailer for	220	33	253
Retailer sells to end consumer for	300	45	345
	780	117	897

The total tax payable by the end consumer is £45 although it is collected at each stage of the chain as each trader pays over the difference between the amount he has charged and suffered. The above example may be analysed as follows:

	£
Original supplier of materials	15
Manufacturer £24 less £15	9
Wholesaler £33 less £24	9
Retailer £45 less £33	12
Paid by end consumer	45

Thus the tax is progressive and is levied on the *added value*.

25.4   Input and Output VAT

VAT which is paid on goods and services purchased by a business is known as *input* tax whilst VAT charged on goods and services sold by a business is known as *output* tax.

When output tax charged by a business exceeds input tax suffered, the balance is paid over to the Customs and Excise.

When input tax suffered by a business exceeds output tax charged, Customs and Excise will refund the difference to the registered trader.

In all cases the trader is merely acting as an unpaid collector of revenue; it is not costing him anything in monetary terms, only his time.

25.5   Some VAT is Not Reclaimable

In most cases, the registered trader may claim a credit for input tax suffered. There are certain items where input tax cannot be reclaimed and must be borne by the business, e.g. entertainment expenses (unless a foreign customer), cars bought for company use and not for resale.

25.6   Recording VAT in Analysed Books

VAT does not form any part of a business profit and loss account. Therefore, all sales, purchases and expenses in the accounts of a registered person will be shown net of tax.

VAT will be accounted for in the Sales Day Book, the Purchases Day Book or the Cash Book and in all cases use of analysed books should be made.

An analysed book is one where each page has several vertical columns which enables the main details to be entered in a total column with an analysis of the amount mainly categorised into the main account headings following.

One main function is that the VAT amount can be analysed, thus providing details of gross and net amounts and the related VAT.

25.7 Analysed Purchases Day Book

The following is an example of an analysed Purchases Day Book.

Fig. 25.1

Analysed Purchases Day Book

Date 198–		Fo	Total	VAT	Purchases	Motor	Phone
Jan 2	A. Brown	B1	115	15	100		
3	P. Green	G1	69	9		60	
5	C. Blue	B2	345	45	300		
8	B. Tele com	T1	92	12			80
			621	81	400	60	80

This not only enables each page to be proved but also provides the total to be posted to the control account as well as the columnar analysis to be posted to the nominal accounts. In the above example, the total column is credited to purchase ledger control and the totals of the various analysis columns are debited to their respective accounts. (In this way, double-entry is maintained.)

25.8 Analysed Sales Day Book

The Sales Day Book will normally only contain three columns for the total income, the net amount and VAT. Additional columns may be used if required to give further analysis for management purposes, such as analysis of sales on a geographical basis or between certain types of merchandise.

Fig. 25.2

Analysed Sales Day Book

Columns As Required→

Date 198–		Fo	Total	VAT	Net		
Jan 3	M. Green	G2	230	30	200		
5	P. Pink	P3	115	15	100		
7	F. Watkins	W5	46	6	40		
9	G. Brown	B4	138	18	120		
			529	69	460		

25.9   Analysed Cash Book

When analysed day books are in use, the Cash Book will also incorporate analysis columns. The credit side will consist of a total column, a VAT column (to analyse any VAT which has not passed through the Purchase Day Book), a purchase ledger column to analyse payments for those items to be posted to various purchase ledger accounts and several other columns for sundry amounts, again not part of the day book system. Examples would be wages, PAYE, proprietor's drawings, etc.

Amounts extended into the purchase ledger columns would be the gross amounts because VAT has already been analysed through the day book.

Fig. 25.3

Analysed Cash Book (Credit)

Date 198–		Fo	Total	VAT	Purchases Ledger	Wages	PAYE	Drawings	Sundi
Jan 3	A. Brown	B1	115		115				
5	P. Green	G1	69		69				
10	Telecom	T1	92		92				
20	Drawings	D1	100					100	
20	PAYE (Dec)	P10	50				50		
25	Advert (Non Purchase Ledger)	A6	230	30					200
30	Staff wages	W5	200			200			
			856	30	276	200	50	100	200

The postings would be to the purchase ledger control account for the total of the purchase ledger column whereas the other totals would be to the debit of the respective nominal accounts.

The debit side of the cash book would probably contain at least three columns for the total amount and the analysis between sales ledger receipts and sundry amounts.

There is no need for a separate VAT analysis if the business operates only with credit sales. For businesses making cash sales a VAT column is necessary.

Fig. 25.4

Cash Book (Debit)

Columns As Required →

Date 198–		Fo	Total	VAT	Sales Ledger	Cash Sales	Sundry
Jan 6	M. Green		230		230		
7	Capital Introduced		500				500
10	Cash Sales		690	90		600	
11	G. Brown		138		138		
			1,558	90	368	600	500

Point to Note

The postings would be completed by crediting the relevant control and nominal accounts.

25.10   The VAT Account

Accounting to the Customs and Excise is a relatively simple exercise and is achieved by normal double-entry methods with the use of a VAT account.

Total *input* tax (VAT suffered) is *debited* to the VAT account and total *output* tax (tax charged and collected) is *credited* to the VAT account.

At the end of each VAT accounting period (usually every three months), the VAT account is balanced. A credit balance indicates that more tax has been charged and collected by the trader than suffered by input, and the difference is due to be paid to the Customs and Excise. A debit balance would indicate the opposite and would signify that a refund is due to be received by the trader.

The trader will not send a copy of his ledger account to the Customs and Excise but will complete a standard Return form.

Fig. 25.5

Standard Return Form for VAT

Value Added Tax Return
For the period
to

H M Customs and Excise

Due to reach the VAT Central Unit by
These dates must not be altered.

For Official Use

Registration No | Period

Before you fill in this form please read the notes on the other side. You must complete all boxes — writing "none" where necessary. If you need to show an exact amount of pounds, please write "00" in the pence column. Don't put a dash or leave the column blank. Please write clearly in ink.
You must ensure that the completed form and any VAT payable are received no later than the due date by the Controller, VAT Central Unit, H M Customs and Excise, 21 Victoria Avenue, SOUTHEND-ON-SEA X

An envelope is enclosed for your use.

	For Official Use	£	p

FOR OFFICIAL USE

VAT DUE in this period on OUTPUTS (sales, etc), certain postal imports and services received from abroad	1	
Underdeclarations of VAT made on previous returns (but not those notified in writing by Customs and Excise)	2	
TOTAL VAT DUE (box 1 + box 2)	3	
VAT DEDUCTIBLE in this period on INPUTS (purchases, etc)	4	
Overdeclarations of VAT made on previous returns (but not those notified in writing by Customs and Excise)	5	
TOTAL VAT DEDUCTIBLE (box 4 + box 5)	6	
NET VAT PAYABLE OR REPAYABLE (Difference between boxes 3 and 6)	7	

Please tick only ONE of these boxes:

box 3 greater than box 6 — payment by credit transfer

payment enclosed

box 6 greater than box 3 — repayment due

How to pay the VAT due
Cross all cheques and postal orders "A/C Payee only" and make them payable to "H M Customs and Excise". Make credit transfers through account 3078027 at National Girobank or 10-70-50 52055000 for Bank Giros and keep your payment slip. You can order pre-printed booklets of credit transfer slips from your local VAT office. In your own interest do not send notes, coins, or uncrossed postal orders through the post.
Please write your VAT registration number on the back of all cheques and credit transfer slips.

Value of Outputs (excluding any VAT)	8	00
Value of Inputs (excluding any VAT)	9	00

Please tick box(es) if the statement(s) apply:

box 5 includes bad debt relief | box 8 includes exempt outputs | box 8 includes exports

Retail schemes If you have used any of the schemes in the period covered by this return please tick the box(es) to show all the schemes used.

A	B	C	D	E	F	G	H	J

Remember, you could be liable to a financial penalty if your return and all the VAT payable are not received by the due date.
DECLARATION by the signatory to be completed by or on behalf of the person named above.

I, ... declare that the
(full name of signatory in BLOCK LETTERS)
information given above is true and complete.

Signed .... Date... 19......
*(Proprietor, partner, director, secretary, responsible officer, committee member of club or association, duly authorised person) *Delete as necessary

FOR OFFICIAL USE

VAT 100   F3790 (JULY 1986)

The form is simple to complete and requires the difference between input and output to be calculated. Other boxes are used to supply statistical information (boxes 8 and 9).

The refund would be received in February, debited to the Cash Book and credited to the VAT account to clear the balance.

Fig. 25.6

VAT Account

31 January 198–

198– Jan 31	Purchases Day Book Cash Book	DB1 CB1	81 30	198– Jan 31	Sales Day Book Balance— Refund due	DB2 c/d	69 52
			121				121
Feb 1	Balance— Refund due	b/d	52				

Point to Note

If the accounting date of the business does not coincide with the VAT accounting date, the VAT account will be balanced and the debtor or creditor included as a current asset or current liability.

25.11   Prices Inclusive of VAT

Sometimes VAT is not identified separately on the income received or given. In this case, the VAT included in the gross figure has to be calculated and this is equal to the gross amount multiplied by the VAT percentage over 100 plus the VAT percentage. At current rates, this is 15/115 or simplified to 3/23.

E.g. VAT included in £2,300 is:

$$\overset{100}{\underset{1}{\cancel{£2,300}}} \times 3/\cancel{23} = 300$$

Thus Net	2,000
VAT @ 15%	300
	£2,300

25.12 Examination Hints

(i) Pay particular attention to the rate of VAT given by the examiner. He may not use the standard rate of 15%.

(ii) In order to calculate the amount of VAT in a VAT inclusive (gross) amount, always use the following formula:

$$\frac{\text{VAT rate}}{100 + \text{VAT rate}} \times \text{VAT inclusive amount} = \text{VAT}$$

(iii) An accurate approximation of the VAT included in a gross amount can be obtained by multiplying the gross figure by 13% (0.13). This assumes the standard rate of VAT is 15%.

25.13 What Should I Have Learned in this Chapter?

(i) That VAT is payable by the ultimate consumer.

(ii) That VAT suffered by a registered business is reclaimed by way of input tax as a deduction against output tax (tax on sales or the provision of services), and that only the difference is paid over to the Customs and Excise.

(iii) That analysed books are an important help in producing the necessary VAT account and subsequent return to the Customs and Excise.

Exercise

1 During the quarter ended 31 May 1986, the raw materials purchased by John Henry Limited, manufacturers of furniture, amounted to £181,590 before VAT at the standard rate of 15% and, in addition, the following items of expenditure occurred:

		£	£
March 12	Highway Garage Limited		
	Motor van C478TBR	9,500.00	
	VAT @ 15%	1,425.00	
		10,925.00	
	Vehicle excise duty	100.00	
			11,025.00
March 19	Smith Motors Limited		
	Motor car C379KTA	8,000.00	
	VAT @ 15%	1,200.00	
		9,200.00	
	Vehicle excise duty	100.00	
			9,300.00

		£	£
April 23	Super Machines Limited		
	Used drilling machine Number		
	KXY54	8,200.00	
	VAT @ 15%	1,230.00	
			9,430.00
May 7	Highway Garage Limited		
	Car repairs	210.00	
	VAT @ 15%	31.50	
			241.50
May 20	Machine Repairs Limited		
	Renovation drilling machine		
	Number KXY54	500.00	
	VAT @ 15%	75.00	
			575.00

Note:
This renovation was necessary before the drilling machine could be used in the factory.

The VAT due to the Customs and Excise Department on 28 February 1986 amounting to £84,000 was paid on 20 March 1986.

During the quarter ended 31 May 1986, the company's turnover, before VAT, amounted to £800,000 and analysed for VAT purposes was as follows:

		Turnover
		£
Taxable—	Standard rate	620,000
	Zero rated	120,000
Non-taxable—	Exempt	60,000
		£800,000

The company maintains an analytical Purchases Day Book.

Required:

(a) Prepare the analytical Purchases Day Book for the three months ended 31 May 1986 of John Henry Limited.

(13 marks)

Note:
Raw material purchases for the three months ended 31 May 1986 should be shown as one entry in the Purchases Day Book.

(b) Prepare the account for HM Customs and Excise—VAT for the three months ended 31 May 1986 in the accounts of John Henry Limited.   (12 marks)

(Total 25 marks)

(AAT June '86)

Chapter 26
Wages, Wages Books and Records

26.1 What Topics are Covered in this Chapter?

How wages and salaries are calculated and the deductions employers have to make; completing wage packets; a look at some of the forms required to be kept.

26.2 Wages and Salaries

People in employment receive either wages or salaries. It is generally taken that manual and factory workers who receive wages are paid on a weekly basis, while employees in management, etc who receive salaries are paid on a monthly basis.

26.3 Gross Earnings

Whether the remuneration is by way of wages or salary, the important factor is to start with the correct gross amount and then to subject this to the various statutory deductions for Income Tax and National Insurance, which are deducted under the Pay As You Earn (PAYE) system.

A salary should not present a problem and is usually taken as one twelfth of the annual amount due.

26.4 Time Records

Wages may present a problem in calculating the gross figure as this may be dependent on the amount of time worked or the number of units produced (sometimes referred to as piecework).

If a time basis is used, it is essential that each member of staff has his or her time recorded accurately and that the hourly rate of pay is agreed and understood.

26.5   Clock Cards and Time Sheets

Nowadays, most time records are kept electronically with each staff member using a card which, when inserted into a time clock, will record the exact time of starting and finishing work, thus enabling a detailed time sheet to be produced which is then used to calculate the gross amount due.

The time sheet will include other essential information, such as the employee's name, payroll number (if required), days and hours worked at normal and overtime rates.

An example is as follows:

Fig. 26.1

Example of Time Sheet

Name A. Brown Dept. Paint Shop		Payroll Number B. 345
Day	Normal Hours	Overtime
Monday	7	
Tuesday	7	
Wednesday	7	3
Thursday	7	
Friday	7	
Saturday	—	4
Sunday	—	4
Total Hours 46	35	11
Normal Rates	35 × £3.00	£105.00
Overtime @ 1 ½ × normal	11 × £4.50	£49.50
	46	£154.50
	Checked by_____	___Factory Floor _____Wages Dept.

26.6   Piecework

If piecework rates are used, the units of production will be counted, often by a foreman or supervisor who will enter the amounts on a tally card. This can then be independently checked by taking the total of the day's production according to the tally cards and comparing this to the physical number of units present.

In cases where the production units are despatched immediately, the gatekeeper's records may have to be scrutinised, but this takes the discussion into the realms of auditing which is not being studied at this stage.

The gross figure is taken by multiplying the week's production by the agreed rate per unit. Overtime will not be recognised on a time basis but a production bonus may be paid on unit production over a certain figure.

Once the gross amount has been ascertained, this will be subject to the various statutory deductions applicable.

26.7   Personal Reliefs from Income Tax

In the UK, each person is entitled to various personal reliefs to be offset against gross income and the balance, if any, will be taxed at the rates currently in force.

The main personal allowances are Single Personal Allowance, Married Man's Personal Allowance (higher than single) and Wife's Earned Income Relief (an amount up to that for Single Personal Allowance).

For the tax year 1987/88, the reliefs were:

Single Personal Allowance	£2,425
Married Man's Allowance	£3,795
Wife's Earned Income Relief	up to £2,425

These allowances are annual allowances and thus a proportion is taken each week or month. Each employee will receive notice of a code number from the Inland Revenue which will enable the correct allowances to be taken by reference to tables prepared by the Inland Revenue and distributed free to all employers.

26.8   National Insurance Contributions (NIC)

As well as deductions for Income Tax, National Insurance is also deducted from the gross amount due. The National Insurance deduction is also taken from a book of tables and will vary according to the gross wages or salary and, in certain circumstances, on whether the employee is over 65 (60 for a woman) or a married woman who is entitled to pay a reduced amount.

The following example concerning Mr B. White assumes that

his annual salary is £6,000, his personal allowance £3,000 and
National Insurance is 9% of his gross salary.

	£	£
Annual Salary	6,000	6,000
Allowances	3,000	
Taxable at 27%	3,000	
Tax	810	
National Insurance at 9%	540	
Total Deduction		1,350
Net Annual Salary		4,650

Each month, Mr White will receive a gross salary of £500 and
the deduction calculated will be one twelfth of the total annual
amount.

Mr White will also be entitled to receive a payslip showing his
gross salary deductions and net salary.

26.9   Employers' Contributions

As well as the employee suffering a deduction for National
Insurance, the employer is also required to pay a further sum,
again based on the gross salary, into the National Insurance
Scheme. This is known as employers National Insurance and is
not deductable from the employee. It is rather like a separate tax
levied on the employer for the benefit of having employees.

It should be noted that employees' National Insurance is
calculated by reference to minimum and maximum salaries,
whilst employers' National Insurance shares the same minimum
but has no ceiling.

26.10   Inland Revenue Returns

The PAYE taxation and National Insurance deductions are
collected by the employer and remitted to the Inland Revenue on a
monthly basis. The employer is acting as an unpaid Collector of
Taxes (a situation similar to VAT).

The employer is obliged to keep a record of wages/salaries paid
and the relevant deductions and this is done on a specially
prepared sheet supplied by the Inland Revenue. An example of
the sheet is reproduced opposite.

Fig. 26.2

Deductions Working Sheet

Deductions working sheet P11 (New)	Employee's surname in CAPITAL LETTERS	First two forenames		Year to 5 April
Employer's name	National insurance no	Date of birth Day | Month | Year	Works no etc	19......
Tax District and reference			Date of leaving in figures Day | Month | Year	Tax Code*	Amended code*

National Insurance Contributions*

| | Total of Employee's and Employer's Contributions payable 1a | Employee's contributions payable 1b | Employee's contributions Contracted-out rate included in Col 1c | Statutory sick pay in the week or month included in col 2 1d | **WEEK number** / **MONTH number** | Pay in the week or month including statutory sick pay 2 | Total pay to date 3 | **PAYE Income Tax** — Total free pay to date as shown by Table A 4 | Total taxable pay to date ① 5 | Total tax due to date as shown by Taxable Pay Tables 6 | Tax deducted or refunded in the week or month Mark refunds 'R' 7 | For employer's use |

Week/Month rows:

WEEK	MONTH
1	6 April to 5 May
2	
3	
4	1
5	6 May to 5 June
6	
7	
8	2
9	6 June to 5 July
10	
11	
12	
13	3
14	6 July to 5 Aug
15	
16	
17	4
18	6 Aug to 5 Sept
19	
20	
21	5
22	6 Sept to 5 Oct
23	
24	
25	
26	6
27	6 Oct to 5 Nov
28	
29	
30	7

Total carried forward

* N.I. Contribution Table letter must be entered overleaf beside the N.I. totals boxes – see the note shown there.
This box may be used if the employer wishes to record the N.I. letter what this side of the sheet is in use.

† If amended cross out previous code
● If in any week/month the amount in column 4 is more than the amount in column 3, make no entry in column 5

P11 (New)

26.11   Employer Records

The employer may also want to keep a record of pay and deductions in a separate Wages Book. The example following refers to Mr White for the month of April 198–.

Fig. 26.3

Example of Wages Book

WAGES BOOK APRIL 198–						
Name	Gross	Tax	Nat. Ins.	Total Deductions	Net	Employers Nat. Ins.
B. White Details of other employees→ ↓	500.00	72.50	45.00	117.50	382.50	45.00

26.12   Paying Wages and Salaries; Coin Analysis

It is normal practice for salaried employees to be paid by cheque or bank credit transfer, whereas many weekly paid employees receive their wages in cash.

When cash payments are required, it will be necessary for the cashier to calculate the number and denomination of the bank notes and coins required. He or she will also have to bear in mind that the employee will wish to receive notes that can be readily exchanged, i.e. many people do not like to receive £50 notes in their pay packets but will prefer 5 × £10 notes.

The following example assumes that the highest denomination required are £10 notes.

In order to calculate the breakdown required, it is important to work down from the highest note required. A tabular computation is an easy method to use and this is shown in Fig. 26.4.

26.13   Examination Hints

(i) If required to calculate a breakdown of cash required for wages, always pay particular attention to the examiner's instructions for the maximum denomination of notes required.

(ii) You may not see a complete question on wages but always be prepared for this subject to appear as part of a larger question.

26.14   What Should I Have Learned in this Chapter?

(i) That wages can be calculated by hours or piece work or may be fixed. That salaries are normally fixed by agreement.

(ii) That it is necessary to keep accurate records both of time worked and units produced in order to arrive at gross wages and also that it is equally important (as well as obligatory) to keep adequate records of all deductions, etc. made from gross wages and salaries.

Fig. 26.4

Example of Note and Coin Analysis

	Net wages	£10	£5	£1	50p	10p	5p	2p	1p
L. White	82.50	8		2	1				
R. Brown	98.71	9	1	3	1	2			1
C. Green	57.23	5	1	2		2		1	1
A. Black	74.97	7		4	1	4	1	1	
Notes and coin required		29	2	11	3	8	1	2	2
Agreed	313.41	290.00	10.00	11.00	1.50	0.80	0.05	0.04	0.02

Exercises

1   T. Smith has five employees who are paid weekly every Friday.

The net wages for the week ending 7 July 198– are:

	£
B. Jones	65.21
P. Foster	58.97
P. Blake	61.27
C. Shaw	47.56
J. Griffin	57.74

You are required to prepare a cash analysis of the notes and coins to be collected from the bank. (*Note:* The highest denomination note that will be accepted is £10.)

2   (a) What statutory deductions are calculated under the PAYE
regulations.
(b) Describe briefly how the deductions are calculated.
(c) The following details apply to P. Jones and B. James for
the month of August 198–:

	P. Jones	B. James
Gross Salary	250.00	345.00
Tax	16.25	44.95

National Insurance contributions for P. Jones are: employee
7% of gross salary, employer 7% of gross. B. James: employee
9%, employer 10.45% of gross.

You are required to show how the salaries and deductions
would appear in a wages book and to calculate a breakdown of
the cash required (Notes up to £20 are acceptable).

3   Benjamin and Daniel Limited is a manufacturing company
employing 10 people on the shop floor. The basic working
week is 35 hours with the first 5 hours overtime paid at time
plus a quarter and anything above that paid at time plus a half.
For the week ending 15 September 198– the following details
apply to S. Benson.

Total hours worked 50 hours
Basic rate of pay £4.60p per hour

The 50 hours were recorded as follows:

Monday 8   Tuesday 10   Wednesday 9   Thursday 9½
Friday 8½   Saturday 5.

You are required to give an example of the type of time sheet
that may have been used for S. Benson and to calculate the
gross wages payable.

If free pay for the week taken from the tables supplied by the
Inland Revenue is £150 and employees National Insurance is
9% of gross and the employers proportion is 10.45% of gross
you are required to calculate the net wages payable and to
make a note of the total cost to the company of employing S.
Benson.

Chapter 27

Computers in Accounting

27.1 What Topics are Covered in this Chapter?

We list some advantages and disadvantages of using computers and explain the principal parts of computer systems. We examine the functions of programs followed by some of their applications. The chapter concludes with some of the security aspects of computer systems.

27.2 The Growth of Computer Accounting

Bookkeeping and Accounts has been written to explain the principles of double-entry book-keeping and to this end, the principles have been explained in terms of handwritten books of account. Such systems will probably continue to be employed for many years to come in businesses, especially the smaller ones. However, even in smaller businesses, computers have rapidly been replacing handwritten records. When computers take over, the normal principles of double-entry book-keeping seem to disappear; but they only disappear from our immediate sight. They are still very much there, and are always likely to be so.

> **Remember**
>
> All the basic rules of double-entry apply in
> computerised accounting systems

27.3 Advantages of Computerised Accounting Systems

(i) Computers are highly efficient and can process accurately very large volumes of data at extremely high speeds.

(ii) Computers relieve people of tedious tasks. They perform repetitive tasks such as listing data and routine calculations extremely well.

(iii) Computers may provide management with more information about a business than would otherwise be possible with a manual system because of time, effort and expense.

(iv) Computers release people to do other more useful tasks which might not otherwise be done.

27.4   Disadvantages of Computerised Accounting Systems

(i) The initial cost of installing computers can be very high.

(ii) Alterations to computerised systems can take time and be costly. Manual systems can be changed immediately and at little cost.

(iii) A fault in a computerised system can halt the whole system with possibly catastrophic results to the business. Faults in manual systems will probably only affect the part of the system immediately concerned and the effects may be easily mitigated.

27.5   The Parts of a Computerised System

A computerised system has two main parts. First there is the main computer with its accessories which allow data to be fed into it and information to be communicated by it to the user. Notice that we speak of *inputting data* (a plural word denoting numbers, alphabetic characters, symbols, etc.) into the computer, but speak of *outputting information*. Information is data which have been processed. The computer processes the data by addition and subtraction; it even multiplies by addition and divides by subtraction. It does not automatically know which pieces of data to use nor what to do with them. It has to be instructed at every step.

The second part of the system are the instructions which are called programs. Programs are written by people called programmers in programming language which computers can understand. Some programming languages are simple enough to allow the users of computers to write their own programs.

27.6   Hardware

The first part of the system, the computer and the accessories used for input and output are collectively called *hardware*.

The computer itself consists of the *Central Processing Unit* (CPU). This has three parts:

(i) *Arithmetic Logic Unit* (ALU) which performs arithmetic and logic operations and can store the results of calculations during the processing.

(ii) *Control unit* which, as its name implies, makes the computer carry out in sequence the program instructions.

(iii) *Memory or mainstore.* The capacity of a computer to store data in its memory is expressed as being 'so many K'. K stands for *Kilobytes* (or thousand bytes), a byte being eight bits or digits. A 64K computer has a mainstore which can hold 64,000 bytes. Obviously the bigger the memory, the more a computer can do.

Although a computer memory can be vast, large amounts of data must be held in another store, the *Backing Store,* which may be in the form of magnetic tape or disc. This data can be transferred to the main store by the computer when it is required for processing, and back again when the computer has finished processing it.

Inputting devices

(i) Keyboards (ii) Magnetic tape (iii) Devices to read magnetic characters (such as sorting codes on cheques) (iv) Lightpens to read bar codes like those to be seen on most packaged items in supermarkets.

Output devices

(i) Visual Display Units (VDUs) similar to television screens (ii) Printers to print out information at exceedingly high speeds (iii) Magnetic tape or discs.

A main frame computer is the largest of the computer family and may have many *terminals* (input and output devices) connected to it. The terminals may be located at great distances from the computer and be connected to it by either direct lines or telephone lines.

A microcomputer is the small member of the family and will fit easily on the user's desk-top.

Fig. 27.1

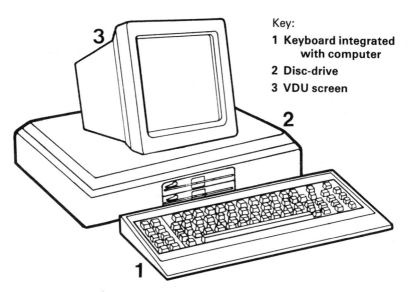

Microcomputer Configuration

Key:
1 **Keyboard integrated with computer**
2 **Disc-drive**
3 **VDU screen**

27.7   Software

Programs are known as software and are stored in magnetic form, usually on discs. The instructions are *loaded* from the discs into the memory store of the CPU. The control unit reads the instructions in sequence. The instructions tells the control unit where in the memory store it will find the piece of datum (singular of data) to be processed and the particular operation to be performed upon that piece of datum. Further instructions will tell the computer to record the result on a magnetic disc, or to display it on a VDU or to print it out to produce a hard copy of the result.

27.8   Some Computer Applications

Software is available to enable computers to perform most of the routine applications contained in the earlier chapters of the book. A few examples are:
   (i) Payroll preparation
  (ii) Postings to Purchases, Sales and Nominal ledger accounts
 (iii) Cash Book
 (iv) Control accounts

(v) Analyses of receipts and expenditure
(vi) Stock records
(vii) Schedules of creditors and debtors, the latter being 'aged' for credit control purposes; this is useful when provisions for bad debts are being calculated
(viii) Forecasts of and budgets for revenue and expenditure.

The formats for forecasts and budgets show monthly figures in columns and analyses of revenue and expenditure item by item in rows down the page. When a format is displayed as a matrix of rows and columns on a VDU so that the user can fill in the figures via the keyboard, it is known as a *spreadsheet*.

Fig. 27.2

Example of Spreadsheet

	JAN	FEB	MAR	APR	TOTAL
REVENUE					
Sales					
Interest R'cble					
Other income					
EXPENDITURE					
Staff costs					
Property exps.					
Office exps.					
Selling exps.					
Depreciation					
PROFIT					

Computers give a lot of assistance to users in the form of messages and instructions displayed on VDU screens. An example of this is a *menu* which is displayed when a user gains access to one of the systems. Fig. 27.3 shows a typical menu for a Sales system.

Fig. 27.3

Example of Menu

```
SALES SYSTEM
    1. OPEN FILES
    2. CLOSE FILES
    3. AMEND FILES
    4. WALK THROUGH FILES
    5. UPDATE FILES
    6. PRINT FILES
ROUTINE REQUIRED_____
```

When data is put into the system and remains available for several applications, it is known as a data-base. A purchase of goods on credit, input to the computer would serve to update the suppliers' account in the Purchases ledger, the Purchases account in the nominal ledger, the Purchases ledger Control Account, the stock records, costing records and management accounting records as well as any other statistical records for which programs may have been written.

Fig. 27.4

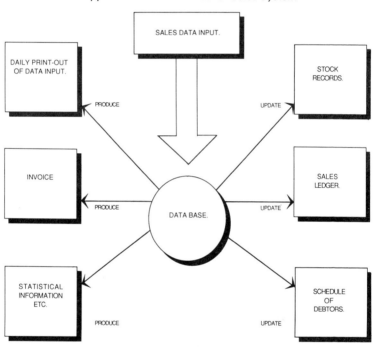

Applications of Data Base for Sales System

27.9   Controls on Accuracy and Security

'Garbage in, garbage out' is a way of saying 'Put rubbish into the computer as data, and the information that comes out will be rubbish'. Complaints about computer errors are invariably the fault of human errors either because programs contain errors, or the data input is incorrect. To protect the system against errors, some checks are built into the system; other checks are made available to the user by means of exception reports.

Checks that can be used are of various kinds of which two are check digits and limit checks.

Check digits

These detect the input of wrong identification numbers to the system. An account number 102645 could be wrongly input as 102465; check digits can be used to detect the error at the input stage. Check digits are often alphabetical characters which are determined by weighting the digits in the account number with the factors 6,5,4,3,2,1 and using a 'modulus' of 11. The check digit for account number 102645 would be found as follows:

$$\frac{(1 \times 6) + (0 \times 5) + (2 \times 4) + (6 \times 3) + (4 \times 2) + (5 \times 1)}{11}$$

$$= \frac{6 + 0 + 8 + 18 + 8 + 5}{11} = \frac{45}{11} = 4, \text{ remainder } 1$$

Subtract the remainder from the modulus: $11 - 1 = 10$.

The tenth letter of the alphabet is J so that the account number would be 102645J. The computer would verify the check digit every time the number was entered. If the operator entered 102465J, the computer would not accept it because the check digit for 102465 should be A, and the user could re-enter the correct account number. (Work it out for yourself.)

Limit tests

These would apply where, for instance, the minimum wage guaranteed to employers is, say, £15, and the maximum number of hours which can be worked in one week is, say, 72. When payroll data is being entered, the computer would detect a wage of less than £15, or the hours for any person in excess of 72 and 'report' such items.

Exception reports take the form of lists of data printed out to show that they do not conform to certain predetermined criteria. The payroll mentioned above is an example. Other examples are: credit notes which have not been authorised by one of a named panel of managers, or those which exceed certain limits; stock levels under or over set limits. Such exception reports should always be examined and acted upon by responsible officials of the firm.

System Security

To stop unauthorised persons from gaining access to computerised systems to gain information or to tamper with the data, programs and files on disc or tape should be kept under lock and key and only issued to authorised users, each occasion being recorded in a register. Access to systems and files on the computer and the ability to enter data is restricted to authorised users who are given confidential *passwords* they must key in on the terminal before they can access a system.

27.10   Examination Hints

This chapter has been written rather to serve as a link between the book-keeping and accounting theory taught in this book and their application in a computerised office, than as an examination topic. The best advice that can be given for both these approaches to the subject is:

(i) Remember that computer systems adhere to all the principles of double-entry.
(ii) Take opportunities to gain 'hands on' experience.
(iii) Keep an enquiring mind to find out all the ways a computer can be used in accounting.

27.11   What Should I Have Learned in this Chapter?

(i) Computer accounting systems adhere to the principles of double-entry.
(ii) Information is data which have been processed.
(iii) The computer with its peripherals, or terminals, as the input and output devices are called, is known as hardware.
(iv) Programs, which instruct the computer in its operations, are known as software.
(v) The main advantages of computers are that they can process vast amounts of data speedily and accurately.
(vi) The disadvantages are that they are initially expensive and systems may only be changed at a cost in time and money.
(vii) Various methods such as check digits, inbuilt 'parameter' tests, etc. are used to check the validity of data.
(viii) Security must be preserved by keeping programs and files under lock and key and the use of passwords.

Exercises

1 A spreadsheet is another name for
  (a) a menu
  (b) the backing store
  (c) a matrix of rows and columns
  (d) a computerised sales ledger.

2 A byte is
  (a) a part of the central processing unit
  (b) a piece of the menu
  (c) an input device
  (d) a group of eight bits or digits.

3 What is an exception report? Give examples.

4 What use should be made of exception reports?

5 What do you understand by 'data base'?

6 Using a data base system, how many ways may a purchase of stock on credit affect the accounting records?

7 What methods have been mentioned in this chapter for ensuring the accuracy of processing data?

8 Name two methods used to ensure the security of computer systems.

9 How many makes and models of microcomputer can you find which would be suitable to perform the accounting function in a small business? (You will need to visit dealers and exhibitions to answer this exercise and the next two.)

10 How much does the most expensive microcomputer in your list for Exercise 9 cost? How much does the least expensive one cost?

11 (a) What accessories are included with the computers you have listed for Exercise 9?
  (b) What other accessories are compatible with (can be used with) those computers?

Answers

Chapter 1

1 (a): (i), (iv); **1** (b):(iii)
2 (a): (iv); **2** (b): (ii)
3 Debits: 4,000, 250, 300, 170. Credits: 100, 1,200, 600, 40, 15, 300, 900
4 Capital Cr. 4,000, Sales Cr. 250, 170; Good (Loan) Cr. 300; Rent Dr. 100; Purchases Dr. 1,200, 300; Shop Fittings Dr. 600; Stationery Dr. 40; Postages Dr. 15; Equipment Dr. 900
5 Debit balances: Bank 2,580; Cash 115; Premises 4,000; Fixtures 700; Purchases 5,400; Motor van 1,000; Motor expenses 35; Wages 60; Drawings 50; Credit balances: Capital 10,000; Sales 3,940
6 (i) Dr. Bank, Cr. P. Singh. Capital; (ii) Dr. Rent, Cr. Bank; (iii) Dr. Shop fittings, Cr. Bank; (iv) Dr. Purchases, Cr. Bank; (v) Dr. Cash, Cr. Bank; (vi) Dr. Wages, Cr. Cash; (vii) Dr. Bank, Cr. Shop fittings. (viii) Dr. Insurances, Cr. Bank; (ix) Dr. Bank, Cr. Sales; (x) Dr. Bank, Cr. Cash

Chapter 2

1 (d)
2 (b)
3 P.D.B. total 1,065; P.R.B. total 100; balances: (Debit) Purchases 1,065; (Credit) Bloom 329; White 402; Lilley 180; Jones 54; Purchases returns 100
4 S.D.B. total 2,378; S.R.B. total 174; balances: (Debit) Singh 304; Massey 716; Matthews 700; Webster 484; Sales returns 174; (Credit) Sales 2,378
5 Debit balances: Bank 5,775; Cash 300; Purchases 4,220; Sales returns 235; A. Briers 518; N. Goodyear 600; L. Cannock 1,120; L. Thorne 360; Credit balances: Capital 6,000; Sales 3,573; Purchases returns 265; C. Williams 1,000; P. Stephens 1,115; D. Tong 1,175
6 Debit balances: Bank 3,320; Cash 84; Motor van 3,000; Equipment 1,500; Coker 340; Purchases 6,110; Callaghan 50; Wages 40; Insurance 30; Snow 120; O'Donnell 100; Sales returns 130; Motor expenses 20; Credit balances: Capital 10,000; Epworth 135; Bickers 1,000; Sandy 850; Sales 2,644; Purchases returns 115; ~~Woolley 300;~~ Stone 100

8 Debits: Shefford 1,122; Bedford 803; Northam 231; Purchases 1,030; Carriage inwards 30; VAT 106; Credits; Bolton 341; Bromley 638; Hastings 187; Sales 1,900; Carriage outwards 60; VAT 196

Chapter 3

1 C
2 C
3 790 Dr.
4 Amended cash book balance 3,732 Cr. (iii) Speak to bank re (b) and (e)
5 (a) 1,596; (b) Dr. balance 1,796, Cr. 168, 306, 15, 1,596 (balance)
6 C.B. and B.S. balances 615
7 C.B. balance 705

Chapter 4

1 Cash Dr. balance 48; Bank Cr. balance 152; Discounts allowed a/c Dr. 9; Discounts received a/c Cr. 13
2 Cash Dr. balance 45; Bank Dr. 55; Discounts allowed Dr. 8; Discounts received a/c Cr. 12
3 (b) April 1 Dr. Cash 150; Cr. Sales 150; Apr 2 Dr. Bank 198 (Discount allowed 2, memo only) Cr. Hyde 198, 2; Apr 3 Dr. Small 234, 6; Cr. Bank 234 (Discount received 6, memo only); Apr 4 Cr. Cash 560, Dr. Wages 560; Apr 7 Dr. Cash, Cr. Bank 50; Discount received a/c Cr. 6; Discount allowed a/c 2 Dr

Chapter 5

3 (ii) Postage 20; Stationery 15.50; Travelling 8; Sundry 9.40; Balance 27.10; Reimbursement 52.90
4 (ii) Postage 10.25; Stationery 7.85; Wages 13.40; Ledger 5.60; Balance 2.90; (iii) Reimbursement 37.10
5 (2) Cleaning 77; Motor expenses 97; Postage 41; Stationery 26; Travelling 45; (3) Reimbursement 286

Chapter 6

1 (c)
2 (b)
3 (a) Adams Dr. 470, Cr. 400; Brown Dr. 260, 260, Cr. 260; Church Dr. 300, 39, Cr. 339. (b) Cash book 10th April Dr. 400.

27th May Dr. 260. 10th April Cr. 20; 20th May Cr. 300; 27th May Cr. 260; (c) Bills receivable Dr. 400, 260, Cr. 400, 260; Bills payable Dr. 300, Cr. 300

Chapter 7

1 (d)
2 (c)
4 T.B. Dr. Bank 10,637, Purchases 830, General expenses 546, Fittings 387, McBay 175; Cr. Capital 10,500, Duckworth 230, Locket 130, Sales 1,665, Purchases Returns 50. Totals 12,575
5 T.B. Dr. Bank 2,380, Hill 380, Nailor 360, Drawings 200, Fixtures and fittings 2,000, Purchases 1,750, Rent 200, Delivery expenses 50, Wages 320; Cr. Kaye 800, Capital 5,000, Sales 1,840. Totals 7,640
6 (i) 15 credited instead of debited; (ii) Credit entry 200 omitted; (iii) Debit entry 550 omitted; (iv) 35 credited instead of debited
7 (a) Corrected items: Debit balances: Purchases 2,960; Returns inward 98; Discount allowed 45; Petty Cash 18; Credit balances: Sales 6,916; Returns outwards 46; Bank overdraft 621. Totals 30,105

Chapter 8

1 (d)
2 (a) Purchases Day Book; (b) Journal; (c) Journal; (d) Sales Returns Book; (e) Cash Book
3 R. Doe Dr. 500, D. Roe Cr. 500; Office equipment Dr. 1,000, Broadwood Office Furniture Cr. 1,000; D. Lowe Dr. 1,400, Motor van Cr. 1,400; Discounts received Dr. 20, L. Walker Cr. 20
4 Dr. Motor van 3,000, Stock 1,600, Equipment 300, Cash 40, Debtors 75; Cr. Bank 150, Creditors 200, Capital 4,665
5 (a) (i) Drawings Dr. 140, Purchases Cr. 140; (ii) Sales Returns Dr. 100, Purchases Cr. 100; (iii) Sales Dr. 200, Equipment Cr. 200
(b) Dr. Balances: Purchases 8,760, Drawings 2,240, Sales returns 500, Premises 10,000, Debtors 2,800, Discounts allowed 375, Cash 25, Bank 1,400, Equipment 1,400; Cr. Balances: Sales 1,400, Purchases returns 500, Creditors 1,700, Discounts received 750, Capital 23,150. Totals 27,500

Chapter 9

1 (b)
2 (c)
3 (d)
4 Cost of sales 3,200, Gross profit 3,800, Net profit 1,410
5 Sales 11,290 – 620; Cost of sales 4,535; Gross profit 6,135; Net profit 755
6 Sales 9,460 – 215; Cost of sales 7,673; Gross profit 1,572; Net loss 454

Chapter 10

1 (d)
2 (a) (i) revenue; (ii) revenue; (iii) revenue; (iv) revenue; (v) capital
(b) Increase both fixed assets (freehold premises) and net profit added to capital account by £1,400
3 (b) Capital expenditure: Van (3,000), seat belts (24), number plates (15); total 3,039. Revenue expenditure: Delivery charges (42), Road tax (90), Insurance (220); total 352. Capital expenditure: Shelves (90). Revenue expenditure: Redecoration shop front (400)
4 Totals: Fixed assets 3,500; Current assets 2,995; Current liabilities 400; Capital 6,095; Grand totals 6,495
5 Totals: Fixed assets 17,600; Current assets 6,177; Current liabilities 7,997; Long term liability 500; Capital 15,280; Grand totals 23,777
6 Totals: Fixed assets 3,400; Current assets 2,550; Current liabilities 610; Capital 5,340. Grand totals 5,950

Chapter 11

1 (b)
2 (c)
4 (a & b) (i) Rent payable: Tfr. P. & L. 1,200; credit balance 100 (shown as accrued expense under current liabilities); (ii) Rent receivable: Tfr. P. & L. 480 (credit); debit balance 150 (shown as rent receivable under current assets); (iii) Electricity: Tfr. P. & L. 363 (debit); credit balance 96 (shown as accrued expense under current liabilities)

5 (a) Rent payable: Dr. 9,600 (c/d) 2,400; Cr. (b/d) 2,400, P/L 9,600. Rent receivable: Dr. P/L 1,600; Cr. b/f 400; 800, c/f 400. Rates: Dr. b/f 600, 2,400; Cr. P/L 2,200, c/d 800
(b) Stationery: Dr. b/f 2,200, 6,100, c/f 520; Cr. b/f 600, P. & L. 6,550, c/f 1,670
6 Cost of sales 27,500. Gross profit 12,500, Net profit 7,000. B/S. Totals: Fixed assets 72,500, Current assets 18,200; Current liabilities 3,700; Capital 87,000. Totals 90,700

Chapter 12

1 (c)
2 (d)
3 (ii) (a) 1984 17,500; 1985 12,500
(b) Dr. balance c/d 250; Cr. balance c/d 175, P. & L. 75
4 (a) (b) (c) 1979: Bad debts (Dr.) 750, Sundry creditors (Cr.) 750; P./L. (Dr.) 750. Bad debts (Cr.) 750. P./L. (Dr.) 700. Prov. (Cr.) 700. 1980: Bad debts (Dr.) 4,085, Sundry creditors (Cr.) 4,085; P./L. (Dr.) 4,085. Bad debts (Cr.) 4,085; P./L. (Dr.) 300, Prov. (Cr.) 300. 1981: Bad debts (Dr.) 2,900, Sundry creditors (Cr.) 2,900, P./L. (Dr.) 2,900. Bad debts (Cr.) 2,900; Prov. (Dr.) 250, P./L. (Cr.) 250
5 Provision for bad debts: 1981: Dr. P./L., Cr. Prov. 205; 1982: Dr. P./L., Cr. Prov. 24 (balance 229); 1983: Dr. Prov. 26 (balance 203), Cr. P./L. 26
6 (a) Provision a/c 1980: Balance c/d 18,500; 1981: Balance c/d 17,500; 1982: Balance c/d 30,000
Balance sheets 1980: 166,500; 1981: 122,500; 1982: 170,000
Charges to P./L. a/c 1980: 7,180 (1,680 + 5,500); 1981: 200 (1,200 − 1,000); 1982: 18,700 (6,200 + 12,500)

Chapter 13

1 (c)
2 (a)
5 (a) Motor vans a/c. Balances 1979: 2,500; 1980: 5,500; 1981: 5,000; 1982: 5,500
Prov. for depn. balances 1979: 500; 1980: 1,600; 1981: 1,600; 1982: 1,500. Disposals 1981: P./L. 500 (loss); 1982: P./L. 200 (profit)
(b) 1979: Dr. 500; 1980: Dr. 1,100; 1981: Dr. 1,000, 500; 1982: Dr. 1,100, Cr. 200
(c) 1979: 2,500 less 500; 1980: 5,500 less 1,600; 1981: 5,000 less 1,600; 1982: 5,500 less 1,500

6 (i) On credit, (ii) Reducing balance, (iii) 10 per cent, (iv) 37,570
7 (a) Wdv at 1981: A 1,350; B 2,940; C 2,520
(b) Machinery a/c at 1981, 13,400; Provision for depreciation at 1981 6,590

Chapter 14

1 Gross profit 7,047; Net profit 2,607; Fixed assets 800; Current assets 4,230; Current liabilities 1,319; Capital 3,711; Totals 5,030
2 (i) Net turnover 61,352; net purchases 31,750; cost of sales 30,956; Gross profit 30,396; net profit 13,746
(ii) Capital: Cr. 38,612; 13,746; Dr. 1,162. Balance 51,196
3 Net turnover 16,910; cost of sales 8,410; Gross profit 8,500; Net profit 3,100; Total fixed assets (N.B.V.) 1,560; Total current assets 7,590; Current liabilities 3,610; Capital 5,540
4 Cost of sales 20,890; Gross profit 21,270; Net profit 12,630. Fixed assets 34,200; Current assets 11,130; Current liabilities 1,300; Capital 44,030

Chapter 15

1 (b)
2 (b)
4 (i) Stock 31.1.81: 900 at £2 = £1,800
(ii) Gross profit 2,550
5 2,971
7 (a) 1979: 35,000; 11,000. 1980: 27,000; 13,600. 1981: 27,600; 15,200. 1982: 32,700; 16,600

Chapter 16

1 Interest on drawings 100, 90, 80; Interest on capitals 800, 480, 320; Salaries 2,600. Profit shares: 2,800; 1,400; 1,400
2 (b) (i) Net profit (24,000 − 2,000) 22,000; Profit shares: Black 1,350; White 900; Grey 450
(ii) Current accounts: Black 950 (Cr.); White 3,600 (Cr.); Grey 8,450 (Cr.)
3 (a) Cash Dr. 27,000. Arthur Cr. 13,500. George Cr. 13,500; P. & M. Dr. 12,000, F. & F. Dr. 1,000; Debtors Dr. 3,800; Stock Dr. 5,200; Goodwill Dr. 6,000. Creditors Cr. 2,000; Harry Cr. 26,000; Harry Dr. 26,000, Cash Cr. 26,000
(b) B.S. totals 29,000

4 (i) Capitals: Hampton 4,800; French 5,370
(ii) Assets: Goodwill 1,200; F. & F. 1,750; Van 900; Stock 3,730.
Debtors: 4,010; Bank 630. Liabilities: Creditors 2,050
5 (a) Appropriation: Profits Day 16,200, Week 10,800
(b) Current accounts: Week credit balance 5,000, Month debit balance 5,000
(c) Balance sheet totals 63,000 (Capital 30,000, Loan 30,000, Bank 3,000)

Chapter 17

1 (b). **2** (c). **3** (c)
4 Total long term capital 88,000; working capital 16,500
5 Profit for year: 3,031; Balance sheet totals: 24,041
6 (a) Fixed assets 62,880; Current assets 14,068; Current liabilities 9,177. Capital and reserves 67,771

Chapter 18

1 Subscriptions (a) 4,827, (b) 4,764, (c) Current asset 84, Current liability 27
Rates (a) 1,300, (b) 875, (c) Current asset 225
2 (i) Surplus 32
(ii) Fixed assets 332; Current assets 272; Acc. Fund 32; Loans 450; Creditors 122
3 (a) 36,759
(b) Surplus 36,759; Fixed assets 33,850; Current assets 3,844; Creditors 194; Accumulated fund 37,500
4 (i) R. & P. balance 87
(ii) Tea bar profit 92
(iii) Surplus 185
(iv) Fixed assets 135; Current assets 103; Creditors 53; Acc. fund 185
5 (a) (i) Surplus 236; (ii) Fixed assets 666; Current assets 264; Creditors 32; Acc. fund 898

Chapter 19

1 (i) (a) 1984: 3,150; 1985: 4,750. (b) Profit 2,960. (ii) Cr. 3,150, 2,960, Dr. 1,250, 110, balance 4,750
2 Profit 6,850
3 (a) Fixed assets 53,000; Current assets 11,710; Creditors 420; Capitals 74,290 – drawings 10,000

(b) Fixed assets 56,000; Current assets 12,170; Creditors 610; Capitals 64,290 + 3,000 + 10,270 − 10,000
4 Fixed assets 3,266; Current assets 6,306; Current liabilities 606; Capital 8,886
5 (a) 1981: 10,400; 1982: 4,200; 1983: 6,600. **6** 729

Chapter 20

1 Net profits: Hardware 13,400; Electrical 17,340; Gardening 10,580

Chapter 21

1 (c) Dr. balance 17,014; Cr. balance 214
2 (a & b) Corrected balances 13,534
3 (a) Drs. control balances 19,000 (Dr.), 670 (Cr.); Crs. control balances 365 (Dr.), 7,187 (Cr.)
(b) Trade Drs. 18,890; Trade Crs. 7,857

Chapter 22

1 (i) 1. Dr. Suspense, Cr. Returns Out 62; 2. Dr. Stationery, Cr. Suspense 3; 3. Dr. Purchases, Cr. Job 300; 4. Dr. Young, Cr. Suspense 9. (ii) Credit 50
2 (i) Debits 420; 852; Credits 70; 188; 792; 222
3 (i) Debits (Diff.) 286; 69; Credits 270; 74; P. & L. 11
(ii) 1. Dr. Purchases, Cr. Suspense 270; 2. Dr. Suspense, Cr. Brown 69; 3. Dr. James, Cr. Jones 50; 4. Dr. Discount allowed, Cr. Suspense 74; 5. Dr. Drawings, Cr. Purchases 65; 6. Dr. P./L.a.c., Cr. Suspense 11
(iii) 19,710
4 (a) (i) Dr. Suspense, Cr. Sales 240; (ii) Dr. Suspense, Cr. Bell 27; (iii) Dr. Discount allowed, Cr. Suspense 498; (iv) Dr. Bank charges, Cr. Suspense 166; (v) Dr. Suspense, Cr. Debtors 97
(b) Debits: (Diff.) 300; 240; 27; 97; Credits: 498; 166
(c) Profit 5,576
5 (a) Dr. Suspense 1,900; Cr. Sales 950, Purchases 950
(b) T.B. totals 145,666

Chapter 23

1 Prime cost 56,968; Factory cost 67,467; Gross profit 14,408; Net profit 6,943

2 Prime cost 155,515; Factory cost 175,000; Stock of finished goods 8,750; Gross profit 68,552; Net profit 11,111
3 Prime cost 182,648; Factory cost 199,046; Gross profit 37,045; Net loss 2,075

Chapter 24

1 (a) (i) 1:4.98; (ii) 1:1.27; (iii) 5,770; Deficiency 1,270; (iv) 12 times
2 (b) 19–3: (i) 1.24:1; (ii) 0.8:1; (iii) 48 days. 19–4: (i) 1.26:1; (ii) 0.73:1; (iii) 70 days
3 (a) R.O.C.E. 24.19%, Net profit/sales 5%; Sales/cap. empl. 484%; Turnover 31.5 times; Current ratio 1.19:1; Quick ratio 0.33:1; Debtors 4.26 days
4 (a) After adjustments for notional salary (GR) and interest (SD), R.O.C.E.: GR 3%; SD 5%; Net profit ratio: GR 3.33%; SD 5.33%; Gross profit ratio GR & SD: 46.67%; Current ratio: GR 3.5:1; SD 5.4:1; Acid test: GR 1.75:1; SD 3.16:1

Chapter 25

1 (a) Purchases Day Book totals: VAT 30,000; Purchases 181,590; Machinery 8,700; Motor vehicles 18,700; Vehicle expenses 410; Total 239,400
(b) Debits: Bank 84,000; Input tax 30,000; balance c/d 65,250; Credits; Balance b/d 84,000; Output tax 93,000; Cost of sales 2,250

Chapter 26

1 26 × £10; 4 × £5; 8 × £1; 3 × 50p; 5 × 20p; 2 × 5p; 6 × 2p; 3 × 1p (Total £290.75)
2 (c) Payroll totals: Gross 595; Tax 61.20; N.I. 48.55; Total deductions 109.75; Net pay 485.25; Employer's contrib. 53.55. Notes & coins: 23 × £20; 1 × £10; 2 × £5; 5 × £1; 1 × 20p; 2 × 2p; 1 × 1p
3 Equivalent hours: 56¼; Gross pay 258.75; Tax (at 27%) 29.36; N.I. 23.29; Net pay 206.10; Employer's contrib. 27.04. Total cost 285.79

Chapter 27

1 (c)
2 (d)

Index